D0804461

TCP/IP

The Cram Sheet

This Cram Sheet contains the distilled, key facts about TCP/IP. Review this information last thing before you enter the test room, paying special attention to those areas where you feel you need the most review. You can transfer any of these facts from your head onto a blank sheet of paper before beginning the exam.

PLANNING

1. Know the proper network configuration for a given scenario. For example, if your new network requires 10 subnets and 50 hosts per subnet, what is the minimum number of Class C addresses needed? By using a mask of 255.255.255.192, you can support 62 hosts on two subnets per Class C address, meaning you will need 5 Class C's.

2. Subnetting/CIDR. Know this like the back of your hand: 2^n-2. The following example should help:
   - 255.255.255.192 gives you 2 networks with 62 hosts per network
   - 255.255.255.224 gives you 6 networks with 30 hosts per network
   - 255.255.255.240 gives you 14 networks with 14 hosts per network
   - 255.255.255.248 gives you 30 networks with 6 hosts per network
   - 255.255.255.252 gives you 62 networks with 2 hosts per network

INSTALLATION AND CONFIGURATION

3. NetBIOS uses the following process to resolve NetBIOS names:

localcache>WINS>b-node broadcast> LMHOSTS>HOSTS>DNS

4. The LMHOSTS file is used to resolve NetBIOS names to IP addresses and is located in the *systemroot*\System32 \Drivers\Etc directory. **#PRE** is used to preload entries into cache. **#DOM** is used to identify a domain controller. **#INCLUDE** is used to include another file in the local LMHOSTS lookup.

5. The HOSTS file is used to resolve host names to IP addresses and is located in the *systemroot*\System32\Drivers\Etc directory. The IP address is in the left column, while the host name is in the right column. Comments begin with a #.

6. Internet Information Server (IIS) is a Windows NT Server service that provides FTP, Gopher, and World Wide Web services. IIS is installed from the Windows NT CD-ROM, not through the Network applet of the Control Panel.

7. Once DNS is installed on a Windows NT Server, the DNS Manager is used to create, configure, and administer DNS zones and DNS resource records.

39. The following utilities (and their applications) can be used to troubleshoot TCP/IP.

Utility	Pertinent Switches	Function
PING		Used to check the connectivity between two hosts. Uses ICMP messages for response.
ROUTE	**-f, -p, add**	Displays the routing table on a computer.
TRACERT		Traces the path a packet takes through the network hop by hop.
NETSTAT	**-e, -r, -s**	Displays IP information for a computer including connected sessions. VERY IMPORTANT.
NBTSTAT	**-c, -R, -r**	Displays NetBIOS over TCP/IP settings. Use **–R** to reload NetBIOS cache.
IPCONFIG	**all, renew, release**	Displays the IP configuration for a computer. Used to release a DHCP lease.
ARP	**-a, -d, -s**	Displays or modifies the ARP cache on a computer.

Certification Insider™ Press

send IP traffic not destined for the local subnet. If the default gateway setting for a computer is blank or invalid, it will not be able to communicate outside the local subnet.

27. Routing Information Protocol (RIP) is a distance-vector routing protocol used by routing devices to determine the best path through the network. RIP routing tables are updated automatically with information received from other routers. RIP is easier to work within large networks than static routing table entries, but it generates network traffic as the routers communicate with each other.

28. IP filtering is enabled by selecting Enable Security from the Advanced IP Addressing window in the TCP/IP Properties section of the Network applet. This setting can filter all incoming IP, TCP, or UDP packets fitting certain criteria.

CONNECTIVITY

29. Because Unix systems cannot use NetBIOS, they cannot resolve names using WINS. They must use DNS or HOSTS files to resolve host names to IP addresses.

30. The PDC is always the Master Browser for its domain; other Master Browsers will exist if the domain spans multiple subnets. The Master Browser is selected by election using the following criteria: OS type, version, current status.

31. The LPR and LPQ utilities can be used to send print jobs to (LPR) and monitor print jobs in (LPQ) Unix print queues.

MONITORING AND OPTIMIZATION

32. SNMP Management Information Bases (MIBs) contain information on the managed objects for an agent. An agent is a software program that monitors the de-

vice and sends the information contained in the MIB to an SNMP Manager.

33. SNMP traps are alerts that are automatically sent by the agent. To define the traps for a managed object, an SNMP Manager is used.

34. SNMP communities provide a minimal level of security on the managed device. An SNMP Manager must use the correct community name to communicate with the device. The default community for a device is Public, which allows any manager access to the device.

35. The Performance Monitor can be used on a Windows NT system to track TCP/IP events over time. It is automatically installed with the operating system. Examples of TCP/IP related counters are: TCP Segments/sec, UDP Datagrams/sec, IP Fragmentation Failures, and ICMP Messages/sec.

36. The Windows NT Network Monitor is installed separately through the Network applet in the Control Panel. It captures all traffic on the network and is used to capture the traffic for analysis. The Network Monitor Agent can be loaded on remote machines to monitor traffic at other locations.

37. The TCP/IP Sliding Window defines the number of segments the sending computer can have on the network without receiving an acknowledgment.

38. The Registry settings that affect TCP/IP performance are:

- TcpWindowSize
- ForwardBufferMemory
- NumForwardPackets
- DefaultTTL

These Registry settings are located in the HKEY_LOCAL_MACHINE\SYSTEM\CurrentControlSet\Services\Tcpip\Parameters subkey.

8. The file CACHE.DNS contains the name-to-IP-address mapping information for the Internet's root DNS servers. If not attaching to the Internet, delete this file and replace with information on the root DNS servers for your private TCP/IP network.

9. DNS files are located in the *systemroot*\System32\dns directory. The zone, cache, reverse-lookup, and arpa-127 files make up the DNS file structure.

10. A DNS boot file controls the startup of a DNS server running under a BIND implementation of DNS. It is not required for the Microsoft implementation, unless porting files from another non-Microsoft RFC compliant DNS server.

11. A primary name server gets the data for its zones from the local DNS database. A secondary name server gets the data for its zones from the primary DNS server for that zone. The sending of the data from primary to secondary is called zone transfer.

12. By supplying the DNS server with multiple IP addresses for a single host, such as a multihomed computer, DNS will automatically distribute the load between the interfaces. This is referred to as a DNS Round-Robin.

13. The Microsoft TCP/IP Print services is installed through the Services tab of the Network applet. This service includes LPD, which is used to provide print services to Unix hosts.

14. DHCP is used to automatically configure IP-related information on a client. The DHCP lease defines the amount of time a client can use a particular address.

15. A DHCP server is installed through the Network applet. Once installed, it is administered through the DHCP Manager, which is accessible through the Administrative Tools (Common) portion of the Start menu.

16. A DHCP scope defines the addresses that can be assigned by the server. To reserve a particular address, choose Add Reservations from the Scope menu of the DHCP Manager.

17. For a router to pass DHCP lease requests, it must be able to handle BOOTP broadcasts. DHCP is based on the BOOTP protocol.

18. DHCP Relay Agents are hardware components (like routers) or software programs (like the DHCP Relay Agent Service) that are able to forward DHCP/BOOTP messages from one subnet to another.

19. When a computer is started, it asks the WINS server if it can use a particular computername. If the name is not in use, the WINS server registers the name to the computer's IP address. The name must be reregistered with the server within the TTL for the registration.

20. WINS is enabled on a computer through the WINS tab of TCP/IP Properties. This configuration includes the IP address of the Primary and Secondary WINS Servers, the Scope ID for the client, and checkboxes to enable DNS for WINS resolution, or enable LMHOSTS lookup.

21. WINS Proxy allows non-WINS-enabled computers to utilize WINS services. A WINS Proxy computer will fulfill a request from a non-WINS computer from its own cache if possible, or it will query the WINS server for the non-WINS client.

22. WINS clients produce a minimum of three name registration requests each time they are started. In large, wide area networks, this traffic should be minimized by placing a WINS server on each remote network and replicating the WINS database between the servers.

23. A multihomed computer has more than one NIC. These are denoted in the LMHOSTS file by #MH.

24. Windows NT supports multiple NICs in one computer. These are configured and managed through the Network applet.

25. Through the Advanced tab of the TCP/IP Properties, you can configure up to five IP addresses for each NIC.

26. The default gateway is the device (usually a router) to which a computer will

Are You Certifiable?

That's the question that's probably on your mind. The answer is: You bet! But if you've tried and failed or you've been frustrated by the complexity of the MCSE program and the maze of study materials available, you've come to the right place. We've created our new publishing and training program, *Certification Insider Press*, to help you accomplish one important goal: to ace an MCSE exam without having to spend the rest of your life studying for it.

The book you have in your hands is part of our *Exam Cram* series. Each book is especially designed not only to help you study for an exam but also to help you understand what the exam is all about. Inside these covers you'll find hundreds of test taking tips, insights, and strategies that simply cannot be found anyplace else. In creating our guides, we've assembled the very best team of certified trainers, MCSE professionals, and networking course developers.

Our commitment is to ensure that the *Exam Cram* guides offer proven training and active-learning techniques not found in other study guides. We provide unique study tips and techniques, memory joggers, custom quizzes, insights about trick questions, a sample test, and much more. In a nutshell, each *Exam Cram* guide is closely organized like the exam it is tied to.

To help us continue to provide the very best certification study materials, we'd like to hear from you. Write or email us (craminfo@coriolis.com) and let us know how our *Exam Cram* guides have helped you study, or tell us about new features you'd like us to add. If you send us a story about how an *Exam Cram* guide has helped you ace an exam and we use it in one of our guides, we'll send you an official *Exam Cram* shirt for your efforts.

Good luck with your certification exam, and thanks for allowing us to help you achieve your goals.

Keith Weiskamp
Publisher, Certification Insider Press

EXAM CRAM™

TCP/IP

Exam #70-059

Microsoft
Certified
Systems
Engineer

Ed Tittel, Kurt Hudson,
and J. Michael Stewart

MCSE TCP/IP Exam Cram

Limits of Liability and Disclaimer of Warranty

Trademarks

The Coriolis Group, Inc.
An International Thomson Publishing Company
14455 N. Hayden Road, Suite 220
Scottsdale, Arizona 85260

602/483-0192
FAX 602/483-0193
http://www.coriolis.com

Library of Congress Cataloging-in-Publication Data
Tittel, Ed
     MCSE TCP/IP exam cram/by Ed Tittel, Kurt Hudson, and J. Michael Stewart.
         p.   cm.
     Includes index.
     ISBN 1-57610-195-9
     1. Electronic data processing personnel—Certification.
2. Microsoft software—Examinations—Study guides.   3. TCP/IP
(Computer Network Protocol)   I. Hudson, Kurt.   II. Stewart, James
Michael.   III. Title.
QA76.3.T58   1997
005.7'13769--dc21   97-32745
                                                                      CIP

Printed in the United States of America
10 9 8 7 6 5 4

Publisher
Keith Weiskamp

Acquisitions
Shari Jo Hehr

Marketing Specialist
Cynthia Caldwell

Project Editor
Jeff Kellum

Production Coordinator
Kim Eoff

Cover Design
Anthony Stock

Layout Design
Jimmie Young
April Nielsen

an International Thomson Publishing company

Albany, NY • Belmont, CA • Bonn • Boston • Cincinnati • Detroit • Johannesburg • London • Madrid
Melbourne • Mexico City • New York • Paris • Singapore • Tokyo • Toronto • Washington

(From L. to R., Ed Tittel, J. Michael Stewart, Kurt Hudson)

About The Authors

Ed Tittel

Ed Tittel recently worked as an instructor and course developer for American Research Group, where he developed and taught from a set of materials on Windows NT 4, both Workstation and Server. Ed is also a regular contributor to *Windows NT* magazine and an instructor for Softbank Forums at its Interop and NT Intranet tradeshows. Prior to going out on his own in 1994, Ed worked at Novell for six years, starting as a field engineer and departing as the director of technical marketing.

Ed has written over 40 computer books, including *HTML for Dummies* (with Stephen N. James, IDG Books Worldwide, 3rd ed., 1997); *Networking Windows NT 4.0 for Dummies* (with Mary Madden and Dave Smith, IDG Books Worldwide, 1996); and a variety of titles on Windows NT, NetWare, networking, and Web-related topics.

Ed has written over 200 articles for publications such as *Byte, InfoWorld, LAN Magazine, LAN Times, The NetWare Advisor, PC Magazine,* and *WindowsUser.* At present, Ed also writes a biweekly column for *Interop Online.* You can reach Ed by email at etittel@lanw.com or on the Web at http://www.lanw.com/etbio.htm.

Kurt Hudson

Kurt Hudson is a technical author, trainer, and consultant in the field of networking and computer-related technologies. For the past six years, he has focused his energy on learning and teaching technical skills. He has written several training manuals and books for government and private industry on topics ranging from inventory control to network administration.

14

As a former trainer for the U.S. Air Force, Kurt worked on high-security government projects employing technologies most people see only in the cinema. During his six-year engagement with the military, he earned three medals for improving systems efficiency, training excellence, and increasing national security. After departing the U.S. Air Force, he worked for a variety of private corporations, including Unisys and Productivity Point International, where he continued to learn and teach technical topics.

Since achieving Microsoft Certified Systems Engineer (MCSE) and Microsoft Certified Trainer (MCT) ratings, he has been writing books and conducting training sessions that have helped many individuals succeed in their pursuit of professional certification. You can reach Kurt on the Internet at kurt@hudlogic.com or on the Web at www.hudlogic.com.

James Michael Stewart

James Michael Stewart is a full-time writer focusing on Windows NT and Internet topics. In addition to working on the *Exam Cram* series, he has recently co-authored the *Intranet Bible* (IDG Books Worldwide, 1997) and the *Hip Pocket Guide to HTML 3.2* (IDG Books Worldwide, 1997). He also contributed to *Windows NT Networking for Dummies* (IDG Books Worldwide, 1997), *Building Windows NT Web Servers* (IDG Books Worldwide, 1997), and *Windows NT, Step by Step* (Microsoft Press, 1995).

Michael has written articles for numerous print and online publications, including C|Net, *InfoWorld*, *Windows NT* magazine, and *Datamation*. He is also the moderator for a Softbank online forum focusing on NT, located at http://forums.sbexpos.com/forums-interop/get/HOS_3.html and a former leader of an NT study group at the Central Texas LAN Association. He is currently an MCP for Windows NT Server 4, Workstation, and Windows 95.

Michael graduated in 1992 from the University of Texas at Austin with a bachelor's degree in Philosophy. Despite his degree, his computer knowledge is self-acquired, based on almost 14 years of hands-on experience. Michael has been active on the Internet for quite some time, where most people know him by his *nom de wire*, McIntyre. You can reach Michael by email at michael@lanw.com or through his Web pages at http://www.lanw.com/jmsbio.htm or http://www.impactonline.com/.

Acknowledgments

Ed Tittel

For starters, great thanks to the Coriolis team, who pulled an amazing series of rabbits out of a single, small, and bedraggled hat. Keith Weiskamp is the man with the vision and the willpower who turned our idea into a true phenomenon. Shari Jo Hehr is the lady who worked the contract magic that brought everything together. We're especially indebted to the production crew, under Sandra Lassiter's able management, including Managing Editor Paula Kmetz, the Project Editor Jeff Kellum, and Production Coordinator Kim Eoff. Thanks also to the outstanding sales staff, including Tom Mayer, Josh Mills, and Anne Tull. Of course, we're also grateful to the interior and cover design folks as well, April Nielsen, Jimmie Young, and Anthony Stock.

The real credit for this book goes to my co-authors, James Michael Stewart and Kurt Hudson. Without their vast knowledge of Microsoft, its testing, and the detailed world of TCP/IP, this book would not have been possible. We couldn't have delivered this baby without the able assistance of our general manager, David (DJ) Johnson, nor without the editorial and heroic efforts of Dawn Rader, our in-house editor, and Mary Burmeister, our Jill of all trades. Thanks for being such a great team, you guys! I'd also like to thank the gremlins at Microsoft, especially the ones who put the MCSE tests together, for giving us a chance to participate in what has turned out to be a great adventure.

Kurt Hudson

A big thank you to Shannon Johnson, his knowledge and textual contributions are greatly appreciated. As always, thanks to Julie Hudson, who also worked hard reviewing our work. I also want to thank the Coriolis team: Shari Jo Hehr, Jeff Kellum, and Paula Kmetz for all their help in getting this series together.

James Michael Stewart

Thanks to my boss and co-author, Ed Tittel, for including me in this book series. Thanks to DJ for his solid efforts in completing this book. Thanks to Dawn for trudging through this techno-dribble. To my parents, Dave and Sue, your belief in me, that I can be and do anything I want, has proved itself true. To Dave and Laura, congratulations to the new member of the family—claws, whiskers, and all. To Mark, when I imagine a world where we are not friends, all I can picture is sorrow, pain, and misery; fortunately we are not there, but at least we still have schauenfreude. To HERbert, I truly envy you and your cat naps. And finally, as always, to Elvis—your dedication, steadfastness, and determinism has encouraged a whole new generation to eat buckets of chicken and watch three T.V.s simultaneously.

Contents

. . . .

Introduction

Welcome to *TCP/IP Exam Cram*! This book aims to help you get ready to take—and pass—the Microsoft certification test numbered Exam 70-059, titled "Internetworking with Microsoft TCP/IP on Microsoft Windows NT 4.0." In this introduction, we introduce Microsoft's certification programs in general and talk about how the *Exam Cram* series can help you prepare for Microsoft's certification exams.

Exam Cram books help you understand and appreciate the subjects and materials you need to pass Microsoft certification exams. The books are aimed strictly at test preparation and review. They do not teach you everything you need to know about a topic. Instead, we (the authors) present and dissect the questions and problems that you're likely to encounter on a test. We've worked from Microsoft's own training materials, preparation guides, and tests, as well as from a battery of third-party test preparation tools. Our aim is to bring together as much information as possible about Microsoft certification exams.

Nevertheless, to completely prepare yourself for any Microsoft test, we recommend that you begin your studies with some classroom training or that you pick up and read one of the many study guides available from Microsoft and third-party vendors. We also strongly recommend that you install, configure, and fool around with the software or environment that you'll be tested on, because nothing beats hands-on experience and familiarity when it comes to understanding the questions you're likely to encounter on a certification test. Book learning is essential, but hands-on experience is the best teacher of all!

The Microsoft Certified Professional (MCP) Program

The MCP Program currently includes four separate tracks, each of which boasts its own special acronym (as a would-be certificant, you need to have a high tolerance for alphabet soup of all kinds):

➤ **MCPS (Microsoft Certified Product Specialist)** This is the least prestigious of all the certification tracks from Microsoft. Attaining MCPS status requires an individual to pass at least one core operating system exam. Passing any of the major Microsoft operating system exams—including those for Windows 95, Windows NT Workstation, or Windows NT Server—qualifies an individual for MCPS credentials. Individuals can demonstrate proficiency with additional Microsoft products by passing additional certification exams.

➤ **MCSD (Microsoft Certified Solution Developer)** This track is aimed primarily at developers. This credential indicates that those who hold it are able to design and implement custom business solutions around particular Microsoft development tools, technologies, and operating systems. To obtain an MCSD, an individual must demonstrate the ability to analyze and interpret user requirements; select and integrate products, platforms, tools, and technologies; design and implement code and customize applications; and perform necessary software tests and quality assurance operations.

To become an MCSD, an individual must pass a total of four exams: two core exams plus two elective exams. The two core exams are the Microsoft Windows Operating Systems and Services Architecture I and II (WOSSA I and WOSSA II, numbered 70-150 and 70-151). Elective exams cover specific Microsoft applications and languages, including Visual Basic, C++, the Microsoft Foundation Classes, Access, SQL Server, Excel, and more.

➤ **MCT (Microsoft Certified Trainer)** Microsoft Certified Trainers are individuals who are considered competent to deliver elements of the official Microsoft training curriculum, based on technical knowledge and instructional ability. It is necessary for an individual seeking MCT credentials (which are granted on a course-by-course basis) to pass the related certification exam for a course and successfully complete the official Microsoft training in the subject area, as well as to demonstrate teaching ability. This latter criterion may be satisfied by proving that one has already attained training certification from Novell, Banyan, Lotus, the Santa Cruz Operation, or Cisco, or by taking a Microsoft-sanctioned workshop on instruction. Microsoft makes it clear that MCTs are an important cog in the Microsoft training channels. Instructors must be MCTs to teach in any of Microsoft's official training channels, including its affiliated Authorized Technical Education Centers (ATECs), Authorized Academic Training Programs (AATPs), and the Microsoft Online Institute (MOLI).

➤ **MCSE (Microsoft Certified Systems Engineer)** Anyone who possesses a current MCSE is warranted to possess a high level of expertise with Windows NT (either version 3.51 or 4) and other Microsoft operating systems and products. This credential is designed to prepare individuals to plan, implement, maintain, and support information systems and networks built around Microsoft Windows NT and its BackOffice family of products.

To obtain an MCSE, an individual must pass four core operating system exams plus two elective exams. The operating system exams require individuals to demonstrate competence with desktop and server operating systems and with networking components.

At least two Windows NT-related exams must be passed to obtain an MCSE: Implementing and Supporting Windows NT Server (version 3.51 or 4) and Implementing and Supporting Windows NT Server in the Enterprise (version 3.51 or 4). These tests are intended to indicate an individual's knowledge of Windows NT in smaller, simpler networks and in larger, more complex, and heterogeneous networks, respectively.

Two more tests must be passed: networking-and desktop operating system-related. At present, the networking requirement can be satisfied only by passing the Networking Essentials test. The desktop operating system test can be satisfied by passing a Windows 3.1, Windows for Workgroups 3.11, Windows NT Workstation (the version must match whichever core curriculum is pursued), or Windows 95 test.

The two remaining exams are elective exams. The elective exams can be in any number of subject or product areas, primarily BackOffice components. These include tests on SQL Server, SNA Server, Exchange, Systems Management Server, and the like. But it is also possible to test out on electives by taking advanced networking topics like Internetworking with Microsoft TCP/IP (here again, the version of Windows NT involved must match the version for the core requirements taken). As you're already aware, this last item happens to be the focus of this book.

Whatever the mix of tests, individuals must pass six tests to meet the MCSE requirements. It's not uncommon for the entire process to take a year or so, and many individuals find that they must take a test more than once to pass. Our primary goal with the *Exam Cram* series is to make it possible, given proper study and preparation, to pass all of the MCSE tests on the first try.

Finally, certification is an ongoing activity. Once a Microsoft product becomes obsolete, MCSEs (and other MCPs) typically have a 12- to 18-month time frame in which they can become recertified on current product versions. (If individuals do not get recertified within the specified time period, their certification becomes invalid.) Because technology keeps changing and new products continually supplant old ones, this should come as no surprise.

The best place to keep tabs on the MCP Program and its various certifications is on the Microsoft Web site. The current root URL for the MCP Program is Certification Online at www.microsoft.com/Train_Cert/mcp/default.htm. Microsoft's Web site changes frequently, so if this URL doesn't work, try using the Search tool on Microsoft's site with either "MCP" or the quoted phrase "Microsoft Certified Professional Program" as the search string. This will help you find the latest and most accurate information about the company's certification programs. There is also a special CD that contains a copy of the Microsoft Education and Certification Roadmap. The Roadmap covers much of the same information as the Web site and it is updated quarterly. To get your copy of the CD, call Microsoft at 1-800-636-7544, Monday through Friday, 6:30 AM through 7:30 PM Pacific Time.

Taking A Certification Exam

Alas, testing is not free. You'll be charged $100 for each test you take, whether you pass or fail. In the United States and Canada, tests are administered by Sylvan Prometric. Sylvan Prometric can be reached at 1-800-755-3926 or 1-800-755-EXAM, any time from 7:00 AM to 6:00 PM Central Time, Monday through Friday. If you can't get through on this number, try 1-612-896-7000 or 1-612-820-5707.

To schedule an exam, call at least one day in advance. To cancel or reschedule an exam, you must call at least 12 hours before the scheduled test time (or you may be charged). When calling Sylvan Prometric, please have the following information ready for the telesales staffer who handles your call:

➤ Your name, organization, and mailing address.

➤ Your Microsoft Test ID. (For most U.S. citizens, this is your social security number. Citizens of other nations can use their taxpayer IDs or make other arrangements with the order taker.)

➤ The name and number of the exam you wish to take. (For this book, the exam number is 70-059, and the exam name is "Internetworking with Microsoft TCP/IP on Microsoft Windows NT 4.0.")

➤ A method of payment must be arranged. (The most convenient approach is to supply a valid credit card number with sufficient available credit. Otherwise, payments by check, money order, or purchase order must be received before a test can be scheduled. If the latter methods are required, ask your order taker for more details.)

On the day of the test, try to arrive at least 15 minutes before the scheduled time slot. You must bring and supply two forms of identification, one of which one must be a photo ID.

All exams are completely closed book. In fact, you will not be permitted to take anything with you into the testing area; you will be furnished with a blank sheet of paper and a pen. We suggest that you immediately write down the most critical information about the test you're taking on the sheet of paper. *Exam Cram* books provide a brief reference—The Cram Sheet, located in the front of the book—that lists the essential information from the book in distilled form. You will have some time to compose yourself, to record this information, and even to take a sample orientation exam before you must begin the real thing. We suggest you take the orientation test before taking your first exam; they're all more or less identical in layout, behavior, and controls, so you probably won't need to do this more than once.

When you complete a Microsoft certification exam, the software will tell you whether you've passed or failed. All tests are scored on a basis of 1,000 points, and results are broken into several topical areas. Even if you fail, we suggest you ask for—and keep—the detailed report that the test administrator prints out for you. You can use the report to help you prepare for another go-round, if necessary. If you need to retake an exam, you'll have to call Sylvan Prometric, schedule a new test date, and pay another $100.

Tracking MCP Status

As soon as you pass any Microsoft operating system exam, you'll attain Product Specialist (MCPS) status. Microsoft also generates transcripts that indicate the exams you have passed and your corresponding test scores. You can order a transcript by email at any time by sending an email addressed to mcp@msprograms.com. You can also obtain a copy of your transcript by downloading the latest version of the MCT Guide from the Web site and consulting the Key Contacts section for a list of telephone numbers and related contacts.

Once you pass the necessary set of six exams, you'll be certified as an MCSE. Official certification normally takes anywhere from four to six weeks, so don't expect to get your credentials overnight. When the package arrives, it will include a Welcome Kit that contains a number of elements, including:

➤ An MCSE certificate, suitable for framing, along with an MCSE Professional Program membership card and lapel pin.

➤ A license to use the MCP logo, thereby allowing you to use the logo in advertisements, promotions, documents, on letterhead, business cards, and so on. An MCP logo sheet, which includes camera-ready artwork, comes with the license. (Note: Before using any of the artwork, individuals must sign and return a licensing agreement that indicates they'll abide by its terms and conditions.)

➤ A one-year subscription to TechNet, a collection of CDs that includes software, documentation, service packs, databases, and more technical information than you can digest in a month. In our minds, this is the best and most tangible benefit of attaining MCSE status.

➤ A subscription to *Microsoft Certified Professional* magazine, which provides ongoing data about testing and certification activities, requirements, and changes to the program.

➤ A free Priority Comprehensive 10-pack with Microsoft Product Support, and a 25 percent discount on additional Priority Comprehensive 10-packs. This lets you place up to 10 free calls to Microsoft's technical support operation at a higher-than-normal priority level.

➤ A one-year subscription to the Microsoft Beta Evaluation program. This subscription gets you all Microsoft beta products for the next year. (This does not include developer products. You must join the MSDN program or become an MCSD to qualify for developer beta products.)

Many people believe that the benefits of MCSE certification go well beyond the perks that Microsoft provides to newly anointed members of this elite group. We're starting to see more job listings that request or require applicants to have an MCSE, and many individuals who complete the program can qualify for increases in pay or responsibility. As an official recognition of hard work and broad knowledge, MCSE certification is a badge of honor in many IT organizations.

How To Prepare For An Exam

At a minimum, preparing for the TCP/IP exam requires that you obtain and study the following materials:

➤ *Microsoft TCP/IP Training*. Microsoft Press, 1997. ISBN 1-57231-623-3. This boxed set lists for $99.99, and although it's a bit pricey, it does a reasonably good job of covering the test materials.

➤ The exam prep materials, practice tests, and self-assessment exams on the Microsoft Training And Certification Download page (www.microsoft.com/Train_Cert/download/downld.htm). Find the materials, download them, and use them!

➤ This *Exam Cram* book! It's the first and last thing you should read before taking the exam.

In addition, you'll probably find any or all of the following materials useful in your quest for TCP/IP expertise:

➤ **Study Guides** Publishers such as Sybex, New Riders Press, Que (in cooperation with Productivity Point, a well-known training company and Microsoft ATEC), and others all offer so-called MCSE study guides of one kind or another. We've looked at them and found the Sybex and Que titles to be fairly informative and helpful for learning the materials necessary to pass the tests.

➤ *Windows NT Resource Kits* Although neither of these publications (nor their supplements, two of which are available for Windows NT Server at this writing) focuses exclusively on TCP/IP, both *Workstation Resource Kit* and *Server Resource Kit* for Windows NT 4 include valuable additional information about TCP/IP and IP-based or focused software. These products—also available from Microsoft Press, are worth their list prices ($69.95 for Workstation, ISBN 1-57231-343-9, and $149.95 for Server, ISBN 1-57231-344-7), if only for the many additional utilities and capabilities they can add to either operating system's base release.

➤ **Classroom Training** ATECs, AATPs, MOLI, and unlicensed third-party training companies (such as Wave Technologies, American Research Group, Learning Tree, Data-Tech, and others) all offer classroom training on Microsoft TCP/IP. These companies aim to help prepare network administrators to understand Microsoft's TCP/IP implementation and utilities and pass the MCSE tests. Although such training runs upwards of $350 per day in class, most of the individuals lucky enough to partake (including your humble authors, who've even taught such courses) find them to be quite worthwhile.

➤ **Other Publications** You'll find direct references to other publications and resources in this book, but there's no shortage of materials available about Microsoft TCP/IP. To help you sift through some of the publications out there, we end each chapter with a "Need To Know More?" section with pointers to more complete and exhaustive resources covering the chapter's subject matter. This tells you where we suggest you look for further details.

➤ **The TechNet CD** TechNet is a monthly CD subscription available from Microsoft. TechNet includes all the Windows NT BackOffice Resource Kits and their product documentation. In addition, TechNet provides the contents of the Microsoft Knowledge Base and many kinds of software, white papers, training materials, as well as other good stuff. TechNet also contains all service packs, interim release patches, and supplemental driver software released since the last major version for most Microsoft programs and all Microsoft operating systems. A one-year subscription costs $299—worth every penny, if only for the download time it saves.

This set of required and recommended materials represents a nonpareil collection of sources and resources for Microsoft TCP/IP topics and software. In the section that follows, we explain how this book works, and give you some good reasons why this book should be in your required and recommended materials list.

About This Book

Each topical *Exam Cram* chapter follows a regular structure, along with graphical cues about especially important or useful material. Here's the structure of a typical chapter:

➤ **Opening Hotlists** Each chapter begins with lists of the terms, tools, and techniques that you must learn and understand before you can be fully conversant with the chapter's subject matter. We follow the hotlists with one or two introductory paragraphs to set the stage for the rest of the chapter.

➤ **Topical Coverage** After the opening hotlists, each chapter covers a series of at least four topics related to the chapter's subject. Throughout this section, we highlight material most likely to appear on a test using a special Exam Alert layout, like this:

> This is what an Exam Alert looks like. Normally, an Exam Alert stresses concepts, terms, software, or activities that will most likely appear in one or more certification test questions. For that reason, we think any information found offset in Exam Alert format is worthy of unusual attentiveness on your part. Indeed, most of the facts appearing in The Cram Sheet (at the front of this book) appear as Exam Alerts within the text.

Occasionally, you'll see tables called "Vital Statistics." The contents of vital statistics tables are worthy of an extra once-over. These tables contain informational tidbits that might well show up in a test question.

Even if material isn't flagged as an Exam Alert or included in a vital statistics table, *all* the contents of this book are associated, at least tangentially, to something test-related. This book is lean to focus on quick test preparation; you'll find that what appears in the meat of each chapter is critical knowledge.

We have also provided tips that will help build a better foundation of networking knowledge. Although the information may not be on the exam, it is highly relevant and will help you become a better test-taker.

> This is how tips are formatted. Keep your eyes open for these, and you'll become a test guru in no time!

➤ **Exam Prep Questions** This section presents a series of mock test questions and explanations of both correct and incorrect answers. We also try to point out especially tricky questions by using a special icon, like this:

Ordinarily, this icon flags the presence of an especially devious question, if not an outright trick question. Trick questions are calculated to "trap" you if you don't read them carefully, and more than once, at that. Although they're not ubiquitous, such questions make regular appearances in the Microsoft exams. That's why we say exam questions are as much about reading comprehension as they are about knowing TCP/IP material inside out and backwards.

➤ **Details And Resources** Every chapter ends with a section titled "Need To Know More?" It provides direct pointers to Microsoft and third-party resources that offer further details on the chapter's subject matter. In addition, this section tries to rate the quality and thoroughness of each topic's coverage. If you find a resource you like in this collection, use it, but don't feel compelled to use all these resources. On the other hand, we recommend only resources we use on a regular basis, so none of our recommendations will be a waste of your time or money.

The bulk of the book follows this chapter structure slavishly, but there are a few other elements that we'd like to point out: the answer key to the sample test that appears in Chapter 17 and a reasonably exhaustive glossary of TCP/IP-specific and general Microsoft terminology. Finally, look for The Cram Sheet, which appears inside the front cover of this *Exam Cram* book. It is a valuable tool that represents a condensed and compiled collection of facts, figures, and tips that we think you should memorize before taking the test. Because you can dump this information out of your head onto a piece of paper before answering any exam questions, you can master this information by brute force—you need to remember it only long enough to write it down when you walk into the test room. You might even want to look at it in the car or in the lobby of the testing center just before you walk in to take the test.

How To Use This Book

If you're prepping for a first-time test, we've structured the topics in this book to build on one another. Therefore, some topics in later chapters make more sense after you've read earlier chapters. That's why we suggest you read this book from front to back for your initial test preparation. If you need to brush up on a topic or you have to bone up for a second try, use the index or table of contents to go straight to the topics and questions that you need to study. Beyond the tests, we think you'll find this book useful as a tightly focused reference to some of the most important aspects of this essential networking protocol, as implemented in Windows NT 4.

Given all the book's elements and its specialized focus, we've tried to create a tool that you can use to prepare for—and pass—Microsoft Certification Exam 70-059, "Internetworking with Microsoft TCP/IP on Microsoft Windows NT 4.0." Please share your feedback on the book with us, especially if you have ideas about how we can improve it for future test-takers. We'll consider everything you say carefully, and we respond to all suggestions. You can reach us via email at etittel@lanw.com (Ed Tittel), michael@lanw.com (James Michael Stewart), and kurt@hudlogic.com (Kurt Hudson). Please remember to include the title of the book in your message; otherwise, we'll be forced to guess which book you're making a suggestion about. And we don't like to guess—we want to KNOW!

For up-to-date information on certification, online discussions forums, sample tests, content updates, and more, visit the Certification Insider Press Web site at www.examcram.com or the authors' Web site at www.lanw.com/examcram.

Thanks, and enjoy the book!

Microsoft Certification Tests

Terms you'll need to understand:

✓ Radio button

✓ Checkbox

✓ Exhibit

✓ Multiple-choice question formats

✓ Careful reading

✓ Process of elimination

Techniques you'll need to master:

✓ Preparing to take a certification exam

✓ Practicing (to make perfect)

✓ Making the best use of the testing software

✓ Budgeting your time

✓ Saving the hardest questions until last

✓ Guessing (as a last resort)

As experiences go, test-taking is not something that most people anticipate eagerly, no matter how well they're prepared. In most cases, familiarity helps ameliorate test anxiety. In plain English, this means you probably won't be as nervous when you take your fourth or fifth Microsoft certification exam as you will be when you take your first one.

But no matter whether it's your first test or your tenth, understanding the exam-taking particulars (how much time to spend on questions, the setting you'll be in, and so on) and the testing software will help you concentrate on the material rather than on the environment. Likewise, mastering a few basic test-taking skills should help you recognize—and perhaps even out-fox—some of the tricks and gotchas you're bound to find in some of the Microsoft test questions.

In this chapter, we'll explain the testing environment and software, as well as describe some proven test-taking strategies you should be able to use to your advantage. We've compiled this information based on the 40-plus Microsoft certification exams we have taken ourselves, and we've also drawn on the advice of our friends and colleagues, some of whom have also taken more than 30 tests each!

The Testing Situation

When you arrive at the Sylvan Prometric Testing Center where you scheduled your test, you'll need to sign in with a test coordinator. He or she will ask you to produce two forms of identification, one of which must be a photo ID. Once you've signed in and your time slot arrives, you'll be asked to deposit any books, bags, or other items you brought with you, and you'll be escorted into a closed room. Typically, that room will be furnished with anywhere from one to half a dozen computers, and each workstation is separated from the others by dividers designed to keep you from seeing what's happening on someone else's computer.

You'll be furnished with a pen or pencil and a blank sheet of paper, or in some cases, an erasable plastic sheet and an erasable felt-tip pen. You're allowed to write down any information you want on this sheet, and you can write stuff on both sides of the page. We suggest that you memorize as much as possible of the material that appears on The Cram Sheet (inside the front cover of this book) and then write that information down on the blank sheet as soon as you sit down in front of the test machine. You can refer to it anytime you like during the test, but you'll have to surrender the sheet when you leave the room.

Most test rooms feature a wall with a large picture window. This is to permit the test coordinator to monitor the room, to prevent test-takers from talking to one another, and to observe anything out of the ordinary that might go on. The test coordinator will have preloaded the Microsoft certification test you've signed up for—for this book, that's Exam 70-059—and you'll be permitted to start as soon as you're seated in front of the machine.

All Microsoft certification exams permit you to take up to a certain maximum amount of time to complete the test (the test itself will tell you, and it maintains an on-screen counter/clock so that you can check the time remaining anytime you like). Exam 70-059 consists of 58, randomly selected from a pool of questions. You're permitted to take up to 90 minutes to complete the exam.

All Microsoft certification exams are computer generated and use a multiple-choice format. Although this might sound easy, the questions are constructed not just to check your mastery of basic facts and figures about internetworking with Microsoft TCP/IP on Windows NT 4, but they also require you to evaluate one or more sets of circumstances or requirements. Often, you'll be asked to give more than one answer to a question; likewise, you may be asked to select the best or most effective solution to a problem from a range of choices, all of which technically are correct. It's quite an adventure, and it involves real thinking. This book will show you what to expect and how to deal with the problems, puzzles, and predicaments you're likely to find on the test.

Test Layout And Design

A typical test question is depicted in Question 1. It's a multiple-choice question that requires you to select a single correct answer. Following the question is a brief summary of each potential answer and an explanation of why it was either right or wrong.

Question 1

Which of the following correctly describes the function of ARP?

O a. Maps IP addresses to NetBIOS names

O b. Puts frames on the wire

O c. Converts bits into bytes

O d. Maps IP addresses to MAC addresses

The correct answer is d. ARP, the Address Resolution Protocol, is the Internet layer protocol responsible for determining the hardware address (also called a MAC address) that corresponds to a particular IP address. ARP does not map IP addresses to NetBIOS names, put frames on the wire, or convert bits into bytes. Therefore, answers a, b, and c are incorrect.

This sample question corresponds closely to those you'll see on Microsoft certification tests. To select the correct answer during the test, you would position the cursor over the radio button next to answer d and click the left-mouse button to select that particular choice. The only difference between the certification test and this question is that the real questions are not immediately followed by the answer key.

Next, we'll examine a question that requires choosing multiple answers. This type of question provides checkboxes, rather than the radio buttons, for marking all appropriate selections.

Question 2

Which two programming interfaces provide Windows applications with access to the TCP/IP transport protocols? [Choose two]

❑ a. NetBIOS

❑ b. NDIS

❑ c. BSD Sockets

❑ d. Windows Sockets

The correct answers for this question are a and d. NetBIOS and Windows Sockets are the APIs that provide applications with access to the TCP/IP Transport layer protocols. Answer b is incorrect because NDIS (Network Device Interface Specification) is an API designed to facilitate communication between Transport protocol drivers and the underlying network interface drivers. Answer c is incorrect because BSD Sockets was designed to provide Unix applications with access to TCP/IP transport protocols.

For this type of question, one or more answers must be selected to answer the question correctly. As far as we can tell (and Microsoft won't comment), such questions are scored as wrong unless all the required selections are chosen. In other words, a partially correct answer does not result in partial credit when the test is scored. For Question 2, you would have to position the cursor over the checkboxes next to items a and d to obtain credit for a correct answer.

Although there are many forms in which these two basic types of questions can appear, they constitute the foundation upon which all the Microsoft certification exam questions rest. More complex questions may include so-called "exhibits," which are usually screen shots of some Windows NT TCP/IP utility or another. For some of these questions, you'll be asked to make a selection by clicking a checkbox or radio button on the screen shot itself; for others, you'll be expected to use the information displayed therein to guide your answer to the question. Familiarity with the underlying utility is the key to the correct answer.

Other questions involving exhibits may use charts or network diagrams to help document a workplace scenario that you'll be asked to troubleshoot or configure. Paying careful attention to such exhibits is the key to success—be prepared to toggle between the picture and the question as you work. Often, both are complex enough that you might not be able to remember all of either one.

Using Microsoft's Test Software Effectively

A well-known test-taking principle is to read over the entire test from start to finish first, but to answer only those questions that you feel absolutely sure of on the first pass. On subsequent passes, you can dive into more complex questions, knowing how many such questions you have to deal with.

Fortunately, the Microsoft test software makes this approach easy to implement. At the bottom of each question, you'll find a checkbox that permits you to mark that question for a later visit. (Note: Marking questions makes review easier, but you can return to any question by clicking the Forward and Back buttons repeatedly until you get to the question.) As you read each question, if you answer only those you're sure of and mark for review those that you're not, you can keep going through a decreasing list of open questions as you knock the trickier ones off in order.

 There's at least one potential benefit to reading the test over completely before answering the trickier questions: Sometimes, you find information in later questions that sheds more light on earlier ones. Other times, information you read in later questions might jog your memory about Microsoft TCP/IP facts, figures, or behavior that also will help with earlier questions. Either way, you'll come out ahead if you defer those questions about which you're not absolutely sure of the answer(s).

Keep working on the questions until you are absolutely sure of all your answers or until you know you'll run out of time. If there are still unanswered questions, you'll want to zip through them and guess. No answer guarantees no credit for a question, and a guess has at least a chance of being correct. This strategy only works because Microsoft counts blank answers and incorrect answers as equally wrong.

At the very end of your test period, you're better off guessing than leaving questions blank or unanswered.

Taking Testing Seriously

The most important advice we can give you about taking any Microsoft test is this: Read each question carefully! Some questions are deliberately ambiguous; some use double negatives; others use terminology in incredibly precise ways. We've taken numerous practice tests and real tests ourselves, and in nearly every test we've missed at least one question because we didn't read it closely or carefully enough.

Here are some suggestions on how to deal with the tendency to jump to an answer too quickly:

➤ Make sure you read every word in the question. If you find yourself jumping ahead impatiently, go back and start over.

➤ As you read, try to restate the question in your own terms. If you can do this, you should be able to pick the correct answer(s) much more easily.

➤ When returning to a question after your initial read-through, reread every word again—otherwise, the mind falls quickly into a rut. Sometimes, seeing a question afresh after turning your attention elsewhere lets you see something you missed before, but the strong tendency is to see what you've seen before. Try to avoid that tendency at all costs.

➤ If you return to a question more than twice, try to articulate to yourself what you don't understand about the question, why the answers don't appear to make sense, or what appears to be missing. If you chew on the subject for a while, your subconscious might provide the details that are lacking, or you might notice a "trick" that will point to the right answer.

Above all, try to deal with each question by thinking through what you know about the NT TCP/IP utilities, characteristics, behaviors, facts, and figures involved. By reviewing what you know (and what you've written down on your information sheet), you'll often recall or understand things sufficiently to determine the answer to the question.

Question-Handling Strategies

Based on the tests we've taken, a couple of interesting trends in the answers have become apparent. For those questions that take only a single answer, usually two or three of the answers will be obviously incorrect, and two of the answers will be plausible. But, of course, only one can be correct. Unless the answer leaps out at you (and if it does, reread the question to look for a trick—sometimes those are the ones you're most likely to get wrong), begin the process of answering by eliminating those answers that are obviously wrong.

Things to look for in the "obviously wrong" category include spurious menu choices or utility names, nonexistent software options, and terminology you've never seen before. If you've done your homework for a test, no valid information should be completely new to you. In that case, unfamiliar or bizarre terminology probably indicates a totally bogus answer. As long as you're sure what's right, it's easy to eliminate what's wrong.

Numerous questions assume that the default behavior of a particular TCP/IP utility is in effect. It's essential, therefore, to know and understand the default settings for Windows NT TCP/IP. If you know the defaults and understand what they mean, this knowledge will help you cut through many Gordian knots.

Likewise, when dealing with questions that require multiple answers, you must know and select all the correct options to get credit. This, too, qualifies as an example of why "careful reading" is so important.

As you work your way through the test, another counter that Microsoft thankfully provides will come in handy—the number of questions completed and questions outstanding. Budget your time by making sure that you've completed one-fourth of the questions one-quarter of the way through the test period (or 13 questions in the first 22 minutes). Check again three-quarters of the way through (39 questions in the first 66 minutes).

If you're not through with the test after 85 minutes, use the last 5 minutes to guess your way through the remaining questions. Remember, guesses are potentially more valuable than blank answers, because blanks are always wrong, but a guess might turn out to be right. If you haven't a clue with any of the remaining questions, pick answers at random, or choose all a's, b's, and so on. The important thing is to submit a test for scoring that has some answer for every question.

Mastering The Inner Game

In the final analysis, knowledge breeds confidence, and confidence breeds success. If you study the materials in this book carefully and review all of the Exam Prep questions at the end of each chapter, you should be aware of those areas where additional studying is required.

Next, follow up by reading some or all of the materials recommended in the "Need To Know More?" section at the end of each chapter. The idea is to become familiar enough with the concepts and situations that you find in the sample questions to be able to reason your way through similar situations on a real test. If you know the material, you have every right to be confident that you can pass the test.

Once you've worked your way through the book, take the practice test in Chapter 17. This will provide a reality check and will help you identify areas you need to study further. Make sure you follow up and review materials related to the questions you miss before scheduling a real test. Only when you've covered all the ground and feel comfortable with the whole scope of the practice test, should you take a real test.

> **TIP**
> If you take our practice test and don't score at least 75 percent correct, you'll want to practice further. At a minimum, download the Personal Exam Prep (PEP) tests and the self-assessment tests from the Microsoft Training And Certification Web site's download page (its location appears in the next section). If you're more ambitious or better funded, you might want to purchase a practice test from one of the third-party vendors that offers them. We've had good luck with tests from Transcender Corporation and from Self Test Software (the vendors who supply the PEP tests). See the next section in this chapter for contact information.

Armed with the information in this book, and with the determination to augment your knowledge, you should be able to pass the certification exam. But if you don't work at it, you'll spend the test fee more than once before you finally do pass. If you prepare seriously, the execution should go flawlessly. Good luck!

Additional Resources

By far, the best source of information about Microsoft certification tests comes from Microsoft itself. Because its products and technologies—and the tests that go with them—change frequently, the best place to go for exam-related information is online.

If you haven't already visited the Microsoft Training And Certification pages, do so right now. As we're writing this chapter, the Training And Certification home page resides at www.microsoft.com/Train_Cert/ (see Figure 1.1).

> *Note: It might not be there by the time you read this, or it may have been replaced by something new and different, because things change regularly on the Microsoft site. Should this happen, please read the sidebar titled "Coping With Change On The Web," later in this chapter.*

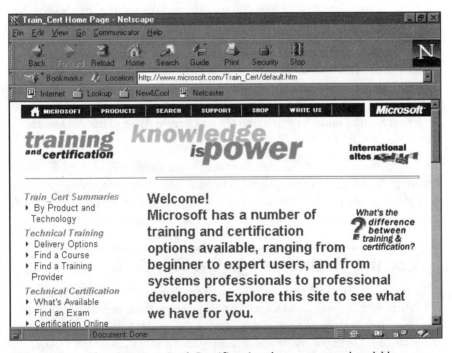

Figure 1.1   The Training And Certification home page should be your starting point for further investigation of the most current exam and preparation information.

The menu options in the left column of the home page point to the most important sources of information in the Training And Certification pages. Here's what to check out:

➤ **Train_Cert Summaries/By Product and Technology** Use this to jump to product-based summaries of all classroom education materials, training materials, study guides, and other information for specific products. Under the heading of Microsoft Windows/Windows NT, you'll find an entire page of information about Windows NT training and certification. This tells you a lot about your training and preparation options, and it mentions all the tests that relate to Windows NT.

➤ **Technical Certification/Find an Exam** This pulls up a search tool that lets you list all Microsoft exams as well as locate all exams pertinent to any Microsoft certification (MCPS, MCSE, MCT, and so on) or those exams that cover a particular product. This tool is quite useful not only to examine the options, but also to obtain specific test preparation information, because each exam has its own associated preparation guide. For this test, be sure to grab the one for 70-059.

➤ **Site Tools/Downloads** Here, you'll find a list of the files and practice tests that Microsoft makes available to the public. These include several items worth downloading, especially the Certification Update, the Personal Exam Prep (PEP) tests, various assessment exams, and a general Exam Study Guide. Try to make time to peruse these materials before taking your first test.

Of course, these are just the high points of what's available in the Microsoft Training And Certification pages. As you browse through them—and we strongly recommend that you do—you'll probably find other things we didn't mention here that are every bit as interesting and compelling.

Coping With Change On The Web

Sooner or later, all the specifics we've shared with you about the Microsoft Training And Certification pages, and all the other Web-based resources we mention throughout the rest of this book, will go stale or be replaced by newer information. In some cases, the URLs you find here might lead you to their replacements; in other cases, the URLs will go nowhere, leaving you with the dreaded "404 File not found" error message.

When that happens, please don't give up! There's always a way to find what you want on the Web—if you're willing to invest some time and energy. To begin with, most large or complex Web sites—and Microsoft's qualifies on both counts—offer a search engine. Looking back at Figure 1.1, you'll see that a Search button appears along the top edge of the page. As long as you can get to the site itself (and we're pretty sure that it will stay at www.microsoft.com for a long while yet), you can use this tool to help you find what you need.

The more particular or focused you can make a search request, the more likely it is that the results will include information you can use. For instance, you can search the string "training and certification" to produce a lot of data about the subject in general, but if you're looking for the Preparation Guide for Exam 70-059, "Internetworking with Microsoft TCP/IP on Windows NT 4.0," you'll be more likely to get there quickly if you use a search string such as this:

```
Exam 70-059 AND preparation guide
```

Likewise, if you want to find the Training and Certification downloads, try a search string such as this one:

```
training and certification AND download page
```

Finally, don't be afraid to use general search tools such as www.search.com, www.altavista.digital.com, or www.excite.com to search for related information. Even though Microsoft offers the best information about its certification exams online, there are plenty of third-party sources of information, training, and assistance in this area that do not have to follow a party line like Microsoft does. The bottom line is this: If you can't find something where the book says it lives, start looking around. If worse comes to worst, you can always email us! We just might have a clue.

Third-Party Test Providers

Transcender Corporation is located at 242 Louise Avenue, Nashville, TN, 37203-1812. You can reach the company by phone at 1-615-726-8779, or by fax at 1-615-320-6594. Trancender's URL is www.transcender.com; you can download an order form for the materials online, but it must be mailed or faxed to Transcender for purchase. We've found these practice tests, which cost between $89 and $179 if purchased individually (with discounts available for packages containing multiple tests), to be pricey but useful.

SelfTest Software is located at 4651 Woodstock Road, Suite 203-384, Roswell, GA, 30075. The company can be reached by phone at 1-770-641-9719 or 1-800-200-6446, and by fax at 1-770-641-1489. Visit the Web site at www.stsware.com; you can even order the wares online. STS's tests are cheaper than Transcender's—$69 when purchased individually; $59 each when two or more are purchased simultaneously—but they are otherwise quite comparable, which makes them a good value.

Concepts And Planning: TCP/IP And Windows NT 4

2

Terms you'll need to understand:

- √ ARPANet
- √ RFC (Request For Comments)
- √ IAB (Internet Architecture Board)
- √ OSI (Open System Interconnection)
- √ Ports
- √ Sockets
- √ TCP Sliding Windows
- √ Application layer
- √ Transport layer
- √ Internet layer
- √ Network Interface layer
- √ NetBIOS
- √ Windows Sockets

Techniques you'll need to master

- √ Explaining IP layers
- √ Comparing IP layers to OSI layers
- √ Describing IP interfaces

This chapter explains the basic concepts of Microsoft's implementation of TCP/IP to provide you with a foundation for further study. Although some of the more conceptual topics that we cover in this chapter may not appear on the exam, they are important to understand to set a solid knowledge of the Microsoft TCP/IP protocol suite. We introduce the major components of the TCP/IP protocol suite and explain how each one works individually. We also discuss the role each component plays within the overall architecture of the Windows NT TCP/IP protocol stack.

TCP/IP: Explored And Explained

TCP/IP is not a single protocol, nor is it, as its name might suggest, a pair of protocols. TCP/IP is actually a suite of protocols. In other words, it's a large group of protocols that work together. The TCP/IP designers' original intent was to create a protocol that could traverse various heterogeneous network environments while having the ability to take multiple routes to a final destination. This flexibility was crucial. TCP/IP, originally called NCP (Network Control Protocol), was a product of an experimental project commissioned by the Department of Defense for ARPANet (Advanced Research Project Agency Network) as an experimental protocol that traveled over packet-switched networks. The goal was to ensure that if a single part of the network became damaged or unreachable, transmission of critical data would continue to reach its destination on the network through alternate routes.

Despite its roots in the defense community, the development and evolution of TCP/IP cannot be attributed to any one group of individuals. TCP/IP is nonproprietary, and it's the accepted communications protocol on the Internet. Like other matters related to the Internet, TCP/IP standards are publicly available and published as RFCs (Request For Comments—see the following section) that are maintained by the Internet Activities Board (IAB).

The IAB allows any individual or company to submit or evaluate an RFC. RFCs can contain a variety of information; one use of RFCs is to publish proposals or new ideas for standards that might add to or change the functionality of the TCP/IP protocol suite in some way. RFCs are posted to the Internet for public review and are also reviewed by the IETF (Internet Engineering Task Force), a division of the IAB. After an appropriate amount of discussion and scrutiny, a newly proposed draft can be made into a standard that will then be adopted by the entire Internet development community. Because TCP/IP is based on open, nonproprietary standards, it has been scrutinized and revised by numerous people from all over the world, and has thus been continuously developed and improved since its inception.

TCP/IP is based on the idea of an open system (nonproprietary) model. With regard to system architecture, TCP/IP's functionality maps loosely to the OSI (Open Systems Interconnection) Reference Model, a basic system architectural reference designed for programmers to provide a common framework and design for network protocols. By using the OSI Model, protocol designers can ensure that the protocols they design meet at least the basic levels of functionality and that there is some degree of standardization between their implementation of a protocol and someone else's. Microsoft's TCP/IP is compliant with RFC-published TCP/IP standards. However, the Microsoft implementation includes support for a number of features not found in other versions of TCP/IP.

Request For Comments (RFCs)

As mentioned earlier, one way that RFCs are used is to document Internet standards. Keep in mind that the RFCs that actually document standards are merely a subset of all the RFCs that exist. In other words, all Internet standards are documented by at least one RFC, but not all RFCs become Internet standards.

A number of different types of RFCs exist, including FYIs, Drafts, and STDs (Standards). Anyone can submit an RFC or make comments in support of, or against, a current RFC. The IETF then makes this documentation available to the public. If the RFC is a proposal for a new Internet protocol or service, it is reviewed by the IETF and recommendations for revisions are made. To allow ample time for review and revision of an RFC, there is a minimum six-month waiting period before a Proposed Standard can become a Draft Standard; there's then an additional four-month time period before a Draft Standard can become a Standard.

RFCs are referenced by a specific number, such as RFC 1880 "Internet Official Protocol Standards." These numbers are issued sequentially and are never reused. If a current Standard is revised, a new number is issued to the revised Standard, and the older version becomes obsolete. Always make sure you have the most recent RFC on any topic you are researching. RFC 1880, for example, contains an index of the most current RFCs for Internet Standards. To locate a specific RFC, or to learn more about RFCs in general, you can visit the InterNIC at www.internic.net or one of the many search engines available on the Web, such as Search.Com at www.search.com, and search for "RFC."

The OSI Model And TCP/IP

Although various protocols are available for computer data transmission, all network communications protocols must provide for certain core functions.

These functions may be implemented differently from vendor to vendor, but they will generally all share a few basic characteristics. The Open Systems Interconnection Reference Model was created by the International Organization for Standardization (ISO) to provide a basic model on which all protocols can be modeled. The OSI Model has been used in practice, but it's generally used as a theoretical prototype that charts and defines the building blocks of a good network protocol system. Most networking protocols in use today—for example, TCP/IP or Novell's IPX/SPX—contain all or part of the basic functions outlined in the OSI Model.

Having this type of standard architectural model provides several benefits. It provides a general framework to guide programmers who develop protocol stacks. It allows all members of the computer networking community, both proprietary and nonaffiliated, to be on the "same page" when discussing the common layers of functionality inherent to all protocol systems. Also, in an ideal situation, the very modularity of a layered protocol concept would allow for one obsolete functional block of code to be replaced with an improved version of the same functional block—without having to rework the entire stack. This interchangeable, modular quality can help to interface networking software supplied by two different vendors.

Before the OSI Reference Model was recognized as a valid model for protocol design, most vendors created their own proprietary protocols with very little concern for interoperability with other vendors' products. However, as more and more consumers began to embrace the idea of open standards, proprietary standards began to lose out in the market. Interoperability became increasingly important; hence, the need for a standard model, such as OSI, became obvious. For example, if two vendors both decided to develop their own versions of a protocol, and they both decided to use the OSI Model as a reference, at the very least, both protocols would be relatively modular in design, with distinct responsibilities assigned to each of the defined functional blocks of both protocols. And, although the OSI Model itself might not guarantee interoperability between two implementations of the same protocol, it is a good framework within which to begin development.

Layer By Layer

The OSI Model is divided into seven layers, and each layer has a specific responsibility. This is not to say that a protocol based on the OSI Model has seven distinct parts, or only seven specific functions. As mentioned earlier, these layers merely represent the types of functions that a protocol should support, and they arrange the functional blocks in a logical fashion, with a top and a bottom. Note that the top of the model represents functions that occur nearest the user or the application, and the bottom of the model represents those functions that occur nearest the physical network or network interfaces.

The following sections provide an explanation of the different roles and responsibilities handled by each layer of the OSI Reference Model, which is shown in Figure 2.1.

➤ **Layer 7: Application** This is the top layer of the OSI Model. It is responsible for allowing applications to gain network access. User applications and system services generally gain network access by interacting with a process running at this layer of the OSI.

➤ **Layer 6: Presentation** This layer of the OSI works closely with the Application layer. Its primary responsibility is to ensure that data being passed up to the Application layer is either converted to, or is already in, a format that will be understood by the Application layer's processes.

➤ **Layer 5: Session** The Session layer is responsible for establishing, maintaining, and terminating communications among applications or processes running across a network.

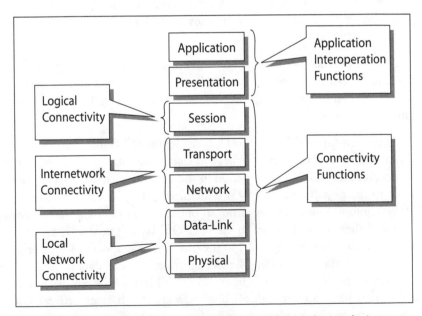

Figure 2.1   The seven layers of the OSI Model and their relative functions.

➤ **Layer 4: Transport** The Transport layer is responsible for the transmission of messages from the sending host to the final receiving destination. It is responsible for creating a virtual circuit between two points on the network as well as ensuring the integrity of the data (if the lower levels or protocols do not provide this service).

➤ **Layer 3: Network** This layer is responsible for routing packets through multiple networks. The Network layer operates without regard to the underlying protocols in use, and because of this, devices, such as routers, operating at this level can be used to connect networks that use different Data Link and Physical layer technologies.

➤ **Layer 2: Data Link** This layer was originally created as a single functional layer. However, the need became apparent to divide the Data Link layer into two sublayers—the Logical Link Control (LLC) sublayer and the Media Access Control (MAC) sublayer. Together, these two sublayers are responsible for moving packets onto and off of the network. The MAC sublayer is specifically concerned with obtaining access to the network at an appropriate time, such as when no other machines are communicating or when permission to access the network has been specifically given. At this layer, bits and bytes are assembled into frames, or vice versa. The LLC sublayer packages the bytes it has received from the MAC sublayer below it into a format readable by the Network layer above it.

➤ **Layer 1: Physical** The Physical layer is concerned with the physical method by which the actual bits and bytes are being sent and received. This is the layer where hardware, connectors, cable length, and signaling specifications are defined.

To simplify how the OSI Model works, consider the following example: When the Application layer receives a package of electronic data from an application or service, it processes that information in some way, adds a header, and passes it down to the next layer of the OSI Model, which is the Presentation layer. The Presentation layer then performs an operation on the data, adds its own header, and then passes it down to the next OSI layer. The data is eventually passed all the way down the model to the physical media, with each layer performing an operation and adding header information. The data is then transmitted across the network to another machine. This machine receives the data and passes it back up through all of the layers. Each layer processes and removes its respective header information and passes the data up to the next layer, as shown in Figure 2.2.

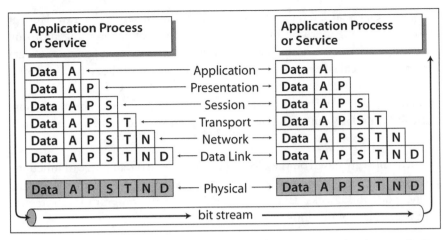

Figure 2.2   The peer-level communication that occurs between similar layers of the OSI Model on separate nodes of the network.

Each layer of the OSI is only aware of the layers directly above and below it. Also, each layer maintains logical communication with a corresponding layer on another machine and is unaware of the underlying processes being performed by other layers.

Communication that occurs near the bottom of the OSI Model occurs as simple bits and bytes or as a stream of bytes. The data near the bottom of the model is generally handled as raw data or as frames of data. However, as the data moves up the model, the payload of numerous frames of data is recombined into a meaningful order. Bits become bytes, bytes become words and complex data, and words and data eventually become whole ideas, sentences, or even documents before they are handed up to the application or user.

The OSI Model's Functionality

As mentioned earlier in this chapter, the layering of functionality helps to make OSI-based protocols very modular. The functions of these types of protocols are very compartmentalized, so that rather than having a programmer write one huge monolithic chuck of code, several separate, smaller pieces of code (functional blocks) can be written to provide the same functionality. Again, this modularity has the benefit of allowing for easy updating and interchanging of specific parts of the code.

For example, consider a case where a programmer develops a new TCP/IP protocol stack using the modular approach of the OSI Reference Model. He then decides, a year later, that there's a more efficient way to lay raw data out onto the network. Because of the modular design of his existing protocol, rewriting and recompiling the parts of the protocol stack that handle the Data Link and Physical layer responsibilities (usually the job of the network adapter driver) is very easy. However, if he had not followed the OSI Model and had created his protocol by writing one huge chuck of code, it would be much more difficult to update the protocol; it might even be necessary to completely rewrite it.

Protocol software based on the OSI Model includes a broad range of functionality, from the NIC driver, to the software that transports the information across the network and checks data integrity, and on to the program that interacts with the actual applications.

Not all software programs written for use with network protocols include all the functions defined in the OSI Model. For example, one company might manufacture only network cards. If this is so, then it will not want to be concerned with how one application speaks to another. The design of the OSI Model allows this company to focus on the development of the hardware and software at the bottom of the model while allowing someone else to design the software that will operate at a higher level of the model.

An OSI Analogy

The OSI Model works much like our modern postal service. Assume for a minute that you are an application running on a computer that needs to speak with another application that resides on a different computer across the network (in this case the network will be the many transports of the U.S. Postal Service). The first step in sending your information to the other application would be to write a letter; place it in an envelope with a name, address, and correct postage; and then drop it in the mailbox. At this point, you probably don't care (and may not know) how the letter gets to its final destination—your primary concern is only that it gets there somehow.

From there, the envelope is picked up by a postal worker and placed into a mail bag for delivery to the local post office. The letter is then routed to another post office by car, truck, van, rail, or air—depending on priority—and re-sorted. From there, it is usually placed in another postal worker's mailbag and delivered to the recipient's door. Again, you generally do not concern yourself with the exact means of transportation of your mail—you just know that when you follow the correct "protocols" and place the mail in your mailbox, it usually arrives at its destination.

In this way, only those responsible for a particular leg of the trip need to be concerned with how information gets from point A to point B. If part of the process needs to be changed to allow for newer technology or a better implementation of a process, only that piece needs to be changed. All the other processes and protocols in place do not need to be modified and can continue to run as normal.

Fortunately, Microsoft has developed its implementation of TCP/IP in accordance with the standards. Because TCP/IP follows a modular reference model much like the OSI, Microsoft's TCP/IP (MS TCP/IP) is modular as well. However, Microsoft has added some extra features and a couple of additional interfaces to its version of TCP/IP. Additions include extended support for NetBIOS (used extensively by Windows applications and services), TDI (Transport Driver Interface), and NDIS (Network Device Interface Specification) interfaces. These add-ins make it easier for independent software vendors (ISVs) and independent hardware vendors (IHVs) to write applications and drivers for MS TCP/IP.

Microsoft's TCP/IP: Architectural Overview

Microsoft's implementation of TCP/IP actually maps to the four-layer TCP/IP Reference Model instead of a seven-layer model like the OSI, as shown in Figure 2.3.

This four-layer model does not leave out any of the functionality of its seven-layer cousin, the OSI Model. It simply includes more functionality within fewer layers. You can see from Figure 2.3 that the Application layer of the TCP/IP Reference Model maps to the Application, Presentation, and Session layers of the OSI Model. The Transport layer of the TCP/IP Reference Model maps to its respective layer of the OSI Model. The Internet layer of the TCP/IP Reference Model and the Network layer of the OSI Model perform the same functions. The Network Interface layer of the TCP/IP Reference Model maps to the Data Link and the Physical layers of the OSI Model.

Application Layer

The Application layer of the TCP/IP Reference Model is where applications and some services gain access to the network. It's their window to the rest of the world. Two different APIs (Application Programming Interfaces) provide access to the TCP/IP transport protocols—Windows Sockets and NetBIOS,

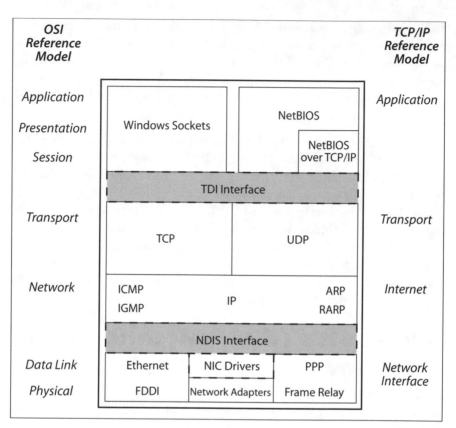

Figure 2.3 The layers of the OSI Model and how they map to different areas of Microsoft's TCP/IP, and the four layers of the TCP/IP Reference Model and how they map to Microsoft's TCP/IP.

which are discussed in the following sections. We also discuss the Transport Driver Interface (TDI), which lets application programmers create components for the Session layer without having direct knowledge of the underlying Transport components.

> An API is used to provide a common interface that programmers can use when they write applications. For example, if one programmer writes a protocol that works with the Windows Sockets interface and another writes an application that works with the Windows Sockets interface, both the protocol and the application can work together through that common interface, which is Windows Sockets.

Windows Sockets Interface

Windows Sockets, or WinSock, as it is commonly called, is a networking API designed to facilitate communication among different TCP/IP applications and protocol stacks. As mentioned previously, many people develop applications for use with TCP/IP or their own specific implementations of TCP/IP. Windows Sockets is based on the original sockets API created for the BSD Unix operating system. It's designed to provide a common ground for applications and protocols existing near the top of the TCP/IP Reference Model.

NetBIOS Interface

Most of the services and applications that run within the Windows operating system use the NetBIOS interface for IPC (Interprocess Communications) to allow for the use of NetBIOS names. For example, when you want to connect to the Accounts share on SALES1, you type "\\SALES1\Accounts". This naming convention is known as the UNC (Universal Naming Convention), and it uses NetBIOS names and resolution as opposed to Internet domain names and DNS (Domain Name Service—covered in detail in Chapter 9) for name resolution.

NetBIOS performs three primary functions:

➤ NetBIOS name resolution

➤ NetBIOS Datagram service

➤ NetBIOS Session service

NetBIOS names are either resolved by broadcast queries to the local network or through the use of a NetBIOS Name Server (NBNS). Most larger networks utilize WINS (Windows Internet Name Service), Microsoft's implementation of NBNS, to perform NetBIOS name resolution. This allows for point-to-point resolution of NetBIOS names and reduces the need for broadcasts on the local network. If WINS is not available or if a particular computer is not configured to use WINS for name resolution, then a broadcast is sent out over the local network segment. WINS is discussed in greater detail in Chapter 12, "Windows Internet Name Service."

NetBIOS Datagram services are responsible for sending and receiving information via broadcasts and connectionless datagrams. Because these transmissions are connectionless, they are considered unreliable. There's no guarantee that the destination host will receive the information. This sender will not wait for an acknowledgment of receipt nor will it try to resend the information.

NetBIOS Session services are responsible for sending and receiving information through the use a reliable two-way connection, called a *session*. When a session is established, both machines involved in the communication agree to communicate with one another and decide what port or socket to use to ensure that all communication is reliable.

Transport Driver Interface (TDI)

The Transport Driver Interface is an actual programming interface that occurs at the boundary between the Session layer protocol(s) components and the Transport layer components. It allows a programmer to create a component for the Session layer without having direct knowledge of the underlying Transport components, and vice versa. This interface is specific to Microsoft's implementation of TCP/IP.

Transport Layer

The Transport layer of the TCP/IP Reference Model is responsible for the establishment and maintenance of end-to-end communication between two hosts. Its primary responsibilities are to provide acknowledgment of receipt, flow control, and sequencing and retransmission of packets.

Depending on the type of service needed by the application, either TCP (Transmission Control Protocol) or UDP (User Datagram Protocol) can be used. TCP is generally used when an application needs to transmit large amounts of data and ensure that the data gets to the recipient correctly and in a timely fashion. Applications and services that are sending smaller amounts of data and do not need an acknowledgment of receipt use UDP, which is a connectionless protocol.

Transmission Control Protocol (TCP)

TCP is responsible for the reliable transmission of data from one node on a network to another. It creates a connection-oriented session, or virtual circuit, between two machines. For TCP to establish a connection with another machine, it creates and sends a packet requesting a connection to the destination machine, and it then waits to see if that machine is available for communication. If the destination machine is online and listening, it responds with a packet of its own saying, "I am available for a conversation and would like to hear more from you." To which the first machine responds with, "Fine, here is the rest of the information." This process of establishing a communication session between two machines is called the three-way handshake. It is referred to as a three-way handshake because three steps must be taken:

1. The requesting client sends a segment (packet) specifying the port number that the client wishes to use and the client's initial sequence number (ISN) to the server.

2. The server responds with a segment containing the server's ISN and a separate acknowledgment of the client's ISN plus 1.

3. The client must acknowledge the server's ISN, plus 1.

The three-way handshake process establishes the port number to be used and the beginning sequence numbers from both sides.

For machines to establish and maintain connections with each other, they must exchange certain vital information. Each TCP packet that is sent contains a source and destination TCP port number, a sequence number for messages that must be broken into smaller pieces, and a checksum to ensure that information is sent without error. Additionally, each packet also contains an acknowledgment number that tells the sending machine which pieces of the message have arrived at their destination. The packet also includes a TCP Sliding Windows metric to allow for flow control between the two machines.

Ports, Sockets, And Sliding Windows

Each process that uses TCP/IP must have a protocol port number to reference the location of a particular application or process on each machine. An application can be configured to run on almost any of the available 65,535 ports. However, the most commonly used TCP/IP applications and services use the first 1,023 of all available ports. These default, or "well-known," ports are assigned to each server-side protocol by the IANA (Internet Assigned Numbers Authority), whereas the client-side port numbers are assigned dynamically by the application initiating communication.

For example, when establishing a Telnet session with another machine, you generally connect to the "well-known" TCP port 23 on the host machine, and your client dynamically assigns a port number for the server to use when communicating with your machine.

A port is actually a subset of a socket. Sockets are used by services and applications that need to establish a connection with another host(s). Sockets consist of both an IP address and a port number.

An application creates a socket by combining an IP address and a protocol port number. If an application needs to guarantee the delivery of information, it will choose the connection-oriented service (TCP); if not, it will choose to use the connectionless service (UDP). This information is then passed down the

TCP/IP layers and sent as a broadcast or directed message (to a specific computer) on the network. If the computer is establishing a session, the connection will be formed using the specified socket.

"Sliding Window" is a term used to describe the variable sizes of the sending and receiving TCP buffers and the mechanism used to control how full each of these buffers gets. The Sliding Window's size can be used to regulate how much information is passed over a TCP connection before an acknowledgment is returned to the sender.

 If your network is used to transfer large amounts of data, such as digital video or audio, you might realize a performance increase by increasing the TCP Window Size. However, if you are running TCP/IP over a slow WAN link, you might want to reduce the TCP Window Size. For more information, see Microsoft TechNet Article Q140552 or search on "TCP Window Size."

User Datagram Protocol (UDP)

UDP is another Transport layer protocol responsible for end-to-end transmission of data on a network. Unlike TCP, UDP is a connectionless protocol. No session is established; it simply makes a best-effort attempt when sending data. UDP does not attempt to verify that the destination host actually receives the information being sent.

UDP is used by applications that send small amounts of data and do not require guaranteed delivery. NetBIOS Name service, which sends very small amounts of data at a time, and NetBIOS Datagram service, both utilize the UDP protocol.

UDP also uses port numbers to identify a particular process at a specified IP address. However, UDP ports are different than TCP ports and can therefore use the same port numbers without interfering with other services.

Internet Layer

The Internet layer is responsible for routing data within and among different networks. Routers, which are protocol dependent, function at this layer of the model and are used to forward packets from one network, or segment, to another.

Internet Protocol (IP)

IP is a connectionless protocol that utilizes datagrams to send data from one network to the next. IP does not expect an ACK (acknowledgment) to ensure the destination host is receiving the packets it is forwarding. Acknowledgments, along with retransmission of packets, are left up to protocols and processes running at higher levels in the model.

For example, when an application uses UDP over IP (neither of these protocols is reliable), it becomes the job of the application or service to ensure that packets arrive at their destination, and in the correct order. This provides for quicker transmission and less overhead for the network, but requires additional overhead for the application.

Each IP packet contains source and destination addresses, a protocol identifier (which helps IP route the packet to the appropriate transport protocol), a checksum, and a TTL (time to live). The TTL is a metric that tells each router between a source and a destination how long the packet has been on the network. Each time the packet crosses a router and is forwarded to another network, the TTL is decreased by one unit (a second) or the time that the packet was queued for delivery on that router, whichever is greater.

This prevents incorrect or damaged packets from looping around a network indefinitely. If such packets were allowed to roam freely, network bandwidth would eventually decrease to a level that would prevent viable communication.

IP uses a process called "ANDing" to determine if an IP address is local or remote. If the destination address is local, IP asks ARP (Address Resolution Protocol) for the hardware address of the destination machine. This address is then used to forward the information directly to its destination, rather than broadcasting it to the local network.

If the IP address has been determined to be a remote address, IP checks its local routing table for a route to the destination host. If one exists, IP uses that route to send the packet. If a route does not exist in the local routing table, IP forwards the packet to the local default gateway. IP routing is discussed in greater detail in Chapter 6, "Implementing IP Routing."

The default gateway examines the destination address. If the address is local to one of the router's interfaces, the router uses ARP to forward the packet to its final destination. If the router determines that the destination address is remote, it decrements the TTL by at least one, calculates a new checksum, and forwards the packet to its own default gateway. This process repeats itself until the packet reaches its destination or the TTL reaches zero.

Address Resolution Protocol (ARP)

Address Resolution Protocol is the Internet layer protocol responsible for determining the hardware address (also called a MAC address) that corresponds to a particular IP address. This process is referred to as "IP address resolution".

Before an IP packet can be forwarded to another host, the hardware address of the receiving machine must be known. ARP first checks its own cache for an IP/hardware address mapping. If one is found, the packet is sent directly to the destination host using its hardware address. All other machines on the network will see this packet, but they will not process it because it is not addressed to them.

If no mapping is found in the ARP cache, ARP sends an ARP request broadcast. Hardware addresses are in a hexadecimal format; the hardware address for a broadcast is FF-FF-FF-FF. The message in this broadcast looks something like, "Hey, is anyone out there using the W.X.Y.Z IP address? If so, please send your hardware address directly to me at A-B-C-D hardware address." Every machine on the local network then processes the packet to determine whether or not it is using the IP address being sought by the host that sent the ARP request. If one of the machines on the local network is using that IP address, it will create and send a response packet indicating that it is the host being sought and that it will include its hardware address in the transmission. This information is then used by the sending host to transmit the rest of the data directly to the recipient.

If the sending machine receives a response, it places the mapping into the ARP cache for future use and then forwards the packet. If no response is received, ARP repeats this entire process to obtain the hardware address of the local default gateway and then forwards the packet for routing to another network. ARP is discussed in greater detail in Chapter 7, "IP Address Resolution."

Internet Control Message Protocol (ICMP)

The Internet Control Message Protocol is used by IP and other higher level protocols to send and receive status reports about the information being transmitted. It is commonly used between two routers to control how fast information flows between the two systems. If a router gets bogged down with traffic from other hosts, it can send a source quench message—an ICMP error that may be generated by a system if it receives datagrams at a rate that is too fast to process—to the router from which it is receiving data. This control message asks the sending machine to send information at a slower rate.

Internet Group Management Protocol (IGMP)

Hosts on a local network use the Internet Group Management Protocol to register themselves in a group. The routers on the local network maintain the group information. The routers on the network use this group information to send multicast data to all hosts registered in a particular group.

"Multicasting," similar to broadcasting, is a method of sending data to multiple hosts simultaneously. This technology is used by applications such as Microsoft's NetShow, a program used to send sound and image streams to a client application, which can be used to simulcast meetings and events over the Internet.

Network Interface Layer

This layer of the TCP/IP Reference Model is responsible for delivery of IP datagrams. It works closely with ARP to determine the appropriate header information to add to each frame. It then creates a frame suitable for the type of network being used, such as Ethernet, Token Ring, or ATM, drops the IP datagram into the payload area of the frame, and sends the data.

Exam Prep Questions

Question 1

Choose the option that best defines TCP/IP.

○ a. A protocol designed by Microsoft to allow information to be routed among heterogeneous network environments.

○ b. A protocol designed by the IAB to allow many different hardware and software vendors to access the Internet.

○ c. A suite of protocols that allows for communication among different types of applications running on various platforms and in various network environments.

○ d. A suite of protocols designed by Microsoft to allow everyday people to access resources on the Internet.

The correct answer for this question is c. TCP/IP allows for network communication among applications and services running on almost any platform, including Unix, Windows, Macintosh and others. TCP/IP was not designed by Microsoft, although Microsoft did create its own implementation of this protocol. Therefore, answers a and d are incorrect. And, although the IAB and its subcommittee, the IETF, are involved in the TCP/IP standards process, they did not design TCP/IP themselves. Therefore, answer b is incorrect as well.

Question 2

Which of the following statements about RFCs are correct? [Check all correct answers]

❑ a. RFCs are referenced by a specific number, such as RFC 1880.

❑ b. RFC numbers are assigned sequentially and are never reused.

❑ c. RFC stands for "Requested Format of Comments."

❑ d. When a standard outlined in an RFC is revised, a new number is issued.

The correct answers for this question are a, b, and d. All RFCs are issued a number by which they can be referenced. These numbers are assigned sequentially by an independent organization and are never reused. When a standing RFC is changed or revised, a new number is issued, and the older documents pertaining to that standard become obsolete. RFC is an acronym for "Request For Comments." Therefore, answer c is incorrect.

Question 3

Each of the following statements list layers of the OSI Reference Model and the respective layers of the TCP/IP Reference Model. Which of the following statements incorrectly maps corresponding layers.

○ a. OSI Application, Presentation, Session, and TCP/IP Application

○ b. OSI Transport and TCP/IP Transport

○ c. OSI Network and TCP/IP Network Interface

○ d. OSI Data Link, Physical and TCP/IP Network Interface

The correct answer for this question is c. The Network layer of the OSI Model corresponds to the Internet (work) layer of the TCP/IP Reference Model. The other answers are all correct. For a review of corresponding layers of the OSI and TCP/IP Reference Models, take another look at Figure 2.3.

Question 4

Which two programming interfaces provide Windows applications with access to the TCP/IP transport protocols? [Check two]

❑ a. NetBIOS

❑ b. NDIS

❑ c. BSD Sockets

❑ d. Windows Sockets

The correct answers for this question are a and d. NetBIOS and Windows Sockets are the APIs that provide applications with access to the TCP/IP transport layer protocols. Answer b is incorrect, because NDIS (Network Device Interface Specification) is an API designed to facilitate communication between transport protocol drivers and the underlying network interface drivers. Answer c is incorrect, because BSD Unix Sockets was designed to provide Unix applications with access to TCP/IP transport protocols.

Question 5

You are thinking about creating an application that will require a constant end-to-end connection with another machine that is running a corresponding service. You do not want to include code in your program to ensure that data is arriving at its destination in an orderly and timely fashion. With these requirements in mind, which of the following protocols is most appropriate for use with your application?

- O a. TCP
- O b. UDP
- O c. ARP
- O d. ICMP

The correct answer for this question is a. The Transmission Control Protocol (TCP) provides a "reliable" connection-oriented session, over IP, with another client or server on the network. Answer b is incorrect, because User Datagram Protocol (UDP) is "unreliable" and only makes a "best-effort" attempt when sending information. Answers c and d are also incorrect. ARP is used by IP to resolve IP addresses to hardware addresses, and it does not provide for the "reliable" transmission of data. ICMP is also used by IP to send error and flow-control messages to a client, and it does not provide for the "reliable" transmission of data.

Question 6

Which of the following statements best describes a socket?

- O a. A number used to identify the location of a process on a remote host.
- O b. A port number used to identify the location of a process on a remote host.
- O c. A random number generated by a server that provides an application with access to a process on a remote host.
- O d. The combination of a port number and an IP address used to provide an application or service with access to a process on a remote host.

The correct answer for this question is d. A socket is created by a local process or application to establish a connection with a remote application. This socket is a combination of the IP address of the machine the remote application is running on, the protocol port number, and the type of service needed. Therefore, answer d is the best option. Answer a is incorrect because a socket is not simply a number used to identify a remote process. Answer b is partially correct, because a socket does include a port number, but the answer is not specific enough. And, finally, a client (not a server) generally chooses a port number "on the fly" when establishing a connection with a remote process. Therefore, answer c does not correctly describe a socket either.

Question 7

The following statements describe individual parts of the three-way handshake used to establish a session. Which of these statements is incorrect?

○ a. "I have information for you. Can we establish communication?"

○ b. "No, I am busy right now and don't have time for you. Try back in few minutes."

○ c. "Yes, I am available for communication. Continue with your transmission."

○ d. "Great, I received your response. Here is the rest of the information."

The correct answer for this question is b. The three-way handshake does not include a "No" response from the recipient machine. If the machine is unavailable, it simply does not respond. If it is available but is getting bogged down with other transmissions, it uses a flow-control mechanism, such as source quench, to ask the sending client to slow the transmission of data. Answers a, c, and d are the correct format of the handshake messages, and they are in the correct order from top to bottom.

Question 8

Which of the following reside at the Internet layer of the TCP/IP
Reference Model? [Check all correct answers]

❑ a. PING

❑ b. ARP

❑ c. ICMP

❑ d. IGMP

The correct answers for this question are b, c, and d. PING is not part of the
Internet layer (it functions as an application); however, it does use ICMP mes-
sages. **The rest of these protocols correspond to the Internet layer of the TCP/
IP Reference Model.** For a review of the Internet layer protocols, take a look at
Figure 2.3.

Question 9

IP resides at which layer of the TCP/IP protocol stack? [Choose
the best answer]

○ a. Network Interface

○ b. Internet

○ c. Transport

○ d. Application

**The correct answer is b. The Internet Protocol (IP) resides at the Internet
layer of the TCP/IP protocol stack.** IP is a connectionless protocol that
utilizes datagrams to send data from one network to the next. IP does not
expect an ACK (acknowledgment), which ensures that the destination host
is receiving the packets it is forwarding. Acknowledgment and retransmission
of packets are left up to protocols and processes running at higher levels in
the Model.

Question 10

> Which of the following correctly describes the function of ARP?
>
> O a. Maps IP addresses to NetBIOS names
>
> O b. Puts frames on the wire
>
> O c. Converts bits into bytes
>
> O d. Maps IP addresses to MAC addresses

The correct answer is d. ARP, the Address Resolution Protocol, is the Internet layer protocol responsible for determining the hardware address (also called a MAC address) that corresponds to a particular IP address.

Need To Know More?

Lammle, Todd, Monica Lammle, and James Chellis. *MCSE: TCP/IP Study Guide*. Sybex Network Press, San Francisco, CA, 1997. ISBN 0-7821-1969-7.

McLaren, Tim and Stephen Myers. *MCSE Study Guide: TCP/IP and Systems Management Server*. New Riders Publishing, Indianapolis, IN, 1996. ISBN 1-56205-588-7.

Search the TechNet CD (or its online version through www.microsoft.com) using the keywords "TCP," "NetBIOS," "Reference Model," and "Windows Sockets," as well as related query items.

The *Windows NT Server Resource Kit* contains a lot of useful information about TCP/IP and related topics. You can search the CD version using the keywords "TCP/IP," "NetBIOS," "Reberence Model," "Windows Sockets." Useful TCP/IP-related materials occur throughout the "Networking Guide" volume of the *Resource Kit*.

Installation
And
Configuration

3

Terms you'll need to understand:

√   DNS (Domain Name Service)

√   WINS (Windows Internet Name Service)

√   DHCP (Dynamic Host Configuration Protocol)

√   IPCONFIG

√   PPTP (Point-To-Point Tunneling Protocol)

√   Default gateway

√   IP address

√   DHCP relay

Techniques you'll need to master:

√   Installing TCP/IP on Windows NT

√   Understanding basic IP configuration

In this chapter, we examine the process of installing and configuring the TCP/IP protocol suite on a computer running Microsoft Windows NT 4. We present the TCP/IP installation process as well as the configuration of required and advanced settings. Configuration of the Windows Internet Name Service (WINS) and Domain Name Service (DNS) is also explained.

Installing TCP/IP On Windows NT 4

When you install TCP/IP on a Windows NT machine, you are installing the core components necessary for TCP/IP to run, as well as a number of very useful connectivity utilities. On a Windows NT server, you can also install and configure the WINS, DNS, and DHCP server services. These services allow your Windows NT server to provide name resolution and TCP/IP configuration parameters for other hosts on your network.

When you install TCP/IP, you also install several client connectivity utilities, such as the File Transfer Protocol (FTP) client and Telnet. These utilities allow you to connect to other TCP/IP hosts on your network or anywhere on the Internet. An FTP client allows you to connect to an FTP server to upload and/or download files to and from that server. Telnet is a utility that can be used to remotely execute shell commands on another machine. These and other utilities will be discussed in greater detail in Chapter 13, "Connectivity."

The Installation Process

Before you can install and configure TCP/IP (or any protocol) on a Windows NT machine, you must be logged on as a member of the local administrators group. Because of the Windows NT security model, only those who are members of the local administrators group can make changes to the configuration of the machine.

 You must be logged on as a member of the local administrators group to make configuration changes to Windows NT.

You will also need to make sure that you have the original installation media available during the installation process. This might be a CD-ROM, or it might simply be a network share to which the installation files have been copied. A network installation or upgrade can be accomplished by copying the contents of the I386 directory from the CD-ROM to a network share. If Windows NT is installed on a RISC (Alpha chip) system, the directory is Alpha.

If you are going to attempt to install or copy files from a network share, you must have some type of transport protocol (such as NetBEUI or NWLink IPX/SPX Compatible Transport) already installed. Make sure that at least one protocol, common to your network, is currently installed.

The following sections describe the installation process for TCP/IP on Windows NT. In this section, we discuss the concepts, cautions, and potential exam items that relate to this process.

You must first access the Network Control Panel to add or remove network components or to make changes to your current network configurations. This is done by accessing the Control Panel applet on the Start menu (Start|Settings|Control Panel) and choosing Network, or you can access the Network Control Panel directly by right-clicking on the Network Neighborhood icon and choosing Properties. Once you have opened the Network properties sheet, select the Protocols tab and then click the Add button.

Next, locate and select the TCP/IP protocol from the list of available protocols and then click OK. This will begin the installation process. You should see the message depicted in Figure 3.1. This message asks if you would like to use DHCP (Dynamic Host Configuration Protocol). A DHCP server can automatically configure the TCP/IP settings for your computer. If the Remote Access Service is installed, you may also be asked whether you want to configure RAS to use the TCP/IP protocol. If the RAS service has been installed on your computer before installing TCP/IP, you will be asked whether you want to configure RAS to use TCP/IP.

DHCP provides for the automatic configuration of TCP/IP host machines. Each machine on which you want to use DHCP must have client software configured to allow it to contact a DHCP server (see Figure 3.1). This server provides the client with an IP address, subnet mask, and a default gateway, as well as numerous other TCP/IP configuration parameters. For additional information about DHCP, read Chapter 11, "Dynamic Host Configuration Protocol."

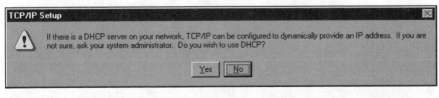

Figure 3.1   TCP/IP Setup message, allowing TCP/IP to be configured for DHCP.

Windows NT must copy the necessary files from the I386 directory of the Windows NT Server CD-ROM, so it prompts you for the location of these files during installation. Type in the path to the CD-ROM in the File location dialog box (for example, "D:\I386") or enter a path to where the files can be found on the network (for example, "\\APPS\I386").

Once Windows NT has finished copying the core TCP/IP networking files and the default connectivity utilities, click OK. Next, you are asked to configure the necessary TCP/IP parameters.

Configuring TCP/IP On Windows NT 4

If you did not choose to use DHCP, you must configure TCP/IP manually. This process includes setting the IP address, the subnet mask, and the default gateway (if you want to communicate with remote subnets). Optionally, you can configure the addresses for WINS and DNS servers that exist on your network. You can also perform more advanced configurations, such as adding multiple IP addresses or configuring multiple network cards.

The IP Address Properties Sheet

In order for a TCP/IP host to function properly on the network, it must be configured with a valid IP address and subnet mask. This information must be entered manually if you are not using DHCP.

If you set an incorrect IP address, you might receive an error message that an address conflict has occurred on the network. This happens when two or more computers on the network are configured to use the same IP address. You should ensure that you have the correct addressing information before configuring the TCP/IP settings on any machine.

A default gateway (router) is also required by a host using TCP/IP if it will be sending or receiving any information outside of the local network segment.

To configure the TCP/IP settings manually, select the Protocols tab from the Start|Settings|Control Panel|Network icon. Then, click the Properties button, select the IP Address tab, and change settings as needed. The following list explains these options:

➤ **Adapter** You can configure the IP addresses for all of the currently installed adapters (see Figure 3.2). You can use the Adapter drop-down list to select each adapter that needs to be configured.

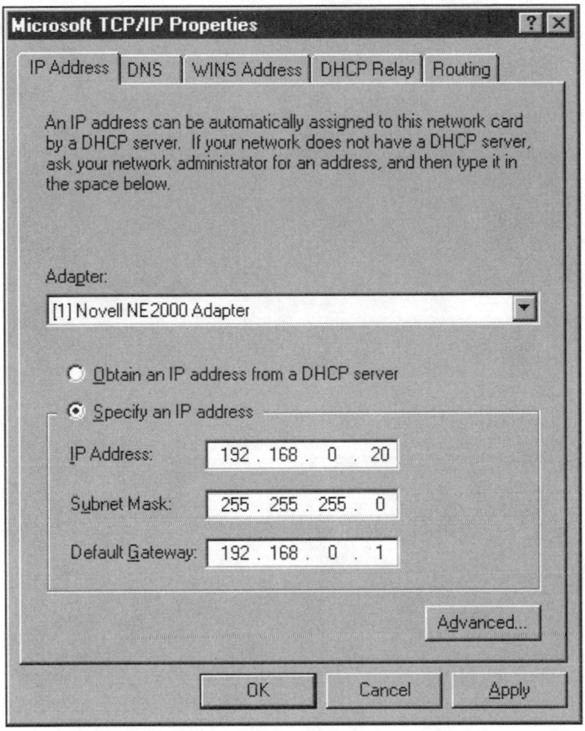

Figure 3.2   IP Address properties sheet for TCP/IP configuration.

➤ **Obtain An IP Address From A DHCP Server** If you have a DHCP
   server on your network, select the Obtain An IP Address From A
   DHCP Server radio button. After doing this, your machine can contact
   a local DHCP server to obtain its IP configuration information. If a
   DHCP server is not available, you must choose the Specify An IP
   Address radio button and enter a valid IP address, subnet mask, and
   default gateway for your network (also shown in Figure 3.2).

Advanced IP Addressing For Windows NT 4

The Advanced button on the Microsoft TCP/IP Properties dialog box
displays the interface shown in Figure 3.3. The Advanced IP Addressing
dialog box allows you to configure multiple IP addresses and multiple
default gateways for each of the currently installed network adapters. Additionally, you can enable the PPTP Filtering or Advanced Security options
for each adapter individually. PPTP filtering is a security measure that

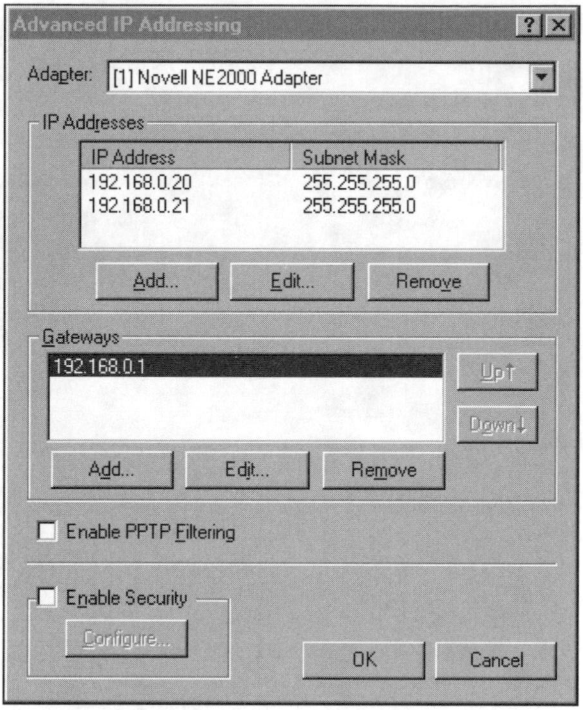

Advanced IP Addressing [?] [X]

Ada_p_ter: [1] Novell NE 2000 Adapter [▼]

IP Add_r_esses

IP Address	Subnet Mask
192.168.0.20	255.255.255.0
192.168.0.21	255.255.255.0

[_A_dd...] [_E_dit...] [Remo_v_e]

_G_ateways

192.168.0.1

[_U_p↑]

[D_o_wn↓]

[A_d_d...] [E_d_it...] [Re_m_ove]

[ ] Enable PPTP _F_iltering

[ ] E_n_able Security

[_C_onfigure...]

[OK] [Cancel]

Figure 3.3   The Advanced IP Addressing dialog box.

prevents all packets, except PPTP packets, from being processed by Windows NT's network interfaces.

You can use the Adapter drop-down list to select the adapters that you want to configure. This interface makes it possible to manage multiple network cards. The individual adapter settings are displayed each time you select a different adapter.

The following list details the settings that you can configure through the Advanced IP Addressing dialog box:

➤ **IP Addresses** You can also specify multiple IP addresses for a single network adapter (see Figure 3.3). You may provide up to four additional addresses through this interface. If you want to add more than five total IP addresses per network card, you'll have to edit the Windows NT Registry. See TechNet article Q149426 "Adding More Than Five IP Addresses to NIC in Windows NT" for more information.

Configuring multiple IP addresses for a single network adapter allows you to host multiple virtual Web sites on a single computer.

➤ **Gateways** In the Gateways dialog box, you may enter a total of five default gateways. The gateway at the top of the list is always used first. If this gateway is not accessible for some reason, TCP/IP tries each of the gateways listed until one of them accepts the information to be transmitted.

➤ **Enable PPTP Filtering** The Enable PPTP Filtering checkbox prevents a network adapter from processing any packets except PPTP packets. This feature is usually restricted to use on machines that are set up specifically as PPTP gateways for a network. Because these gateway machines have at least one adapter interface exposed to the outside world, this feature can prevent intruders from gaining access to the server or the network behind the server's other interfaces.

 PPTP (Point-To-Point Tunneling Protocol) is a new feature of Windows NT 4. It has both a server and a client component that provide for the secure transfer of data from a client to a private network over a TCP/IP network, such as the Internet. By encrypting the data before it is sent, a virtual private network (VPN) is created, allowing a client to send and receive data over an unsecured connection. PPTP supports NetBEUI, IPX, and IP, and it can be used over WAN, LAN, and dial-up connections.

For additional information on PPTP, see the "Windows NT Server Networking Guide" in the *Windows NT Server Resource Kit* (for NT Version 4), Chapter 11, "PPTP", or the Microsoft Knowledge Base article Q161410 (which can be found on the TechNet CD-ROM or the World Wide Web).

➤ **TCP/IP Security** This feature is actually a TCP/IP-based packet filter (see Figure 3.4). This filter allows you to control the flow of incoming TCP/IP traffic based on TCP or UDP ports, or the IP protocol for which the packets are bound. This filtering does not affect outbound traffic, and you can configure the filter separately for each network adapter installed. Select the Permit Only radio button to prevent the processing of all traffic for a specific protocol. Then, add each port or protocol that you want to allow.

Figure 3.4 TCP/IP Security properties sheet.

The DNS (Domain Name Service) Properties Sheet

Microsoft TCP/IP on Windows NT 4 allows you to configure each machine to contact a DNS (Domain Name Service) server for TCP/IP host name resolution. A DNS server resolves friendly DNS host names to IP addresses so that you do not have to remember some arbitrary number (such as 131.107.2.12) to contact another computer. This is similar in functionality to the WINS server (mentioned previously in Chapter 2, "Concepts And Planning: TCP/IP And Windows NT 4"), which resolves NetBIOS names to IP addresses.

DNS and WINS both provide user-friendly name-to-IP address resolution (for example, users can type "www.microsoft.com," rather than having to remember "207.68.156.61"). However, WINS provides for the dynamic registration and resolution of NetBIOS names, whereas DNS uses a static database that must be configured and updated manually. Another difference between DNS and WINS is the namespace (the method used to name computers on the network and the Internet).

The NetBIOS naming convention utilizes a flat namespace, unlike the DNS naming convention, which utilizes a hierarchical namespace. The NetBIOS namespace is flat because NetBIOS names consist of only one part. Administering this type of namespace works fine for a small organization, but as the organization becomes larger, it becomes increasingly difficult to prevent the use of duplicate names. The WINS service assists the administrator by allowing each machine to register its name and IP address into the WINS database each time the machine is booted. If the NetBIOS name requested is already in use, NetBIOS will not properly initialize on the requesting machine.

The DNS namespace is hierarchical—each DNS name consists of a host name and a domain name component. For example, the name www.xerox.com is comprised of the host name "www" and the domain name "xerox.com." This segmentation allows for decentralized administration of the namespace. The entire organization is recognized by a specific domain name, such as xerox.com, and this domain can contain subdomains, such as servers.xerox.com. Host names can then be assigned to machines within these subdomains, by each local authority, without concern for duplicate names within the organization. The combination of the host name, the subdomain, and the domain name produces a fully qualified domain name (FQDN), such as servers.xerox.com.

Unlike WINS, DNS does not currently allow for the dynamic registration and resolution of DNS names. This means that each time a DNS name changes or a host is moved to another subnet (requiring a new IP address), an administrator must change the entry in the DNS database manually. For additional information about DNS, read Chapter 8, "Host Name Resolution," and Chapter 9, "DNS."

> **TIP** In Windows NT 4, DNS and WINS are closely integrated with one another. The close relationship of these two services provides a form of dynamic DNS (a proposed standard that will allow a host to dynamically register its DNS name and IP address with the DNS server). Although this relationship does not provide true dynamic DNS, it does allow a Microsoft Windows NT 4 DNS server to contact a WINS server when it cannot resolve a host name on its own.

The following list details the fields you set to configure Windows NT to access a DNS server (see Figure 3.5):

➤ **Host Name** By default, the Host Name field should be the current NetBIOS name of the machine. Unless you have a specific need to change this information it should be left as it is.

➤ **Domain** In order for the host to be able to communicate properly on an IP network, you must enter the correct domain name for your organization (if you do not know the correct domain name for your organization or group, contact your network administrator). The combination of these two fields produces an FQDN, which becomes the DNS name by which this machine is known.

➤ **DNS Service Search Order** Enter the IP address of the DNS server(s) for your network in this field. You may enter up to three IP addresses through this interface, and you can change the order in which these

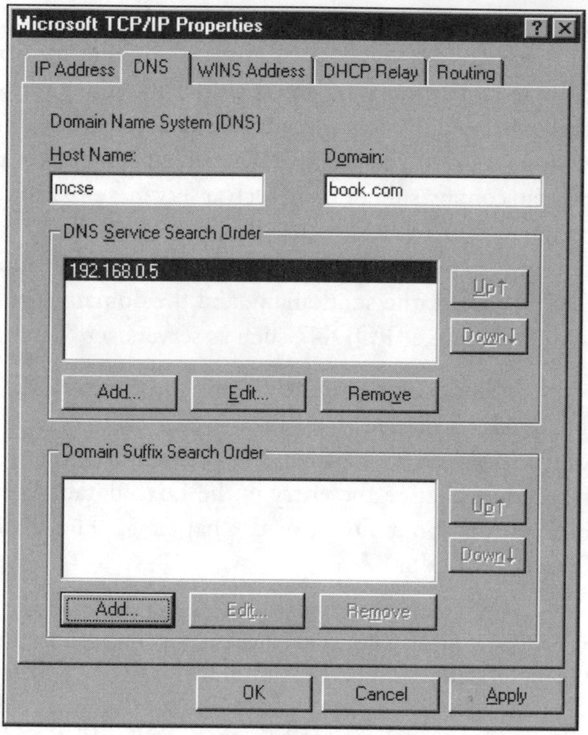

Figure 3.5 DNS configuration properties

servers are contacted for host name resolution by using the up- and down-arrows in the dialog box.

➤ **Domain Suffix Search Order** Enter additional domain suffixes for use during host name resolution in this field. When attempting to resolve simple host names to fully qualified domain names, these suffixes will be appended to the host name, starting with the local domain suffix and then continuing down the list.

The WINS Address Properties Sheet

WINS provides Windows machines with the capability to dynamically register and resolve NetBIOS names to IP addresses. WINS clients must be configured with the IP address of the WINS server. Once the IP address of the WINS server is configured on the client, clients contact the WINS server directly for name resolution. There is no need to broadcast for name resolution with WINS. This reduces the amount of network traffic needed for name reso-lution. This is also useful for computers that lease IP addresses temporarily or change IP addresses frequently (as is the case when using DHCP). The dynamic database in the WINS server adjusts automatically when clients change their IP addresses. Figure 3.6 shows the WINS Address properties sheet.

The following information explains the process of configuring Windows NT to resolve NetBIOS names:

➤ **Adapters** WINS can be configured separately for each network adapter that is installed. Use the Adapter drop-down list to select each adapter that needs to be configured for WINS.

➤ **Primary WINS Server and Secondary WINS Server** Enter an IP address for a primary and secondary WINS server in each of these fields. If Windows NT does not receive a response from the primary WINS server, it will contact the secondary server.

➤ **Enable DNS For Windows Resolution** This checkbox allows for the use of DNS host names and FQDNs with Windows-based applications. These applications usually expect a NetBIOS name, but with this feature enabled, they can resolve DNS type host names as well.

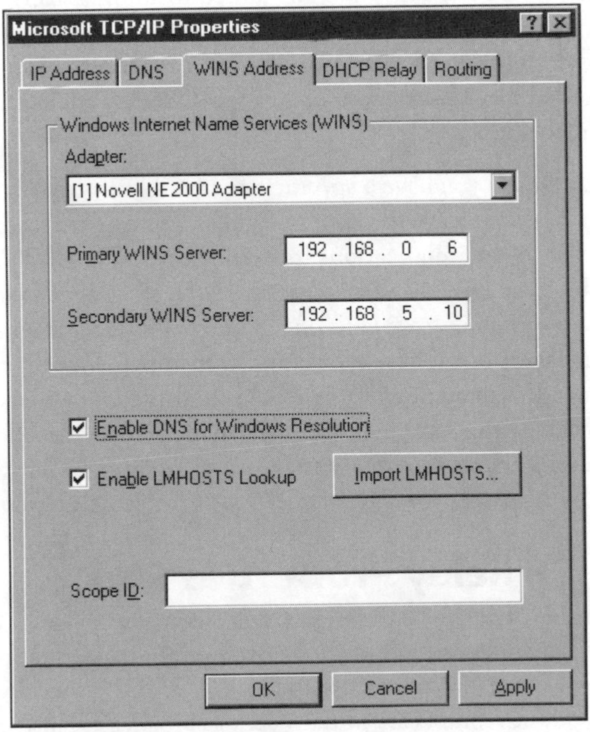

Figure 3.6 WINS Address properties sheet.

An example of this feature can be seen by using the **NET USE** or **NET VIEW** command. The **NET USE** command typically takes the form **NET USE T: ***NetBIOS name\share name*. However, when the Enable DNS For Windows Resolution feature is enabled, the command can take this form: **NET USE T: ** *IP address or FQDN \share name*.

➤ **Enable LMHOSTS Lookup** This checkbox allows for the use of a static NetBIOS name-to-IP address mapping file, called the LMHOSTS file. This file can be used to supplement the naming resolution provided by the WINS server. However, this file is static and must be updated manually whenever name or IP address changes occur. A sample of the LMHOSTS and the HOST files can be found in the \winnt\system32\drivers\etc directory. The LMHOSTS file will be discussed in greater detail in Chapter 8, "Host Name Resolution," and Chapter 10, "NetBIOS Name Resolution."

➤ **Import LMHOSTS** This function is used to automatically import an already existing copy of the LMHOSTS file from another location. Click the Import LMHOSTS button and provide Windows NT with the path to the needed file. This can either be a local file or a file residing on another machine.

➤ **Scope ID** Unless you have a specific need (and know what you are doing), it is best to leave the Scope ID field empty. This feature segregates NetBIOS communications from the normal NetBIOS broadcast traffic. However, only machines that share the same scope can use NetBIOS to communicate with one another. This can be a helpful security measure if you have a machine(s) to which you would like to limit access. But remember: Only machines that share a scope can communicate with each other over NetBIOS. To provide a Scope ID, simply enter a character string value, such as "resource." Be aware that a Scope ID is case sensitive: "Resource" is not the same as "resource."

The DHCP Relay Properties Sheet

DHCP (mentioned at the beginning of this chapter) provides TCP/IP hosts within a local network or subnet with the configuration information they need. However, because the machines that contact the DHCP server do not yet have an IP address, these requests are initially sent as broadcasts, and broadcasts are generally not forwarded by routers to other subnets.

If your organization has more than one subnet, but does not have DHCP servers on each local network, Windows NT machines can be configured as DHCP Relay Agents. A DHCP Relay Agent can be configured to accept and forward DHCP requests directly to a DHCP server on another network. The DHCP server on the other network will process the request and forward the response to the machine that originated the request.

To enable the DHCP relay option, the DHCP Relay Agent software must be installed. If you have not already installed this software, Windows NT will allow you to install it after you have modified the settings on the DHCP Relay Properties sheet.

The following information explains the process of configuring the DHCP Relay Properties sheet:

1. Click the DHCP Relay tab at the top of the TCP/IP Properties sheet to bring this dialog box to the foreground.

    You can keep the default settings for the seconds threshold and the maximum hops, which is four seconds. The seconds threshold will prevent the Relay Agent from forwarding the DHCP request until the client has waited for at least four seconds for the local DHCP server to reply to the request. The maximum hops setting provides the same type of functionality by preventing packets with a hop count greater than the specified number from being forwarded. This feature is a function of the TTL (Time To Live) for the packet that is received.

2. Enter the IP addresses of the DHCP server(s) to which requests should be forwarded.

3. Once you have completed configuring the Relay Agent, confirm the settings, and tell Windows NT whether to install the Relay Agent (if it has not been installed already).

The Routing Properties Sheet

This properties sheet has only one option. It simply toggles the IP routing function for the machine off or on. If the machine is currently configured with multiple network adapters (multihomed), enabling this feature allows IP packets to be forwarded from one network interface to another. This turns your Windows NT machine into a simple router. If you do enable this feature, you might need to add route entries in the routing table for this machine or enable RIP (Routing Information Protocol). You do not need to modify the routing table or add RIP routing if you are physically connecting the Windows NT computer to all segments and no other routers are present on the network.

However, in an environment where multiple routers and segments exist, it is necessary to configure a static routing table or install RIP. More information on routing and RIP is presented in Chapter 6, "Implementing IP Routing."

Reboot The Machine

Once you are finished configuring TCP/IP, Windows NT will need to be rebooted for the new settings to take effect. The Network Control Panel application will save the settings and review all the bindings for the adapters and services that are now installed. If Windows NT does not automatically reboot, you must reboot it manually.

Verifying And Testing The Configuration

Now that you are done installing and configuring TCP/IP, you need to make sure that everything is in working order. Two tools are very helpful in this process: the IPCONFIG and PING utilities.

IPCONFIG is a Windows NT command-line utility that provides you with most TCP/IP configuration information, without requiring you to access the Network Control Panel (see Figure 3.7). Use this command with the /ALL modifier to view host name, DNS, routing, and IP information about each adapter that is configured.

Use this command to verify that the information you entered during configuration is correct. If everything looks okay, you should use the PING (Packet InterNet Groper) utility to verify that the configuration actually works.

```
Command Prompt - ipconfig /all                              _ □ ×

E:\>ipconfig /all

Windows NT IP Configuration

        Host Name . . . . . . . . . : mcse.book.com
        DNS Servers . . . . . . . . : 192.168.0.5
        Node Type . . . . . . . . . : Hybrid
        NetBIOS Scope ID. . . . . . :
        IP Routing Enabled. . . . . : No
        WINS Proxy Enabled. . . . . : No
        NetBIOS Resolution Uses DNS : Yes

Ethernet adapter NE20001:

        Description . . . . . . . . : Novell 2000 Adapter.
        Physical Address. . . . . . : 00-C0-F0-19-DD-47
        DHCP Enabled. . . . . . . . : No
        IP Address. . . . . . . . . : 192.168.0.20
        Subnet Mask . . . . . . . . : 255.255.255.0
        Default Gateway . . . . . . : 192.168.0.1
        Primary WINS Server . . . . : 192.168.0.6
        Secondary WINS Server . . . : 192.168.5.10
```

Figure 3.7   IPCONFIG /ALL command output.

PING is a utility that utilizes the ICMP protocol (mentioned in Chapter 2) to request a reply from a TCP/IP host. This ensures that communication is possible between two hosts. The format of the **PING** command looks like this:

```
ping IP address or host name
```

When using the Microsoft PING utility, the response generally consists of four echo requests, followed by their corresponding reply messages on the screen (see Figure 3.8).

Although the PING utility will accept the use of host names, FQDNs, and IP addresses, it is recommended that you use IP addresses when troubleshooting a connectivity problem. This separates name resolution problems from other possible causes.

The first step in testing the configuration is to PING the adapter loopback address, which is 127.0.0.1. By doing this, the program will not actually contact another machine, but it will test the local TCP/IP configuration down to the network adapter software and back up the protocol stack. If you receive a response from this address, you know that at least the local host is properly configured with TCP/IP.

The next step is to PING the IP address that you have assigned to this machine. If you receive a response from both of these addresses, you can assume that your IP address is properly configured.

Next, PING the address of another machine on the local network segment. If you don't know of a specific IP address, you can try PINGing an address close to the one you are using or have been assigned. If your current IP address is 192.168.0.66, try PINGing 192.168.0.67 or 192.168.0.68.

Once you have confirmed that your machine can function properly within its own subnet or local network, you need to confirm that information from your machine can make it across the router.

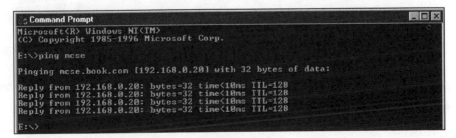

Figure 3.8   PING command output.

First, PING the IP address of the router's interface that is connected to your local subnet. If you receive a response, try PINGing the IP address of one of the router's other interfaces (one not connected directly to your local network). If that works, the final step is to try PINGing a host that resides on another subnet (that is, on the other side of the router).

If you are not able to successfully PING any of these IP addresses, use the information you have obtained up to this point to locate the source of the problem. If you cannot PING your own IP address, the problem is with your machine. If you can PING other machines on your local network, but not any that are behind a router, the problem may be your IP settings, the router itself, or the machine you are trying to contact. As you can see, in order to pinpoint the problem, you'll need to be thorough, patient, and troubleshoot in a linear fashion.

Exam Prep Questions

Question 1

> You are getting ready to install and configure TCP/IP on your Windows NT Server. Which of the following items are not requirements to complete the installation? [Check all correct answers]
>
> ❑ a. You must be a member of the local administrators group for the machine you're configuring.
>
> ❑ b. You must be a domain administrator for the domain in which the machine is installed.
>
> ❑ c. You must have some type of access to the original installation files.
>
> ❑ d. You must have a good understanding of the required settings and configurations.

The correct answer for this question is b. You do not need to be a domain administrator when installing or configuring TCP/IP on a standard NT Workstation or Server. However, the statements made in a, c, and d are all necessary requirements. You need to read each question carefully. A quick once-over of this question may cause you to choose a, c, and d because they are requirements. But the question asks which answers are not requirements, which, of course, is answer b.

Question 2

> Which of the following statements about DHCP are correct? [Choose two]
>
> ❑ a. DHCP is a service that provides TCP/IP configuration information to machines that request it.
>
> ❑ b. DHCP is a service that provides for the resolution of friendly names to IP addresses.
>
> ❑ c. Each TCP/IP client must be configured to access a DHCP server if you want it to use this service.
>
> ❑ d. When configuring a client to use DHCP, you must supply the client with the IP address of the DHCP server.

The correct answers for this question are a and c. DHCP is a service that provides TCP/IP clients with configuration information, and each client must be configured to use this service. DHCP does not provide for name resolution. Therefore, b is incorrect. There is no need to supply the device with an IP address for the DHCP server; because the machine is without an IP address for itself, it would have no means of transmission, other than a broadcast. Therefore, d is incorrect.

Question 3

On the Advanced IP Addressing Properties sheet, how many IP addresses per network card can you configure?

○ a. 4

○ b. 5

○ c. 10

○ d. Unlimited

The correct answer for this question is b. Windows NT will allow you to configure up to five IP addresses through the Advanced IP Addressing interface. It is possible to add more, but this must be done through the Registry. Therefore, a, c, and d are incorrect.

Question 4

Which of the following statements about PPTP are correct? [Check all correct answers]

❑ a. It has both a server and a client component.

❑ b. It uses a form of encryption.

❑ c. It can be used to send data securely over TCP/IP networks.

❑ d. It supports IP and IPX, but not NetBEUI.

The correct answers for this question are a, b, and c. PPTP (Point-To-Point Tunneling Protocol) is used to send encrypted data over TCP/IP-based networks, both public and private. In order to use this feature, you must have the client software installed on one machine and the PPTP server software installed on the other. PPTP supports tunneling for IP, IPX, and NetBEUI. Therefore, d is incorrect.

Question 5

You are attempting to resolve a communication problem with a computer named bob15 on a remote subnet. You can success-fully PING other computers on the same subnet as bob15; how-ever, when you try to PING bob15, you get no response. Which of the following could be the problem? [Check all correct answers]

❑ a. Your default gateway is configured incorrectly.

❑ b. Bob15 has an incorrect default gateway.

❑ c. Bob15 has a NetBIOS Scope ID that is different than the other computers, including yours.

❑ d. Bob15 is offline.

The correct answers are b and d. Your default gateway is already configured correctly if the other computers on the same subnet as bob15 can respond to you. However, if bob15 has an incorrect default gateway, the reply from the PING could not be returned to you. Bob15 could have a NetBIOS Scope ID set in its WINS Configuration tab that is different from yours. Only computers with the same NetBIOS Scope ID can communi-cate with one another. Therefore, if bob15 were configured with one Scope ID and the other computers' Scope IDs were left blank (or configured with a different set of characters than bob15), bob15 could not communicate with the others. Of course, if a computer is offline or shutdown, it will also not be able to communicate on the network. The NetBIOS ScopeID has no bearing on the success or failure of a PING. Therefore, answer c is incorrect.

Question 6

You want to install a Windows NT computer to route IP traffic between two segments. These will be the only two segments on your small network. Which of the following must be done in order to make this possible? [Check all correct answers]

❑ a. The Windows NT computer must be configured with two network cards.

❑ b. Each network card must be attached to the same subnet.

❑ c. IP forwarding must be enabled on the multihomed computer.

❑ d. RIP routing must be configured on the Windows NT router.

The correct answers to this question are a and c. You must put two network cards in the Windows NT computer and enable IP forwarding in order to make it route (multihomed means "configured with multiple network adapters"). You would not want to connect both network adapters to the same segment; instead, you must connect each card to a different segment in order to route traffic between them. You won't need RIP routing or a static routing table in this scenario, because your computer is going to be attached to both segments. One item not mentioned in the answer set is that you will have to configure each network adapter for a different network segment. This is important because it is how the Windows NT router knows where to send incoming packets.

Question 7

You have been asked to configure several Windows NT Workstations for your company's network that uses DNS and WINS for name resolution.

Required Result:

- The computers must be able to communicate with each other via a computer name, Internet-style name, and IP address.

Optional Desired Results:

- Keep the broadcast traffic to a minimum.

- Give the clients a level of fault tolerance for name resolution if the primary WINS server is unavailable.

Proposed Solution:

- Place an LMHOSTS file on each computer that has mappings for the computer names and IP addresses.

Which results does the proposed solution produce?

- ○ a. The proposed solution produces the required result and produces both of the optional desired results.

- ○ b. The proposed solution produces the required result and produces only one of the optional results.

- ○ c. The proposed solution produces the required result but does not produce any of the optional desired results.

- ○ d. The proposed solution does not produce the required result.

The answer to this question is d. This does not meet the required result. An LMHOSTS file is not used to resolve Internet-style names, such as www.microsoft.com. You would need a DNS server or HOSTS file for that purpose. Remember, if a question like this does not meet the required results, you don't even have to worry about the optional results.

Question 8

You have been asked to configure several Windows NT Workstations for your company's network that uses DNS and WINS for name resolution.

Required Result:

- The computers must be able to communicate with each other via a computer name, Internet-style name, or IP address.

Optional Desired Results:

- Keep the broadcast traffic to a minimum.

- Give the clients a level of fault tolerance for name resolution if the primary WINS server is unavailable.

Proposed Solution:

- Configure the TCP/IP protocol for each NT Workstation and configure each Workstation with the IP address of the WINS server and the DNS server.

Which results does the proposed solution produce?

- ○ a. The proposed solution produces the required result and produces both of the optional desired results.

- ○ b. The proposed solution produces the required result and produces only one of the optional results.

- ○ c. The proposed solution produces the required result but does not produce any of the optional desired results.

- ○ d. The proposed solution does not produce the required result.

The answer to this question is b. By configuring the clients with the address of the WINS and DNS server, all the computers should be able to resolve NetBIOS names and Internet-style names to IP addresses. You should always be able to communicate via IP addresses. One of the major benefits of WINS is that it reduces broadcast traffic. The fact that you have configured

WINS should be enough to safely say that broadcast traffic will be kept to a minimum. The only thing that is missing is the configuration of a secondary WINS server, in case the primary goes down. In order for answer a to be the correct selection, you would have had to configure each Windows NT Workstation for the address of one primary and one secondary WINS server. This means that you would have to have at least two WINS servers available on the network.

Need to Know More?

 McLaren, Tim and Myers, Stephen. *MCSE Study Guide: TCP/ IP and Systems Management Server*. New Riders Publishing, Indianapolis, IN, 1996. ISBN 1-56205-588-7.

 Lammle, Todd, Monica Lammle, and James Chellis. *MCSE: TCP/IP Study Guide*. Sybex Network Press, San Francisco, CA, 1997. ISBN 0-7821-1969-7.

 Search the TechNet CD (or its online version through www.microsoft.com) using the keywords "IP addressing" and related query items.

The *Windows NT Server Resource Kit* contains lots of useful information about TCP/IP and related topics. You can search the CD version, using the keywords "TCP/IP" and "IP address- ing." Useful TCP/IP-related materials occur throughout the "Networking Guide" volume of the *Resource Kit*.

IP
Addressing

Terms you'll need to understand:

√   IP address

√   Dotted-decimal notation

√   Octet

√   Binary

√   Network ID

√   Host ID

√   InterNIC

√   Classes

√   Subnets

√   Subnet masks

Techniques you'll need to master:

√   Understanding the components of an IP address

√   Converting numbers from binary to decimal and back

√   Understanding how an IP address class can indicate the number of hosts on a network

√   Using a subnet mask to determine the destination of a packet

In this chapter, we examine the major components of an IP address and how IP addresses are used to send information from one network to another. We discuss the network and host ID components of an IP address, as well as address classes, subnets, and subnet masking. Additionally, we review binary-to-decimal conversions as they relate to understanding IP address formation.

IP Addressing: Explored And Explained

An "IP address" is, quite simply, a number that uniquely identifies a TCP/IP host on the Internet or an intranet. In TCP/IP terminology, a "host" is any machine with a network interface configured to use TCP/IP. A host, for example, could be a Windows NT Server, a Unix workstation, or one of the many routers used to pass information from one network to another.

> **TIP**
> Although the term "host" is used here to describe any device configured to access a TCP/IP network, it is also used when discussing DNS names versus NetBIOS names. For example, www.microsoft.com is a host name, whereas SERVER2 is a NetBIOS name; yet, both machines are considered hosts on a TCP/IP network. This can be confusing, but you can usually determine the meaning of the word "host" by the context in which it is used.

The Internet or IP addressing scheme is much like the addressing scheme used by the U.S. Postal Service to deliver mail to your home. An IP address is comprised of a network ID component and a host ID component. In this analogy, the Internet corresponds to your neighborhood, the network ID corresponds to the name of your street, and the host ID corresponds to the address of your home.

The term "Internet" actually refers to a collection of interconnected networks, not just one network. The boundaries of each of these interconnected networks are created by routers, which are used to segment and subdivide network traffic. Each interface on a router signifies a separate network (or subnet) and is therefore assigned a separate network ID. When the interfaces of two separate routers connect to the same physical network segment, they share the same network ID and are identified by unique host IDs.

The network ID identifies the particular network (or segment) on which a host physically resides. It is much like the name of the street where a house is located. This address must be unique across the entire TCP/IP network—whether the network is a part of the global TCP/IP network we call the Internet or just a small company LAN that has implemented TCP/IP. The network ID is used to forward information to the correct network interface on a router (that is, street). Once the information reaches the correct network (or network segment), the data is then delivered to the appropriate host using the host ID portion of the address. All hosts that share the same network ID must be located on the same physical network segment for information to reach them properly. If a host is moved from one network segment to another, it must be assigned a new network address.

A unique network or subnet ID is required for each physical network segment. Network and subnetwork boundaries are created by using routers. Therefore, every interface on a router must have a unique network ID assigned to it. Two routers with interfaces connected to the same physical network segment share network IDs but have unique host IDs.

The host ID identifies a specific host on a particular network. This is much like your street address, which identifies your home from all the others on your street. This portion of the address must be unique within each network (or subnet), just as each home on your street must be identified by a unique street address. Hosts are usually configured with a single network interface or NIC, but some hosts, such as routers, are configured with multiple network interfaces. Each network interface on a host must be configured with a separate and unique IP address, like the one shown in Figure 4.1.

IP Address Formats

IP addresses can be represented in both binary and decimal format. Because we humans tend to have a more difficult time with numbers than our silicon counterparts, we usually prefer to deal with IP addresses in their decimal format.

When an IP address is written in a decimal format, it is comprised of four groups of numbers, called octets, each separated by a dot (.). This way of representing an IP address is called "dotted-decimal notation".

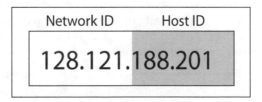

Figure 4.1 Network and host ID components of a Class B IP address.

When written as a decimal number, it may not be immediately apparent why a three-digit number would be referred to as an octet (eight digits), but when each of these numbers is converted to a binary format, this concept starts to make more sense.

Computers, unlike humans, see the world in a binary fashion. For a computer, everything is either on or off, true or false, ones or zeros. This somewhat simplistic view of the world is a function of the computer's architecture, which is well-suited to binary computation.

Computers see IP addresses as 32-bit numbers (or four bytes, eight bits each). Each octet in the decimal format ranges from 0 to 255 and can be represented by eight bits in the binary format, thus the name "octet".

For instance, in the following example, the number on the left represents the binary version of an IP address and the number on the right represents its decimal counterpart:

Binary IP Address   **Dotted-Decimal IP Address**

11000000 10101000 00000000 00000001   192.168.0.1

You can easily see why these binary numbers are converted into a decimal format.

Converting Binary And Decimal Numbers

Before you can truly understand IP addressing, you must have a good understanding of binary numbers and how they equate to decimal numbers. This review of binary-to-decimal conversions assumes that you already have an understanding of the process.

You'll be allowed to use the Microsoft scientific calculator on the exam. This calculator will allow you to convert numbers from decimal to binary or from binary to decimal, by switching the mode of the calculator. This can be very helpful if you are stuck on a particular problem. However, you should not depend heavily on the calculator, because your time to complete the exam is limited. Instead, you should make sure you are comfortable with converting these numbers quickly in your head, and only rely on the calculator when necessary.

The values listed in Table 4.1 are good numbers to memorize for the exam. These are the most commonly occurring values and knowing them beforehand will speed your question answering time. Thus, a combination of memorization of common binary/decimal equivalents and understanding the conversion process for the non-standard numbers (which appear infrequently on the exam) will be a beneficial preparation for the exam.

As previously mentioned, each IP address is broken down into four octets. An octet is comprised of eight bits. In a binary format, each bit has a value of either 1 or 0. These ones and zeros correspond to decimal values that can be found by using the equation 2^{n-1}, where n is the position of the binary digit from the right of the octet. A one indicates that the decimal value of the bit should be used, and a zero is used as a placeholder when the decimal value of the bit is not needed.

Remember, the decimal value of an octet ranges from 0 to 255, so the sum of the decimal values of all bits in an octet does not exceed 255. Table 4.1 illustrates this point.

In the last row, you can see that even with all of the bits in an octet set to 1, the total decimal value of the octet still does not exceed 255. You might have noticed that the decimal value sequence contains some large gaps. These gaps can be filled in by recombining the bits that are set to 0 or 1 in ways other than the nine examples shown here. For example, to generate the decimal value 197, you would need a binary value of 11000101. Table 4.2 gives additional examples of binary values and their decimal equivalents.

Where Do IP Addresses Come From?

Every IP address on the Internet or an intranet must be unique. This is true whether the network has 1,000 or 1,000,000 hosts. If your company

Table 4.1	A sample of octets and their corresponding bit and decimal values.	
Binary Octet	**Octet Bit Value**	**Octet Decimal Value**
00000000	0	0
10000000	128	128
11000000	128+64	192
11100000	128+64+32	224
11110000	128+64+32+16	240
11111000	128+64+32+16+8	248
11111100	128+64+32+16+8+4	252
11111110	128+64+32+16+8+4+2	254
11111111	128+64+32+16+8+4+2+1	255

Table 4.2   Additional binary and decimal numbers within an octet.

Binary Octet	Octet Bit Value	Octet Decimal Value
11000101	128+64+0+0+0+4+0+1	197
11000110	128+64+0+0+0+4+2+0	198
11000111	128+64+0+0+0+4+2+1	199
11001000	128+64+0+0+8+0+0+0	200

has configured its network to use TCP/IP, and it is not connected to the Internet, then the allocation and use of nonduplicate addresses from the IP address space is not a big issue. You can select your IP addresses from the entire IP address space to suit your particular needs. Depending on the size of the company, one or more people will be able to handle the task of assigning unique IP addresses to each subnetwork and host on the company's network. However, if your organization needs to be connected to the Internet, it becomes much more difficult to ensure that the IP addresses you're using are not also being used by someone else.

The InterNIC (Internet Network Information Center) is responsible for allocating and assigning IP addresses to those who want to connect their networks with the Internet. Because only one group assigns all the IP addresses for the Internet, it is easier to ensure the proper distribution of nonduplicate addresses. The InterNIC does not, however, keep track of every IP address that it allows an organization to use. Rather, it uses classes to assign an organization a network ID that corresponds to an appropriate number of host IDs, as discussed in the following section. The organization is then free to assign the host IDs however it sees fit.

Address Classes

So far, you have seen that IP addresses are numbers that uniquely identify each and every host or network interface on an IP network. These addresses are comprised of a network ID component and a host ID component, both of which determine the network that a packet is bound for and the specific host on that network the information needs to reach. You have also seen that IP addresses can be represented in dotted-decimal and binary format. People prefer to work with IP addresses in their decimal format, whereas computers work with IP addresses in their binary format.

Now that we have discussed the process of converting binary numbers to decimal numbers, you can begin to see that there is a relationship between the number of bits in an address space and the total number of addresses that can be created from those bits.

When the Internet was just beginning to emerge, the governing bodies decided that an address space comprised of 32 bits was sufficient to handle all the potential networks and hosts that would ever be connected to the Internet. This 32-bit address space equates to approximately 4.3 billion (or 2^{32}) different addresses. These Internet founders never imagined the incredible growth the Internet would experience in subsequent years. Had they known, they could have easily added a couple of extra bits to the address space, increasing the number of hosts that could be supported exponentially.

Although they did not anticipate the need for additional addresses, they did devise a method using address classes that allows for an appropriate allocation of the available address space. Address classes range from Class A through Class E, although addresses in Class D and Class E are reserved for special use. These classes correspond to the number of network IDs and host IDs allowed within a range of the total IP address space.

By dividing the available address space into classes, it is possible to allocate blocks of the address space to organizations according to the total number of hosts that the organization needs to support.

Table 4.3 shows, from left to right, each class of the address, the value of the high-order bits (the first bits of the first octet), the range of decimal values allowed in the first octet of each class, and the number of networks and hosts supported by each class.

 Table 4.3 contains information you should memorize for the exam. Being able to look at an IP address and to know its class, number of networks, and number of hosts is an invaluable asset on the exam.

Table 4.3	Address classes and corresponding network and host IDs available.			
Address Class	**High-Order Bits**	**First Octet Decimal Range**	**Networks Available**	**Hosts Available**
Class A	0	1-126.x.y.z	126	16,777,214
Class B	10	128-191.x.y.z	16,384	65,534
Class C	110	192-223.x.y.z	2,097,152	254

In a Class A address, the first octet represents the network ID component of the address. In a Class B address, the first two octets are used for the network ID, and in a Class C address, the first three octets are used for the network ID. This creates a subdivision of the address space that is represented by Table 4.4.

Class A Addresses

Class A only uses the first octet to designate the network ID, and it uses the remaining three octets for the designation of the host ID. The high-order bit (first bit of the first octet) of this address class is always set to 0 (zero), indicating a Class A address (see Table 4.5). Because the high-order bit is always set to 0, only seven bits remain to represent the network ID. These 7 bits provide a maximum of 127 possible network addresses, but the network ID 127 is reserved for the network adapter loopback function (explained later in the section on IP addressing guidelines). Therefore, only 126 possible Class A addresses are available.

The remaining 24 bits are available for use in the host ID portion of the address. This provides for 16,777,214 or (2^{24})-2 hosts per network. Because this address class allows for such a large number of possible hosts per network, these addresses are only given to organizations that need to provide access to an extremely large number of hosts. In fact, few, if any, of these addresses remain, because they were assigned to organizations (mostly universities and the military) years ago.

Table 4.4   Division of IP address component octets according to class.

Address Class	IP Address	Network ID Component	Host ID Component
Class A	w.x.y.z	w	x.y.z
Class B	w.x.y.z	w.x	y.z
Class C	w.x.y.z	w.x.y	z

Table 4.5   Class A address—network and host ID components.

Address Class	IP Address	Network ID	Host ID
Class A	124.29.88.7	124	29.88.7

Class B Addresses

Class B uses the first and second octets to designate the network ID, and it uses the remaining two octets for the designation of the host ID. The high-order bits (first two bits of the first octet) of this class of address are always set to 10 (one-zero), indicating a Class B address (see Table 4.6). Because the high-order bits of the first octet are always set to 10, only 14 bits remain to represent the network ID. The remaining 14 bits provide a maximum of 16,384 network addresses.

The remaining 16 bits are available for use in the host ID portion of the address. This provides for 65,534 or (2^{16})-2 hosts per network. This class of address is designed for medium- to large-size networks, and, although they are not easy to come by, a few of these addresses are probably still left.

Class C Addresses

Class C uses the first three octets to designate the network ID, and it uses the remaining octet for the designation of the host ID (see Table 4.7). The high-order bits (first three bits of the first octet) of this class of address are always set to 110 (one-one-zero), indicating a Class C address. Because the high-order bits of the first octet are always set to 110, only 21 bits remain to represent the network ID. The remaining 21 bits provide a maximum of 2,097,152 network addresses.

The remaining eight bits are available for use in the host ID portion of the address. This provides for 254 or (2^{8})-2 hosts per network. This class of address is designed for small networks that only need to support a limited number of hosts. Because so many Class C addresses are available, they are the easiest type to obtain. However, because of the recent growth of the Internet, even organizations that want to obtain Class C addresses must be able to show that they have a need for the entire block of 254 host addresses.

Table 4.6   Class B address—network and host ID components.

Address Class	IP Address	Network ID	Host ID
Class B	130.29.88.7	130.29	88.7

Table 4.7   Class C address—network and host ID components.

Address Class	IP Address	Network ID	Host ID
Class C	192.29.88.7	192.29.88	7

If your organization is in need of valid IP addresses to connect to the Internet, smaller blocks of addresses can usually be obtained from third parties, such as ISPs (Internet Service Providers). ISPs usually receive larger portions of the IP address space, with the intention of assigning those to customers who may only need a few IP addresses each.

If an organization happens to need more IP addresses than a Class C will allow, but not enough to justify issuing a Class B address, multiple Class C address blocks can be issued. However, this unnecessarily adds complexity to the routing tables on the Internet. One organization is usually identified by a single entry in a routing table. This entry identifies an organization's entire network through the use of the network ID of the IP address. Once information is routed to the network ID/IP address for a particular organization, it becomes the job of the local routers within the private network to maintain routes for all the hosts within the network.

The need to make efficient use of the available address space (as well as the need to cut down on the size of the routing tables of the Internet backbone routers) has recently spurred the creation of a new IP addressing scheme called CIDR (Classless Inter-Domain Routing). CIDR allows for the aggregation of multiple routes to a particular organization, created by using several Class C addresses. It also allows for the distribution of only part of a larger address class (such as a Class A address). CIDR does not recognize the class of an IP address as indicated by the high-order bits of the address; instead, it uses a variable-length network identifier similar to a subnet mask. For additional information on subnet masks, see the section titled "Subdividing A Network: Subnets And Subnet Masks," later in this chapter.

Class D Addresses

Class D is used for multicasting. As mentioned in Chapter 2, multicasting is used to send information to a number of registered hosts. These hosts are grouped by registering themselves with local routers, using a multicast address from the Class D range of addresses. The high-order bits for Class D addresses are always set to 1110 (one-one-one-zero); the remaining bits are used to logically group hosts on the network.

Class E Addresses

Class E is an experimental class of addresses that is reserved for future use. Addresses in this class are identified by their high-order bits, which are set to 1111 (one-one-one-one).

IP Addressing Guidelines

To connect your network to the Internet, you must obtain a network ID and a corresponding block of IP addresses from the InterNIC. You are not allowed to select a particular network ID. Your network ID is based on the class of address necessary to support the number of hosts on your network. In this instance, selecting the appropriate network ID is a nonissue. However, if you are configuring a private TCP/IP network or intranet, you need to follow some guidelines when deciding which class of address to use—assuming that you'll not be subnetting your network. Subnetting is discussed later in this chapter in the section titled "Subdividing A Network: Subnets And Subnet Masks."

Proper Network Addressing

Consider the following suggestions when selecting and assigning IP addresses:

➤ **Plan for the future.** First and foremost, select a class that will allow for the future growth of your network.

➤ **Ensure uniqueness.** When assigning network IDs for an intranet, it's important to make sure that each network has a unique network identifier. In other words, every segment of your network that is bordered by two router interfaces must have its own unique network ID.

➤ **Avoid restricted addresses.** Certain addresses are not allowed for normal use in the network ID portion of an IP address. The Class A network address 127 is reserved for network adapter diagnostic purposes. It is called the loopback address and is used to test the TCP/IP protocol stack within a computer without sending information out onto the network. For a list of restricted addresses, visit the InterNIC's site at http://ds.internic.net.

Additionally, the use of the numbers 0 (represented in an octet by all zeros) and 255 (represented in an octet by all ones) is restricted in network IDs. A network ID cannot be composed of all ones or zeros. The use of all zeros in a network ID indicates that the host resides on the local network and the transmission will not be routed, whereas the use of all ones in a network ID is used to indicate a broadcast.

Proper Host Addressing

When deciding how to assign host IDs within a particular network, you only need to remember a few rules:

➤ **Ensure uniqueness.** Each host ID within a network or subnet must be unique.

➤ **Avoid restricted addresses.** The use of the numbers 0 (represented in an octet by all zeros) and 255 (represented in an octet by all ones) is restricted in host IDs. In other words, a host ID cannot be comprised of all ones or zeros. The use of all zeros in a host ID indicates that the information is intended for a particular network without specifying a host, whereas the use of all ones in a host ID indicates that the information is intended for all hosts on a particular network.

➤ **Have a method.** Host IDs can be assigned consecutively and without regard to the type of machine that needs the address. However, you can save yourself a lot of time when troubleshooting by allocating host IDs in some predetermined way. For example, many network administrators use low ID numbers to indicate router interfaces and high ID numbers to indicate servers. The rest are allocated to workstations within the network. (See Table 4.8 for an example.)

Subdividing A Network: Subnets And Subnet Masks

Now that we've examined the different classes of available IP addresses, you can see that the IP address space has already been subdivided into three major groups: Class A, B, and C addresses. However, additional subdivision of a range of addresses into subnets is sometimes necessary, because the block of addresses assigned to an organization by the InterNIC might not work well with the current network topology. Remember, each network ID corresponds to one physical segment of a network. If you receive a Class C address, but already have two physical networks, then further segmentation of your Class C address is desirable. The act of further subdividing an already existing network ID is called "subnetting".

Table 4.8	Method for assigning host IDs within a network.
Network Device	**Address Range**
Routers	192.168.0.1 - 192.168.0.5
Workstations	192.168.0.6 - 192.168.0.245
Servers	192.168.0.246 - 192.168.0.254

Before we continue, it is necessary to review for a moment. Recall that the entire IP address space is already subdivided into three address classes, and each of these classes supports a predetermined number of hosts. The number of network IDs or host IDs that a class can support is a function of the number of bits available to each portion of the address. For example, in a Class B address, the two high-order bits are set to 10 (one-zero), leaving 14 bits available to the network ID and 16 bits available to the host ID. In this scenario, by examining the high-order bits, you can easily determine which portion of the address indicates the network ID and which portion of the address indicates the host ID.

However, if it becomes necessary to further subdivide the address space given to you by the InterNIC, you'll need to borrow some of the bits assigned to the host ID and loan them to the network ID portion of your address. However, once you do this, you can no longer easily determine the length of the network ID by simply looking at the IP address. The subnet mask was designed to aid in this process.

Subnet Masks

The subnet mask is a 32-bit address that indicates how many bits in an address are being used for the network ID. The subnet mask indicates the length of the network ID by using all ones in the portion of its address that corresponds to the network ID of the address it is being used with. Table 4.9 clarifies this point.

The default subnet mask for a Class A address is 255.0.0.0, because only the first octet of the address is used to indicate the network ID. Similarly, a Class C address uses the first three octets to represent the network ID; therefore, the default subnet mask for this type of address is 255.255.255.0.

When a TCP/IP host is initialized, it compares its own IP address to its given subnet mask through a process called ANDing (see Table 4.10), and it stores the result in memory. When the host needs to determine whether a packet is

Table 4.9 Default subnet masks for Classes A, B, and C.		
Address Class	**Mask Decimal Value**	**Mask Binary Value**
Class A	255.0.0.0	11111111.00000000.00000000.00000000
Class B	255.255.0.0	11111111.11111111.00000000.00000000
Class C	255.255.255.0	11111111.11111111.11111111.00000000

Table 4.10   The ANDing process.

Address	Dotted-Decimal Equivalent
IP Address 11000000.10101000.00000010.01000010	192.168.2.66
Subnet Mask 11111111.11111111.11111111.00000000	255.255.255.0
ANDing Result 11000000.10101000.00000010.00000000	192.168.2.0

bound for a local network or a remote network, it compares the destination IP address of the packet with its own subnet mask and then compares the result to the original result it obtained during initialization. If these two results are the same, the packet is bound for a local host and is not routed from the network. If the results are different, the packet is bound for a remote host and is routed to the appropriate network. This process is discussed in greater detail in Chapter 5, "Subnet Addressing."

During the ANDing process, corresponding ones and zeros are combined. The result of two ones is a one. The result of a zero and any number is a zero.

If you decide to subnet your Class C address into two separate networks, you must extend the subnet mask to indicate the bits that are being added to the network ID. To obtain two additional subnets from a Class C address, most people use the mask 255.255.255.192. The number 192 in the last octet of the subnet mask is obtained by borrowing the first two bits of the host ID. These two bits actually give a total of four networks, but because a network ID cannot be comprised of all ones or all zeros, we are left with two remaining subnets (the 64 and the 128 subnets). An example of the resulting subnet mask is shown in Table 4.11.

Table 4.11   The ANDing process revisited.

Address	Dotted-Decimal Equivalent
IP Address 11000000.10101000.00000010.01000010	192.168.2.66
Subnet Mask 11111111.11111111.11111111.11000000	255.255.255.192
ANDing Result 11000000.10101000.00000010.01000000	192.168.2.64

Troubleshooting IP Addressing Problems

The two most common IP addressing problems are incorrect network IDs for hosts that share the same network and duplicate host IDs on a network.

If a host is using the incorrect network ID, the information it is expecting is forwarded to another network. This can occur when a machine is moved from one network to another.

When two hosts on the same network try to use the same host ID, communication errors can occur. Either of the two hosts can hang or crash. This is supposed to be prevented in Windows NT machines, because they broadcast the address they intend to use during the initialization of TCP/IP and will fail to initialize if a duplicate host ID exists on the network. However, not all hosts use this method of initialization.

Exam Prep Questions

Question 1

> By default, the first ___ octet(s) of a Class B address are used to identify the network ID.
>
> ○ a. 1
>
> ○ b. 2
>
> ○ c. 3
>
> ○ d. 4

The correct answer for this question is b. By default, the first two octets of a Class B address represent the network ID. The default for a Class A address is the first octet, and the default for a Class C address is the first three octets. Although you can change the number of octets that represent the network ID by changing the subnet mask, this question is asking for the default values. Therefore, answers a, c, and d are incorrect.

Question 2

> What class would the address 13.245.88.23 fall under?
>
> ○ a. Class A
>
> ○ b. Class B
>
> ○ c. Class C
>
> ○ d. Class D

The correct answer for this question is a. Remember that the class of an IP address can be determined by the value of the first octet. The first octet of a Class A address ranges from 1 to 126. Class B ranges from 128 to 191 and Class C ranges from 192 to 223. Class D is reserved for multicasting; its addresses range from 224 to 239. Therefore, answers b, c, and d are incorrect.

Question 3

> Which of the following addresses are used for special purposes?
> [Check all correct answers]
>
> ❑ a. 127, when used in the first octet of a Class B address
>
> ❑ b. 255, when used in the last octet of a Class C address
>
> ❑ c. 0, when used in the first octet of a Class A address
>
> ❑ d. 192, when used in the last octet of a Class C address

The correct answers for this question are a, b, and c. The use of 127 in the first octet is restricted. It does not matter whether it is a Class A address. 127 is the loopback address that is used for testing. Therefore, answer a is correct. This network number is reserved for network adapter diagnostics. The use of 255 in the host ID component of a Class C address has a special meaning. It indicates that a packet should be broadcast to all hosts on the specified network. The use of 0 (zero) in the network ID of a Class A address indicates that the packet being sent is for a local host and should not be routed from the network. The use of 192 in the host ID of a Class C address does not necessarily have any special purpose. However, when used as the last octet of a subnet mask, it indicates that the bits have been borrowed from the host ID and given to the network ID for the purposes of subnetting.

Question 4

> What is the decimal value of the octet 11111001?
>
> ○ a. 224
>
> ○ b. 225
>
> ○ c. 248
>
> ○ d. 249

The correct answer to this question is d. By taking the sum of the resulting numbers, you have the decimal value for the entire octet. Thus, 11111001 becomes 128+64+32+16+8+0+0+1, which totals 249. To answer this question correctly, you must be able to convert binary digits to decimal numbers. This can be done by memorizing the sequence 128+64+32+16+8+4+2+1 and then replacing any ones in the octet with their corresponding decimal value. If you can't remember the decimal value for a particular bit within an octet, it can be determined by using the formula 2^{n-1}, where n is the position of the bit from the right of the octet.

Question 5

What is the binary value of the decimal number 225?

O a. 11100000

O b. 11100001

O c. 11111000

O d. 11111001

Trick! question

The correct answer to this question is b. To answer this question correctly, you must be able to convert decimal numbers to binary digits. This can be done by memorizing the sequence 128+64+32+16+8+4+2+1 and then choosing the largest number that will go into the decimal number without exceeding it. **For this question, the number you would select first is 128. Now, choose the largest number remaining that when added to the original selection will not exceed the decimal value being sought. Continue this operation from left to right (largest to smallest values) until you obtain the decimal value you are seeking. For this question, the value would be 128+64+32+0+0+0+0+1, which equals 225. Now that you have the decimal value being sought, replace each nonzero number with a 1. What you are left with is the binary value for the decimal number that you began with. For this question, this would be 11100001.**

Question 6

You have just been promoted to network administrator, and your company is ready to implement TCP/IP on its network. Your company network is composed of two separate networks, containing three Windows NT servers and approximately 35 workstations each. Which of the following address classes would be most appropriate for this size network?

O a. Class A

O b. Class B

O c. Class C

O e. Cannot be determined from the information given

The correct answer to this question is c. Although a Class A or Class B address will certainly support the given scenario, a Class C address will provide for an address space that meets the company's current needs and gives room for the future expansion of the network. At the same time, the company will not be required to maintain an inappropriately large address space within its network.

Question 7

> Which of the following are commonly existing addressing problems? [Check all correct answers]
>
> ❑ a. The host is configured with an incorrect network ID.
>
> ❑ b. The host has not been configured to use DNS.
>
> ❑ c. The host has the same host ID as another host on the same network.
>
> ❑ d. The host has the same network ID as other hosts on the same network.

The correct answers for this question are a and c. Hosts configured with an incorrect network ID are fairly commonplace in the world of TCP/IP. When machines are moved from one physical network to another, it is important to remember that the network ID must be changed on those machines. Answer b is incorrect because DNS is not used for addressing, but rather host name resolution. **Answer c is correct because no two hosts on the same network are allowed to share (have duplicate) host IDs.** Answer d is incorrect because all hosts that reside on a particular network share a network ID.

Need To Know More?

 Lammle, Todd, Monica Lammle, and James Chellis. *MCSE: TCP/IP Study Guide.* Sybex Network Press, San Francisco, CA, 1997. ISBN 0-7821-1969-7. Chapter 2, "Identifying Machines with IP Addressing," contains information about subnet masks.

 McLaren, Tim and Stephen Myers. *MCSE Study Guide: TCP/ IP and SMS.* New Riders Publishing, Indianapolis, IN, 1996. ISBN 1-56205-588-7. Chapter 3, "IP Addressing," contains information regarding binary and decimal number conversions.

Search the TechNet CD (or its online version through www.microsoft.com) using the keywords "subnet mask," "address classes," "ANDing," and related query items.

The *Windows NT Server Resource Kit* contains a lot of useful information about TCP/IP and related topics. You can search the TechNet CD (or its online version) or the *Resource Kit* CD using the keywords "TCP/IP," "address classes," and "subnet mask." Useful TCP/IP-related materials can be found throughout the "Networking Guide" volume of the *Resource Kit.*

Subnet
Addressing

Terms you'll need to understand:

√ Subnet

√ Subnet mask

√ Default subnet mask

√ Custom subnet mask

√ ANDing

√ Network ID

√ Host ID

√ CIDR

Techniques you'll need to master:

√ Determining the number of network IDs needed for an organization

√ Determining the number of host IDs required per network or subnetwork

√ Defining an appropriate subnet mask for a given situation

√ Defining the appropriate network or subnetwork IDs for a given subnet mask

√ Defining the appropriate host IDs for each network or subnetwork

A good deal of the Microsoft TCP/IP exam will test your knowledge of subnets and subnetting. You'll be asked to determine the correct subnet mask for a particular organization, figure out on which subnet a host resides, and trouble-shoot issues concerning the use of incorrect subnet masks.

Many feel that subnetting is the most difficult part of the TCP/IP exam, and, in fact, it is probably the least understood part of administering a TCP/IP network. This is likely due to a lack of understanding of binary numbers and how they convert to decimal numbers. The concept of subnetting would be more straightforward if it were easier for humans to work with and understand large binary numbers, eliminating the need to convert them to a decimal for-mat. This chapter strives to explain the relation between IP addresses in their binary format and the decimal equivalent of those binary numbers, as it per-tains to subnetting. If you consistently think of IP addresses as binary num-bers, even while looking at them in their decimal format, you are well on your way to becoming a proficient TCP/IP administrator.

Subnet Addressing: Explored And Explained

As mentioned in the previous chapter, an "IP address" is a 32-bit number com-prised of four octets (groupings of eight bits). An IP address can also be repre-sented in a dotted-decimal format (for example, 128.13.134.45), and is divided into network ID and host ID components. This division of an IP address aids routers in forwarding packets across a TCP/IP network by decreasing the com-plexity of the routing tables needed to locate a particular host.

The routers between any two hosts do not need to know the exact location of the host on a given network. Instead, they use the network ID portion of the address to forward packets to a router connected to the correct network; then, that router takes care of determining to which host on the network the infor-mation is sent.

By default, the boundary between the network and host IDs for a given IP address falls between two of the four octets. See Table 5.1 for an example of default network and host IDs for a Class B address.

Table 5.1	Class B address—network and host ID components.		
Address Class	**IP Address**	**Network ID**	**Host ID**
Class B	130.29.88.7	130.29	88.7

The default boundaries between the network ID and the host ID correspond to one of the three default address classes. Classes are used to subdivide the entire 32-bit IP address space into arbitrary groups of addresses that can support different numbers of hosts. Table 5.2 illustrates address classes and the number of hosts each class can support. The InterNIC (Internet Network Information Center) uses classes to assign to an organization a network ID that corresponds to an appropriate number of host IDs. The organization is then free to assign the host IDs as it sees fit.

However, the InterNIC assigns only one network ID to an entire organization. This might be fine for a small organization that is assigned a Class C address (which supports up to 254 hosts), if it currently has one network and will not need to add additional network segments in the future. However, most organizations will likely have a number of networks already present and will need to provide for additional networks in the future; therefore, one network ID will not be sufficient. Additional network IDs can be provided by "subnetting" the assigned address space.

What Is A Subnet?

Before trying to grasp the concept of a subnet, it is important to understand that each organization connected to the Internet is usually identified by one unique network ID that is assigned to it by the InterNIC. This network ID may not be changed or modified in any way. You can, however, use any of the host IDs assigned to your organization as you see fit, including using some of the host IDs you are assigned to subdivide your network into "subnetworks."

A "subnet" is a network or network ID that is created by borrowing bits from the host portion of an IP address and using them as part of the network ID. If your network currently has four physical networks separated by routers, additional network IDs are needed to correctly route information among those networks.

Table 5.2	Address classes and the corresponding network and host IDs available.			
Address Class	**High Order Bits**	**First Octet Decimal Range**	**Networks Available**	**Hosts Available**
Class A	0	1-126.x.y.z	126	16,777,214
Class B	10	128-191.x.y.z	16,384	65,534
Class C	110	192-223.x.y.z	2,097,152	254

This can be accomplished by changing the default "subnet mask" (explained in greater detail in the next section) to allow additional bits from the host ID portion of your address class to be added to the network ID component.

If your organization is not connected to the Internet, you really don't need to subnet a given address class, because you are free to use the entire TCP/IP address space for your organization. This means you can use as many of the default network IDs as you want. This is also true for networks that are connected to the Internet by a proxy or firewall. These devices hide the internal structure of a network by servicing all requests for information through one IP address. In other words, every packet that leaves the network appears as if it came directly from the proxy, rather than from the host that actually sent the information. The proxy takes care of mapping incoming and outgoing packets to the correct hosts.

Default Subnet Masks

In Chapter 4, "IP Addressing," we introduced the concept of a subnet mask. The "subnet mask" is another 32-bit address that helps TCP/IP determine which portion of the IP address is the network ID and which is the host ID. Each bit that is set to 1 in the subnet mask corresponds to a bit in the IP address that is to be used as the network ID. Each bit that is set to 0 in the subnet mask corresponds to a bit in the IP address that is to be used as the host ID.

By default, each address class has a predetermined number of bits allocated to the network and host ID components of the address. A Class B address uses the first 16 bits to designate the network ID and has a default subnet mask of 255.255.0.0, whereas a Class C address uses the first 24 bits to designate the network ID and has a default subnet mask of 255.255.255.0. Table 5.3 shows the default subnet masks for address Classes A through C.

As mentioned earlier, the InterNIC assigns a single network ID to represent your organization's entire network. If your network requires more than one network ID, you can extend the default subnet mask to include additional bits from the host ID. This allows for additional network IDs within the network.

Table 5.3   Default subnet masks for Classes A, B, and C.

Address Class	Mask Decimal	Mask Binary Value
Class A	255.0.0.0	11111111.00000000.00000000.00000000
Class B	255.255.0.0	11111111.11111111.00000000.00000000
Class C	255.255.255.0	11111111.11111111.11111111.00000000

For example, assume you work for a company that currently has three physical networks. You have been assigned a Class C address with the network ID 192.168.24.0. You need to provide at least three network IDs within this address space to support the current network configuration. You can do this by extending the default subnet mask (255.255.255.0) to include three bits from the host ID component, which will result in the subnet mask 255.255.255.224. These three bits provide a total of six additional network IDs within your company, because the three bits can be recombined in six—that is, $(2^3)-2$—different ways: 001, 010, 011, 100, 101, and 110. Remember that a network ID cannot contain all ones or all zeros; therefore, the combinations 000 and 111 are not valid subnet IDs. Figures 5.1 and 5.2 show the effects of extending the default subnet mask. Don't worry if you do not fully understand this example right now; the rest of the chapter will further explain this process.

By extending the default subnet mask to include three of the bits from the host ID portion of the address, you are able to create additional network or subnet IDs. In this case, the host at 192.168.24.65 has gone from being the sixty-fifth host on the 192.168.24.0 network to being the first host on the 192.168.24.64 network, because the three bits that were added to the subnet mask now provide the subnetwork numbers 192.168.24(.32), (.64), (.96), (.128), (.160), and (.192). Table 5.4 lists the first IP address of each new subnet.

		Network ID			Host ID
IP Address	192.168.24.65	11000000	10101000	00011000	01000001
Default Subnet Mask	255.255.255.0	11111111	11111111	11111111	00000000

Figure 5.1   Before extending the default subnet mask to allow additional network IDs.

		Network ID			Subnet ID	Host ID
IP Address	192.168.24.65	11000000	10101000	00011000	010	00001
Default Subnet Mask	255.255.255.224	11111111	11111111	11111111	111	00000

Figure 5.2   After extending the default subnet mask to allow additional network IDs.

Table 5.4	First host address of each new subnet.	
IP Address	**Network ID**	**Host ID**
192.168.24.33	11000000.10101000.00011000.001 (32)	00001
192.168.24.65	11000000.10101000.00011000.010 (64)	00001
192.168.24.97	11000000.10101000.00011000.011 (96)	00001
192.168.24.129	11000000.10101000.00011000.100 (128)	00001
192.168.24.161	11000000.10101000.00011000.101 (160)	00001
192.168.24.193	11000000.10101000.00011000.110 (192)	00001

These subnet IDs are gained, however, at the expense of some of the available host IDs. Using the example subnet mask 255.255.255.224, you now have a maximum of 30 hosts per subnet (or 180 hosts on the entire network) instead of the 254 hosts that the default subnet mask allows. To derive the number of valid host IDs remaining after subnetting, use the following equation: 2^n-2 where n is the number of octet digit left after the subnet mask. For Table 5.4, this would be $2^5-2 = 30$.

Once the correct subnet mask is determined and configured, the TCP/IP host uses this value to determine whether the recipient of an IP packet is on the local network or a remote network through a process called ANDing.

How ANDing Works

When a TCP/IP host initializes, it uses a process called "ANDing" to compare its own IP address to the subnet mask it is configured to use and then stores this value in memory. ANDing is a mathematical process that compares the IP address to the subnet mask in their binary forms. Each of the 32 bits of the IP address is combined with its corresponding bit in the subnet mask. The result of two ones being combined is 1, and the result of a zero combined with any number is 0. This process informs the TCP/IP host of its own network ID. Table 5.5 gives an example of this process, using the subnet mask obtained from the previous example.

In Table 5.5, a 27-bit subnet mask is used, and the original ANDing result produced during initialization tells this host that its network ID is 192.168.24.64. This number is stored for future use in determining whether or not to route packets from the local network.

Whenever this host needs to send information to another host, it will AND the IP address of the destination host with the configured subnet mask and

	IP - Decimal Value	Network ID - Binary Value	Host ID - Binary Value
IP Address of Source Host	192.168.24.65	11000000.10101000.00011000.010	00001
Subnet Mask	255.255.255.224	11111111.11111111.11111111.111	00000
Original ANDing Result	**192.168.24.64**	**11000000.10101000.00011000.010**	**00000**
IP Address of a Local Host	192.168.24.91	11000000.10101000.00011000.010	11011
Subnet Mask	255.255.255.224	11111111.11111111.11111111.111	00000
Second ANDing Result	**192.168.24.64**	**11000000.10101000.00011000.010**	**00000**
IP Address of a Remote Host	192.168.24.97	11000000.10101000.00011000.011	00001
Subnet Mask	255.255.255.224	11111111.11111111.11111111.111	00000
Third ANDing Result	**192.168.24.96**	**11000000.10101000.00011000.011**	**00000**

Table 5.5   The ANDing process.

compare this result to the result obtained during start-up. If the two results are the same, the destination host resides on the same network as the sending host, and the information is sent directly to the destination host. The second ANDing result of Table 5.5 illustrates this point. If the two results are different, the destination host resides on a different network than the sending host, and the information is sent to the local default gateway for routing to the correct network. The third ANDing result of Table 5.5 illustrates this point.

Implementing A Subnetwork Architecture

Now that you have an understanding of all of the components and processes involved in subnetting, it's time to put that knowledge to practical use. The remainder of this chapter focuses on the benefits of subnetting a given network ID, the steps involved in correctly assessing the number and size of the subnets needed, and how to implement the subnets correctly once they have been determined.

All Things Considered

The benefits of subnetting are many. Subnetting allows networks that use different media access methods to be interconnected. For example, a router can connect an Ethernet network to a Token Ring network. Subnetting also provides the ability to overcome the physical limitations of a network's capacity. One Ethernet network can only support a limited number of hosts. By subnetting, you allow a greater number of hosts to be supported on the entire network. This segmentation also increases the effective bandwidth of any one network by reducing the amount of broadcast traffic a network receives. And, finally, subnetting allows physically isolated networks, such as wide area networks, to communicate with one another.

Here are the five major steps involved in properly subnetting a network:

1. Determine the total number of network IDs required. This includes planning for the addition of future networks.

2. Determine the total number of host IDs that each network must support. Again, you should assume that additional hosts will be added to each network in the future.

3. Define a subnet mask that will support the number of networks and hosts needed per network.

4. Define the network or subnet IDs to be used.

5. Define each of the host IDs to be used on each network.

Number Of Network IDs Required

The first step in subnetting a network is to determine the number of network (or subnetwork) IDs required. Remember that you'll need to assign a separate network ID to every segment of your network bordered by a router, including WAN connections bordered by routers. Figure 5.3 shows a sample network configuration and the different segments that require unique network IDs.

In Figure 5.3, you can see that there are four distinct networks within this organization and one network outside of the organization that is used to provide access to the Internet. Each local network segment and the remote network segment requires a unique network ID, as does the segment of the network connecting this organization to the Internet. However, you will not be required to create a network ID for the segment of the network outside of your default gateway (which connects to the Internet). This network ID is assigned by the InterNIC because it must be unique to the entire Internet. Additionally, this segment is usually under the control of your ISP (Internet Service Provider), which will ensure that proper addressing is being used.

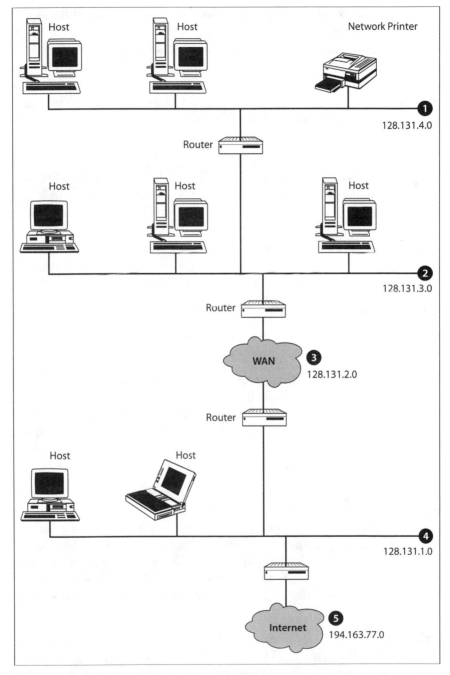

Figure 5.3   A sample network requiring five network IDs.

Remember that you are creating a subdivision of your logical IP address space that corresponds to each physical segment of your network. You want to use the same subnet mask for the entire organization, and you don't want to have to change the subnet mask in the future. With this in mind, it is important to plan for the creation of additional networks in the future. In Figure 5.3, there are currently four subnets within the organization's entire network. In this example, you should plan on adding at least four to eight more networks in the future, depending on anticipated growth.

Number Of Host IDs Required Per Subnet

Once you have determined the number of individual network IDs needed, you must determine the number of host IDs that will be required per subnet. A host ID is required for every network interface card (NIC) on a given network segment. This includes every workstation or server configured to access the TCP/IP network, any printers that access the network directly, and every router interface. Some routers, such as multihomed Windows NT Servers or Workstations, require only two host IDs; however, most enterprise routers require between 8 and 24 host IDs. Remember that each router interface will have a unique network ID as well. Figure 5.4 shows a sample network configuration and the different devices that require unique host IDs.

When determining the correct number of host IDs required per subnet, you should again plan for the future. If your largest subnet currently requires 35 unique host IDs, you might want to allow for a total of 60 hosts in the future. Choose a subnet mask that will support this configuration so that it will not have to be changed later. Imagine the difficulty of reconfiguring every workstation and router on your network with a new subnet mask.

Defining The Subnet Mask

Now that you've determined the number of network and host IDs needed, you must define a subnet mask that will support your requirements. Defining the subnet mask is something of a balancing act. You must borrow enough bits from the host ID to provide the additional network IDs needed, but you cannot borrow so many that each subnet will not support the desired number of hosts.

Let's assume that your company has been assigned the Class C network ID 192.169.220.0. This network ID supports up to 254 hosts on a single network. However, your company already has six networks, the largest of which currently supports nine hosts. Your goal is to determine a subnet mask that supports your current network configuration while providing some room for future growth.

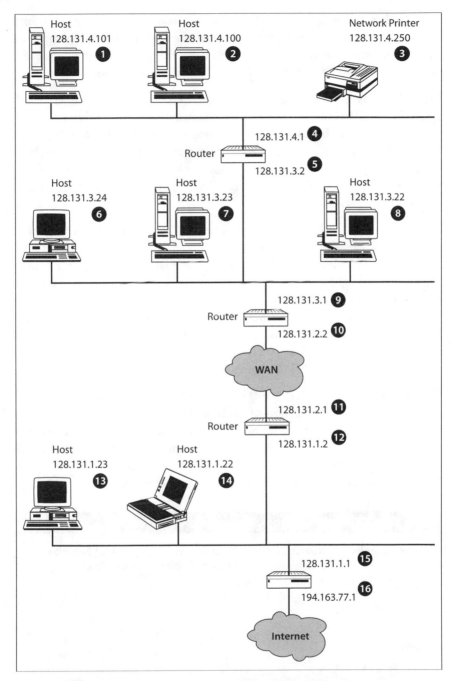

Figure 5.4   A sample network requiring 16 host IDs.

Because there are a limited number of subnet masks that can be used for a Class C network, it can be helpful to examine them all. Table 5.6 illustrates the trade-off between the number of network IDs a subnet mask will provide and the number of hosts that can be supported by each new subnet.

Table 5.6 leaves out the default subnet mask for a Class C network (255.255.255.0) because it provides only one network ID. The table also leaves out the .128 subnet because it uses only one extra bit for the subnets, and a subnet ID cannot be all ones or all zeros. Additionally, the .254 and .255 subnet masks provide numerous subnets, but they don't allow for the presence of any hosts on those subnets. Therefore, you are left with five potential subnet masks from which to choose.

Your company network already has six networks to support, so at the very least, you need to assign the subnet mask 255.255.255.224. This mask provides up to 6 subnets of 30 hosts each. However, your goal when selecting a subnet mask is to provide room for future growth, and the subnet mask 255.255.255.224 will not allow for the addition of any new networks in the future. Therefore, it would be better to select the mask 255.255.255.240. This mask borrows four bits from the host ID, and it allows for a total of 14 subnets on the network. The remaining 4 bits can be used to provide up to 14 host IDs on each network.

The subnet mask 255.255.255.240 is your best choice for this particular scenario. It allows for the addition of up to eight new subnets, and it provides room for even the largest subnet to grow by as many as five hosts. Now that you have seen the relationship between the number of subnets on a network and the number of hosts that each subnet can support, let's see how a subnet mask can be determined without the aid of a subnet table.

Table 5.6   Valid subnet masks for a Class C address.

Subnet Mask	Number of Subnets	Number of Hosts/Subnet	Total Number of Hosts
255.255.255.192	2	62	124
255.255.255.224	6	30	180
255.255.255.240	14	14	196
255.255.255.248	30	6	180
255.255.255.252	62	2	124
255.255.255.254	126	—	—
255.255.255.255	254	—	—

Manually Calculating A Proper Subnet Mask

The first step in manually calculating a subnet mask is to determine the currently needed number of networks. Once this number has been determined, you need to find out how many bits must be borrowed to create this number. For instance, if your network currently has six networks, then the minimum number of subnets needed is six. The number 6 in its binary form is 110 (one-one-zero); therefore, you'll need to borrow a minimum of three bits from the host ID to create the six subnets needed.

This subnet mask meets the current needs of the network, but it does not allow for the addition of any new networks in the future. If you borrow one additional bit from the host ID for use in subnetting, you have a total of four bits to use in creating network IDs. With four bits at your disposal, you can create up to 14—that is, 2^4-2 (2^n-2, where n is the number of host bits)—subnets. Remember, you must subtract 2 of the 16 possible combinations because your network ID cannot be all ones or all zeros.

The last step of the manual process is to determine whether or not the remaining host ID bits will support the maximum number of hosts needed per subnet. Again, with four bits, you can create up to 14 host IDs. Because your largest subnet needs to support only nine hosts, this subnet mask will suit your needs while allowing for growth on each of the new subnets.

Defining The Network And Subnet IDs To Use

Now that you have determined a subnet mask that will support the needs of your network, you must define the individual subnet IDs that will be used. This is an important part of the process because subnetting causes many previously valid IP addresses to become invalid. If you assign any of these invalid IP addresses to hosts on your network, communication errors will occur.

Step 1 in determining which network IDs to use is to list all the binary combinations possible with the borrowed bits. The subnet mask 255.255.255.240 borrows four bits from the host ID. Table 5.7 lists all of the possible binary combinations of four bits.

Table 5.7	All possible binary combinations of four bits.						
0-1	**2-3**	**4-5**	**6-7**	**8-9**	**10-11**	**12-13**	**14-15**
0000	0010	0100	0110	1000	1010	1100	1110
0001	0011	0101	0111	1001	1011	1101	1111

Step 2 in determining which network IDs to use is to discard any combinations containing all ones or zeros. It might help to remember that the first and last network or host ID of any range cannot be used. Once you have removed the invalid combinations, you are left with the binary values 1 to 14.

Step 3 is to append the four remaining bits of the host ID to the valid combinations of subnet IDs and convert the values to decimal format. Table 5.8 demonstrates this process.

Step 4 is easy; simply append the decimal subnet value to the default subnet mask for the class of address being used, and *voilà*, you have the subnet ID and the corresponding subnet mask for each of the required subnets.

Because calculating all of the possible binary combinations for a particular subnet mask can be tiresome, many network administrators use a shortcut. They simply calculate the decimal equivalent of the lowest binary value that can be made with the available subnet bits and then add that value to itself. By doing this as many times as there are valid binary combinations to use, they can obtain all of the subnet IDs for the network, with much less effort.

Table 5.8   Appending remaining host ID bits to the valid subnet values.

Binary Subnet	Decimal Subnet	Decimal Subnet Mask
0001 0000	.16	255.255.255.16
0010 0000	.32	255.255.255.32
0011 0000	.48	255.255.255.48
0100 0000	.64	255.255.255.64
0101 0000	.80	255.255.255.80
0110 0000	.96	255.255.255.96
0111 0000	.112	255.255.255.112
1000 0000	.128	255.255.255.128
1001 0000	.144	255.255.255.144
1010 0000	.160	255.255.255.160
1011 0000	.176	255.255.255.176
1100 0000	.192	255.255.255.192
1101 0000	.208	255.255.255.208
1110 0000	.224	255.255.255.224

Using the previous example, begin by calculating the decimal equivalent of the binary combination with the value. In this case, this would be 0001 plus the four remaining host bits, which gives you 0001 0000, or 16. Use this value (called the *delta*, which means change) to incrementally find the value of each of the subsequent subnet IDs. The first subnet ID is .16, which added to .16 becomes .32, which added to .16 becomes .48, and so on. This method of computing subnet ID values can save you a lot of time when numerous subnets need to be defined within a network. Additionally, you can find many different types of tables that will aid you in the subnetting; however, you are not allowed to use such tables on the Microsoft TCP/IP exam.

Defining The Host IDs To Use

The final step in properly subnetting your network is to define the correct host IDs for each of the subnets you create. Begin by assigning the first host ID for each subnet using the remaining bits of the host ID.

The first host ID on any network is always 1. Using the previous example, the first value you can create from the four remaining bits is 0001. Add this to the subnet ID of the first subnet (which is 16) and you get 0001 0000 plus 0000 0001, which equals 0001 0001, or 17. Because only 14 valid host IDs can be obtained by using four bits, the subsequent steps involve incrementing the host ID value by 1, until the host ID value reaches 14. Again, because a host ID cannot be all ones, a host ID of 15, or 1111, becomes invalid. Table 5.9 shows all valid host IDs for the .16 subnet of the previous example. You can repeat the process shown for each of the remaining subnet IDs.

Table 5.9   Appending remaining host ID bits to the valid subnet values.

Binary Subnet ID	Binary Host ID	Decimal IP Address
0001 0000 (16)	0000 0001 (1)	w.x.y.17
0001 0000 (16)	0000 0010 (2)	w.x.y.18
0001 0000 (16)	0000 0011 (3)	w.x.y.19
0001 0000 (16)	0000 0100 (4)	w.x.y.20
0001 0000 (16)	0000 0101 (5)	w.x.y.21
0001 0000 (16)	0000 0110 (6)	w.x.y.22
0001 0000 (16)	0000 0111 (7)	w.x.y.23
0001 0000 (16)	0000 1000 (8)	w.x.y.24

(continued)

Table 5.9	Appending remaining host ID bits to the valid subnet values *(continued)*.	
Binary Subnet ID	**Binary Host ID**	**Decimal IP Address**
0001 0000 (16)	0000 1001 (9)	w.x.y.25
0001 0000 (16)	0000 1010 (10)	w.x.y.26
0001 0000 (16)	0000 1011 (11)	w.x.y.27
0001 0000 (16)	0000 1100 (12)	w.x.y.28
0001 0000 (16)	0000 1101 (13)	w.x.y.29
0001 0000 (16)	0000 1110 (14)	w.x.y.30

CIDR: Classless Inter-Domain Routing

As mentioned in Chapter 4, CIDR (Classless Inter-Domain Routing) is used to reduce the size of the routing tables used by the routers on the backbone of the Internet. These routers maintain entries for each individual network ID that is assigned by the InterNIC. In general, each of these entries corresponds to a separate organization. However, when the InterNIC assigns multiple network IDs to the same organization, it adds unnecessary complexity and size to these routing tables.

If one organization is assigned three Class C network IDs, three additional entries will need to be added to the routing tables in order for information to correctly reach the network of this one organization. CIDR allows the aggregation of multiple routes to an organization; these routes are created by using several network ID addresses in the opposite way to subnetting. CIDR provides a form of supernetting. Instead of increasing the number of bits used to mask an address, supernetting actually reduces the number of bits used in the subnet mask.

This was not previously allowed because each class of address also had a corresponding default subnet mask. If you reduce the subnet mask beyond the default, you are in effect saying that the boundary for that class of address no longer exists; hence, the term "classless" routing. CIDR also allows for only part of the addresses within one network ID to be assigned to an organization; for example, only part of a Class B address will be assigned to an organization, whereas the remaining addresses within that network ID can be assigned elsewhere. CIDR only works for contiguous network IDs.

To see how this works, assume your organization has been assigned the network IDs 192.169.220.0, 192.169.221.0, and 192.169.222.0. If you look at these network IDs in their binary form, you can see that the only difference in these numbers occurs in the last two bits of the third octet. Therefore, by reducing the subnet mask by two bits, you can effectively lump all the host IDs in these three network IDs together. Table 5.10 illustrates this point.

As you can see, the result of ANDing any IP address that falls within one of these network IDs produces the network ID 192.169.220.0. Therefore, you can reduce the number of entries needed to represent these three networks to a single entry. However, CIDR does not work with all routers, so before you can implement CIDR in your organization, you'll need to verify that your routers support it.

Table 5.10	Using CIDR to supernet a group of Class C addresses.	
	Dotted-Decimal Values	**Binary Values**
Network ID	192.169.220.0	11000000 .10101001 .110111-00 .00000000
Network ID	192.169.221.0	11000000 .10101001 .110111-01 .00000000
Network ID	192.169.222.0	11000000 .10101001 .110111-10 .00000000
New Subnet Mask	255.255.252.0	11111111 .11111111 .111111-00 .00000000
ANDing Result	192.169.220.0	11000000 .10101001 .110111-00 .00000000

Exam Prep Questions

Question 1

> Choose from the following options the answer that best describes the purpose of a subnet mask.
>
> ○ a. The subnet mask is used to mask a portion of an IP address for TCP/IP.
>
> ○ b. The subnet mask aids in determining the location of other TCP/IP hosts.
>
> ○ c. The subnet mask is used to help TCP/IP distinguish the network ID from the host ID. This aids in determining the location of other TCP/IP hosts.
>
> ○ d. The subnet mask is used to help TCP/IP distinguish the network ID from the host ID. This aids in determining the IP address of other hosts.

The best answer for this question is c. The subnet mask is used by a TCP/IP host to help it determine its own network ID during initialization. It then uses this information to determine whether the destination host resides on the local network or a remote network. Answer a is partially correct (thus, the "trick"), but it not the best answer because it does not give enough information. Answer b is not correct for the same reason. Answer d is incorrect because the subnet mask does not help TCP/IP determine the IP address of another host. The remote host's IP address must be known before the subnet mask will be of any use.

Question 2

> Which of the following options is the default subnet mask for a Class B network ID?
>
> ○ a. 255.0.0.0
>
> ○ b. 255.255.0.0
>
> ○ c. 255.255.255.0
>
> ○ d. 255.255.255.255

The correct answer for this question is b. Remember that the default subnet mask for a particular class of address corresponds to the number of octets that each class uses to designate its network ID and its host ID. A Class B address uses the first two octets of the IP address to designate the network ID. Therefore, the default subnet mask would require two full octets of all ones (or 255 in decimal form) to indicate that the network ID stopped just before the third octet. Answer a is the default subnet mask for a Class A address. Answer c is the default subnet mask for a Class C address, and answer d is actually a broadcast address.

Question 3

Which of the following are benefits of subnetting a given network ID? [Check all correct answers]

❑ a. Subnetting allows for the interconnection of networks that use different network technologies.

❑ b. Subnetting allows you to overcome the physical limitations of a network's capacity.

❑ c. Subnetting allows for the arbitrary allocation of IP addresses, regardless of host location.

❑ d. Subnetting allows for an effective increase in network bandwidth, by cutting down on the amount of broadcasts a network must process.

The correct answers for this question are a, b, and d. Because routers can often transfer information from Ethernet networks to Token Ring networks, and vice versa, subnetting your network can allow hosts to use different network technologies to communicate with one another. Subnetting also allows you to overcome the inherent physical limitations of a particular network technology such as an Ethernet, which can support only a limited number of hosts per physical network segment. If you currently have more hosts than your Ethernet can support on a single network segment, subnetting allows you to spread those hosts out over multiple physical network segments. Finally, because subnetting physically isolates each segment of a network from the other segments, the number of broadcasts that must be processed by any one network is reduced substantially. This effectively increases the available bandwidth of each subnet. Answer c is incorrect, because the act of subnetting requires that IP addresses be assigned to hosts in a very specific manner, according to which subnet the host resides on.

Question 4

Which of the following does not require a unique host ID?

○ a. A Windows NT Workstation enabled to use TCP/IP and IPX/SPX

○ b. A Windows NT Server configured to use NetBEUI only

○ c. A network printer configured to use TCP/IP

○ d. Every interface on a TCP/IP router

The correct answer for this question is b. Any host configured to use TCP/IP on an IP network or subnet requires a unique host ID. This includes any workstations, servers, network printers, and IP routers. **Answer b does not require a unique host ID, because this machine is not configured to communicate with other TCP/IP hosts.**

Question 5

By default, how many hosts will a Class B address support?

○ a. 254

○ b. 16,384

○ c. 65,534

○ d. 2,097,152

The correct answer for this question is c. The formula for determining the host IDs any number of bits will support is 2^n-2, where n is the number of bits available for use in the host ID. By default, a Class B address uses 16 bits for the host ID. Therefore, $2^{16}-2$ equals 65,534. Answer a is incorrect because 254 is the number of hosts that a Class C address supports, by default. Answer b is incorrect because 16,384 is the number of network IDs available in the Class B address space, by default. Answer d is incorrect because 2,097,152 is the number of network IDs available in the Class C address space, by default.

Question 6

The host David is configured with the IP address 202.121.74.37 and the subnet mask 255.255.255.224. David needs to send information to the host Goliath, which is configured with the IP address 202.121.74.66 and the subnet mask 255.255.255.224. Use the ANDing process to determine which of the following options is correct.

○ a. Goliath is on the 202.121.74.64 subnet; therefore, David and Goliath are on separate subnets. David will need to forward the information to its default gateway.

○ b. Goliath is on the 202.121.74.224 subnet; therefore, David and Goliath are on the same subnets. David will not need to forward the information to its default gateway.

○ c. David and Goliath are both using the same subnet mask and are therefore on the same subnets. These two hosts can communicate directly with one another without using the default gateway.

○ d. David and Goliath are both using the same subnet mask and are therefore on different subnets. These two hosts must communicate with one another through at least one router.

The correct answer for this question is a. Goliath is configured with the IP address 202.121.74.66 and the subnet mask 255.255.255.224. By ANDing these two values, you can see that Goliath is in fact on the (.64) subnet. David, on the other hand, is configured with the IP address 202.121.74.37 and the subnet mask 255.255.255.224. By ANDing these two values, you can see that David is on the (.32) subnet. Both hosts are using the same subnet mask, and each machine has a different network ID. Therefore, for the host David to send information to Goliath, it will have to forward the information to the default gateway. Answer b is incorrect because 202.121.74.224 is not a valid subnet. The value .224 is actually part of the subnet mask. Answer c is incorrect because the mere fact that two hosts are configured with the same subnet mask does not mean that they both reside on the same subnet. Answer d is incorrect for the same reason.

Question 7

Shannon is getting ready to subnet his IP network and must determine the number of network IDs required before he can calculate an appropriate subnet mask for his network. Which of the following options would help him properly calculate the number of necessary network IDs? [Check all correct answers]

❑ a. Calculate a unique network ID for each segment of the network bordered by a router.

❑ b. Calculate a unique network ID for each interface of a router.

❑ c. Calculate a unique network ID for each network printer on a segment.

❑ d. Calculate only one unique network ID for network segments bordered by two or more routers.

The correct answers to this question are a and d. When determining the number of unique network IDs needed for a network, you need to calculate one unique network ID for each segment of your network bordered by at least one router. A closed network (one without outside access) that has two routers with two interfaces each would require three separate network IDs. Answer b is incorrect because only three network IDs are needed, not four as would be calculated by multiplying the interfaces (2) by the number of routers (2). Answer c is incorrect because each network printer or host on a network segment requires a unique host ID, but they all share the same network ID.

Question 8

You work for the Signature Widget Company, which has recently been assigned the Class B network ID 128.131.0.0. Your company currently has 45 individual network segments or subnets. You have been told that new offices will be added in Rome, Paris, and Chicago over the next 12 months, and your network will need to support at least 50 new subnets. What subnet mask should you use for your network to support the largest number of hosts per subnet?

○ a. 255.255.0.0

○ b. 255.255.240.0

○ c. 255.255.252.0

○ d. 255.255.254.0

The correct answer for this question is d. The .254 value in the third octet of the subnet mask allows for a total of 126 subnets on this network. This is the minimum subnet mask that will meet the requirements of the needed network IDs, and it will therefore provide the largest number of host IDs possible per subnet. The subnet mask in answer a is the default subnet mask for a Class B address and only supports a single network ID. The subnet mask in answer b only supports 14 individual subnets and is therefore invalid. The subnet mask in answer c supports up to 62 individual subnets. This meets the current needs of the company's network, but it does not allow for the anticipated need of 95 subnets.

Question 9

The Billington Steambath Company currently has nine divisions, and each one requires its own subnet. It has been assigned the network ID 130.121.0.0. Billington anticipates the need to support up to 3,000 hosts in each division. Which subnet would you recommend it use?

○ a. 255.255.224.0

○ b. 255.255.240.0

○ c. 255.255.248.0

○ d. 255.255.252.0

The correct answer for this question is b. The .240 value in the third octet of the subnet mask allows for a total of 14 subnets on this network. This subnet mask meets the requirements of the currently needed network IDs and allows for future growth. Additionally, this subnet will allow for a maximum of 4,094 hosts per subnet. This subnet meets the requirements of the Billington Steambath Company. Answer a is incorrect because it does not provide enough subnets to meet the current needs of the company. Answers c and d are incorrect because, although they do provide the required number of subnets, they do not allow for the anticipated number of hosts per subnet.

Question 10

Mary works for a new Internet Service Provider (ISP) that has a customer who has been assigned seven Class C addresses ranging from 223.68.168.0 to 223.68.174.0. Her employer would like for her to limit the number of routing table entries for this customer to one. If the routers at the ISP support CIDR, which of the following subnet masks should Mary use to achieve her objective?

○ a. 255.255.224.0

○ b. 255.255.240.0

○ c. 255.255.248.0

○ d. 255.255.254.0

The correct answer for this question is c. The subnet mask 255.255.248.0 reduces the subnet mask by the least number of bits needed to point all traffic bound for any of these subnets to the default network ID for this organization, which is 223.68.168.0. The Table 5.11 illustrates this point.

Table 5.11   Question ANDing results.

	Dotted-Decimal Values	Binary Values
Network ID	223.68.168.0	11011111 .01000100 .10101-000 .00000000
Network ID	223.68.169.0	11011111 .01000100 .10101-001 .00000000
Network ID	223.68.170.0	11011111 .01000100 .10101-010 .00000000

(continued)

Table 5.11   Question ANDing results *(continued)*.

	Dotted-Decimal Values	Binary Values
Network ID	223.68.171.0	11011111 .01000100 .10101-011 .00000000
Network ID	223.68.172.0	11011111 .01000100 .10101-100 .00000000
Network ID	223.68.173.0	11011111 .01000100 .10101-101 .00000000
Network ID	223.68.174.0	11011111 .01000100 .10101-110 .00000000
New Subnet Mask	255.255.255.248	11111111 .11111111 .11111-000 .00000000
ANDing Result	**223.68.168.0**	**11011111 .01000100 .10101-000 .00000000**

The ANDing result of any of these network IDs produces the network ID 223.68.168.0. Therefore, Mary can reduce the number of entries needed to represent these seven networks to a single entry. Answers a and b are incorrect because they do not mask enough of the network ID. Answer d is incorrect because it masks too much of the network ID.

Need To Know More?

Lammle, Todd, Monica Lammle, and James Chellis. *MCSE: TCP/IP Study Guide*. Sybex Network Press, San Francisco, CA, 1997. ISBN 0-7821-1969-7. Chapter 2, "Identifying Machines with IP Addressing," contains information about subnet masks, the benefits of subnetting, and implementing subnetting.

McLaren, Tim and Stephen Myers. *MCSE Study Guide: TCP/ IP and Systems Management Server*. New Riders Publishing, Indianapolis, IN, 1996. ISBN 1-56205-588-7. Chapter 5, "Subnet Addressing," contains information regarding binary and decimal number conversions, default subnet masks, and the steps needed to properly subnet a network ID.

Microsoft TechNet Information Network. September, 97. PN99367. Contains numerous articles on IP addressing and subnet masks. Search for "subnets," "subnet masks," "ANDing," and "CIDR."

The *Windows NT Server Resource Kit* contains a lot of useful information about TCP/IP and related topics. You can search the TechNet (CD or online version) or the CD that accompanies the *Resource Kit* using the keywords "CIDR," "ANDing," "subnet mask." Useful TCP/IP-related materials can be found throughout the "Networking Guide" volume of the *Resource Kit*.

Implementing IP Routing

6

Terms you'll need to understand:

√ Router

√ Host

√ Remote host

√ Multihomed hosts

√ Routing table

√ Gateway

√ Hardware address (HWA)

√ Static routing

√ Dynamic routing

√ Routing Information Protocol (RIP)

√ Open Shortest Path First (OSPF)

√ MultiProtocol Router (MPR)

Techniques you'll need to master:

√ Understanding Microsoft TCP/IP routing

√ Knowing the differences between static and dynamic routing

√ Learning the functions and parameters of the ROUTE and TRACERT commands

√ Implementing and configuring multihomed computers

As you've already discovered in the previous chapters, Microsoft's way of implementing TCP/IP features and functions is not always exactly like those described in the Internet RFCs that define the standards. Some of Microsoft's constructions are far simpler, whereas others are fairly pointless diversions. IP routing is no exception. The most difficult part of routing with Microsoft's version of TCP/IP is learning the terminology and methods. The issues covered in this chapter are far from exhaustive and may not be complete enough to implement IP routing in reality, but we have included more than adequate detail to aid you in mastering this topic as covered by the certification exam.

IP Routing: Explored And Explained

Routing is the process whereby data transmitted from a computer on one network is directed to its intended recipient, when that recipient is a computer located on another network. A router's sole network role is to examine packets directed to its attention, and to forward incoming packets to an appropriate destination, or to inform the sender that the specified destination is unknown and unreachable. A "router" is a device whose sole purpose is to direct network traffic. A router can be a standalone device or a service of a computer (such as Windows NT Server). Because routers give one network the capability to contact hosts in another network, they are sometimes called "gateways." A gateway is a TCP/IP host that is attached to two or more networks; that is, it connects to several networks simultaneously. Such devices are sometimes called "multihomed hosts" (see the section titled "Multihomed Computers And IP Routing," later in this chapter).

A router forwards or relays packets based on the communication pathways defined in its "routing table." A routing table is simply a database that correlates network segment IP addresses with the IP address of the router's interfaces. When data is transmitted from a host, the routing table is consulted. If the remote or destination host (or its network segment) is not listed in the routing table, it is sent to a default gateway. A default gateway, if defined, is where all data packets sent to unknown addresses are sent. If the destination is found, the data is delivered. If the destination is not found, an error is returned to the source host.

The Routing Process

The process of routing a data packet from one network to another neighboring network is not too difficult to describe or understand. The following routing example uses the layout and number assignments displayed in Figure 6.1.

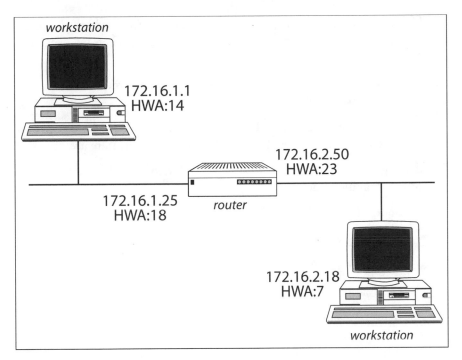

Figure 6.1   Simple routing.

1. The 172.16.1.1 workstation checks the destination address 172.16.2.18 against its local subnet mask.

2. Because 172.16.2.18 is not part of the local subnet, the data must be routed.

3. ARP is called to determine the hardware address (HWA) of the default gateway. The IP address of the default gateway is contained in the TCP/IP configuration 172.16.1.1, but the HWA of the gateway must be obtained through ARP.

4. 172.16.1.1 sends out its data packet to the default gateway 172.16.1.25 with the following information in the header of each packet:

    ➤   Source HWA: 14

    ➤   Source IP address: 172.16.1.1

    ➤   Destination HWA: 18

    ➤   Destination IP address: 172.16.2.18

5. The router, located at the gateway address 172.16.1.25 and HWA 18, determines that it is not the final destination of the packets by inspecting the packet headers.

6. The router determines that the packets must be forwarded to the 172.16.2 network.

7. The router makes an ARP call to determine the HWA of the destination host 172.16.2.18. The HWA is added to its cache for future use.

8. The router sends the packets to the 172.16.2 network with the following information in the header:

   ➤ Source HWA: 23

   ➤ Source IP address: 172.16.1.1

   ➤ Destination HWA: 7

   ➤ Destination IP address: 172.16.2.18

9. The data travels into the 172.16.2 network; the destination host's NIC recognizes its HWA and IP address and retrieves the packets.

You should note that the source IP address in the header when the packet reaches its destination is that of the original transmitting computer. However, the HWA is that of the last gateway (that is, the router interface) encountered. As a packet "hops" between different networks (that is, traverses a router), the IP addresses of the source and destination remain constant, but the HWAs change to match that of the hardware needed to complete the transmission.

Any routing scenario becomes more complex and difficult to follow when multiple networks are involved, or when the destination host is not directly attached to the router. Routing tables help to solve these problems, and other delivery issues that routers must address. Routing tables enable routers to determine where to relay a packet when its final destination is not included in the table. Remember also that a routing table contains only a list of the locations of or pathways to networks, not individual hosts.

Static Vs. Dynamic Routing

The two types of routing tables are static and dynamic (see Table 6.1). System administrators must manually maintain and update static routing tables, because these tables cannot change without explicit intervention. A dynamic routing table is constructed and maintained automatically by the routing protocol. Until Windows NT 4, dynamic routing was only available through expensive third-party add-on products. Now, through MPR and RIP, dynamic routing is part of NT Server 4.

Table 6.1 Dynamic and static routing compared.	
Dynamic Routing	**Static Routing**
A routing protocol function	An IP function
Routers share data	Routers do not share data
Table automatically maintained	Table manually maintained
Requires RIP or OSPF	Multihomed hosts supported
Used on large and complex networks	Used on smaller or simpler networks

Static IP Routing

Static routing is a built-in function of IP and does not require any additional services to function. A static routing table must be created and maintained by hand on each router. A static router can be a standalone routing device or a multihomed NT Server (discussed later, in the section titled "Multihomed Computers And IP Routing").

A static routing table defines the relationships between known networks and the gateway or router interfaces used to access them. A static routing table is composed of the following five columns of data:

➤ **Network Address** The address of each known network, including the local address (0.0.0.0) and broadcasts (255.255.255.255)

➤ **Netmask** The subnet mask used for each network

➤ **Gateway Address** The IP address of the entrance point (router interface) for each network

➤ **Interface** The IP address assigned to the network's interface point

➤ **Metric** The number of hops to reach the network

Table 6.2 provides an example of a routing table.

 Remember the following, whenever you work with static routing tables:

➤ A static router can only communicate with networks for which it is configured.

➤ A static route can be defined as a gateway address or as an entry in a routing table.

Table 6.2   A sample static routing table.

Network	Netmask	Gateway	Interface	Metric
0.0.0.0 (default route)	0.0.0.0	10.57.11.169	1	10.57.8.1
127.0.0.0 (loopback address)	255.0.0.0	127.0.0.1	1	127.0.0.1
10.57.8.0 (local subnet address)	255.255.248.0	10.57.11.169	1	10.57.11.169
10.57.11.169 network card address)	255.255.255.255	127.0.0.1	1	127.0.0.1
10.57.255.255 (subnet broadcast address)	255.255.255.255	10.57.11.169	1	10.57.11.169
224.0.0.0 (multicast address)	224.0.0.0	10.57.11.169	1	10.57.11.169
255.255.255.255 (limited broadcast address)	255.255.255.255	10.57.11.169	1	10.57.11.169

Gateways

A gateway is a dedicated computer or router that has a more complete list of the surrounding networks than does each host device within a single network. When data is destined for a computer outside of the current network, it is passed to the gateway. The gateway (router) reads the delivery header and determines if the destination is local (that is, if it resides on any of the subnets to which the router is physically attached), or if it needs to relay the packet onto its defined default gateway. Ultimately, a packet will either reach its destination, or an error message that explains why it can't be delivered will be relayed until it returns to its sender.

More than one default gateway can be defined, but only the first one is used for routing. The others are only used when the primary gateway is offline or unreachable. This can improve a network's performance, especially should a communication failure occur or when bandwidth usage is high.

The ROUTE Command

The **ROUTE** command is the TCP/IP utility that must be used to create or modify any static IP routing tables maintained by a Windows NT Server machine. Its syntax is as follows:

```
route [-f] [-p] [command [destination] [mask subnetmask]
[gateway] [metric costmetric]]
```

The parameters are as follows:

➤ **-f** Removes all entries. If used with other commands, the flush action is performed first.

➤ **-p** Makes **add** changes persistent (by default, routes are not preserved when the system is restarted). Displays all persistent routes when used with the **print** command (see Figure 6.2).

➤ *command* Specifies one of four commands: **print** (prints a route), **add** (adds a route), **delete** (deletes a route), or **change** (modifies an existing route).

➤ *destination* Identifies the destination network for the route.

➤ **mask** *subnetmask* Defines a subnet mask for this route entry. The default is 255.255.255.255.

➤ *gateway* Specifies the gateway for the route.

➤ **metric** *costmetric* Defines a hop cost ranging from 1 to 9999.

Important! Remember that all the information in any static routing table will be lost following any system reboot, unless the **-p** parameter is used to make the entries persistent.

```
Command Prompt                                                      _ □ ×

    gateway        Specifies gateway.

    METRIC         specifies the metric/cost for the destination

All symbolic names used for destination are looked up in the network database
file NETWORKS. The symbolic names for gateway are looked up in the host name
database file HOSTS.
If the command is print or delete, wildcards may be used for the destination
and gateway, or the gateway argument may be omitted.


E:\>route print

Active Routes:

  Network Address          Netmask  Gateway Address        Interface  Metric
        127.0.0.0        255.0.0.0        127.0.0.1        127.0.0.1       1
       172.16.0.0      255.255.0.0       172.16.1.1       172.16.1.1       1
       172.16.1.1  255.255.255.255        127.0.0.1        127.0.0.1       1
   172.16.255.255  255.255.255.255       172.16.1.1       172.16.1.1       1
        224.0.0.0        224.0.0.0       172.16.1.1       172.16.1.1       1
  255.255.255.255  255.255.255.255       172.16.1.1       172.16.1.1       1
E:\>
```

Figure 6.2   An example of the **ROUTE** command.

The *TRACERT* Command

TRACERT is another useful TCP/IP routing command-line utility (see Figure 6.3). This utility is a route verification and timing tool. Its syntax is as follows:

```
tracert [-d] [-h maximum_hops] [-j computer-list]
[-w timeout] target_name
```

The parameters are:

➤ **-d** Specifies not to resolve addresses to computer names.

➤ **-h maximum_hops** Specifies maximum number of hops to search for target.

➤ **-j computer-list** Specifies loose source route along **computer-list**.

➤ **-w timeout** Waits the number of milliseconds specified by **timeout** for each reply.

➤ **target_name** Specifies the name of the target computer.

 TRACERT is an excellent tool to determine if a route is valid or no longer accessible. You can also use the time feedback to weigh the speed of each route.

```
Command Prompt                                                    _ □ ×
Tracing route to 172.16.1.151 over a maximum of 30 hops

  1   <10 ms    <10 ms    <10 ms   172.16.1.151

Trace complete.

E:\>tracert 206.224.95.1

Tracing route to www.lanw.com [206.224.95.1]
over a maximum of 30 hops:

  1    70 ms     60 ms     90 ms   max1.realtime.net [205.238.128.23]
  2    60 ms     60 ms    110 ms   router3-128.realtime.net [205.238.128.1]
  3    81 ms     80 ms     80 ms   GW1.AUS1.ALTER.NET [137.39.232.41]
  4    80 ms     81 ms    100 ms   186.Hssi5-0.CR2.HOU1.Alter.Net [137.39.31.161]
  5    70 ms    110 ms    101 ms   Fddi0-0.SR1.HOU1.Alter.Net [137.39.37.6]
  6   210 ms     90 ms    120 ms   insync-gw.customer.ALTER.NET [137.39.32.194]
  7    90 ms    111 ms     90 ms   206-66-135-102.insync.net [206.66.135.102]
  8   120 ms    111 ms    130 ms   204.157.152.1
  9   160 ms    140 ms    171 ms   www.lanw.com [206.224.95.1]

Trace complete.

E:\>_
```

Figure 6.3 An example of the **TRACERT** command.

Dynamic IP Routing

Dynamic routing is usually preferable to static routing on large or complex networks, primarily to eliminate the tedium of manually maintaining a plethora of routing tables. The administrative overhead involved in dynamic routing is minimal, and is often limited solely to defining a default gateway for each router. All remaining configuration information, and routing table construction, is handled automatically by the routing protocol itself.

The two most common TCP/IP-related routing protocols are RIP (Routing Information Protocol) and OSPF (Open Shortest Path First). Both of these routing protocols generate network traffic as router tables are updated, but only RIP qualifies as a "chatty" protocol (it propagates entire copies of routing tables at regular intervals across a network, whereas OSPF only propagates changes to routing tables as they need to be updated). For that reason, OSPF is becoming more common on large networks, especially those that include WAN links, and RIP is usually confined for "local routing" use for a single site. OSPF can link multiple RIP domains together, so this creates a kind of protocol hierarchy that occurs on many networks where OSPF is not completely pervasive.

Routing Information Protocol (RIP)

RIP is a distance vector routing protocol. This means that RIP identifies the number of hops for each defined route and uses this information to select the most efficient pathway.

 A routing table maintained by RIP includes the following information:

➤ IP destination address

➤ Hop measurement (1 to 15)

➤ IP address of next router in each path

➤ Delivery time for each route

➤ Time of route information changes

The problem of counting to infinity might occur with RIP if a hop count governor were not in place. For some network connections, when a link becomes inactive, RIP's subsequent attempts to locate the best alternative path will create a logical routing loop. Because such a loop can be traversed an arbitrary number of times yet always returns to itself, a looped path repeats to infinity. To prevent runaway behavior like this, RIP supports a hop-limit counter that may be set anywhere from 1 to 15. Whenever a path's associated hop count hits this limit, the path is judged to be infinite, and will be removed from the routing table. For large networks, setting the hop limit too low will cause delivery problems. Likewise, no pathway longer than 15 hops will work with RIP (to all extents, 16 and infinity are synonymous for RIP). RIP only permits one pathway between any two points to exist at any time, so it can't do any load balancing or load splitting.

Another drawback of RIP is the routine broadcasting of its routing table. This enables each router to compile its routing table from its own data as well as from data elsewhere on the network. If numerous routers are present in a network, this traffic can severely degrade the network's performance. It is common for this default broadcast to occur every 30 seconds.

One of RIP's most troublesome characteristics is its regular broadcasts of routing table information (which also contributes to the protocol's chatty nature). Such broadcasts permit routers to compile their routing tables from internal data, as compared with data from other routers elsewhere on the network. But when numerous routers are present on a network, router table broadcasts can severely degrade network performance, when the amount of bandwidth that such broadcasts consume grows to noticeable levels (and beyond). By default, such broadcasts occur at regular intervals (the most common default interval is once every 60 seconds, but Windows NT's default is once every 30 seconds).

Open Shortest Path First (OSPF)

Whereas RIP is nearly "original equipment" as far as TCP/IP is concerned, OSPF is a second-generation TCP/IP routing protocol. As such, OSPF offers numerous advantages over RIP. As the following list indicates in greater detail: OSPF involves less overhead, supports much larger networks, is significantly less chatty, and supports multiple paths between senders and receivers.

Following is a more detailed look at OSPF's features and functions:

➤ Each link may be assigned its own specific associated cost.

➤ The hop cost limitation is 65,535.

➤ Each node maintains a tree-database of the network paths, with itself as the root.

➤ If equal cost paths exist, load balancing occurs between those paths.

➤ Route tables are only broadcast when changes occur.

➤ Only adjacent or neighboring routers are sent update packets; the "tell a friend" method limits network impact.

Because OSPF is based on a link-state algorithm, it is often called a link-state routing protocol. When it's deployed as the only routing protocol on a network (in networking jargon this is called a "homogeneous routing environment or homogeneous routing protocol system"), each router maintains its own routing table, but needs to maintain information only about its directly attached subnets and only those routers that it can directly access (called adjacent gateways).

Windows NT Server 4 does not include support for OSPF, which probably explains why this protocol does not appear in many questions on the TCP/IP exam. The basic information we've provided here should suffice to help you deal with this subject.

Integrating Static And Dynamic Routing

Static and dynamic routing tables may be integrated simply by defining routes in each static routing table to dynamic routers, and by defining routes to devices that use static routing tables on dynamic routers. This two-way referencing permits a dynamic router to act as a gateway to a statically routed network. In fact, this is a common approach to permit small, simple networks to communicate with one another.

Even though the cross-referencing technique we've just described permits a dynamic router to act as a gateway to a statically routed network, static and dynamic routing tables cannot communicate with one another, and they cannot exchange routing information. Because static routing tables can only be changed manually, this would mean that they acted dynamic, and defies their true nature (and basic limitation).

Multihomed Computers And IP Routing

A multihomed computer is a system with two or more network interfaces installed. Each NIC is attached to a different network; thus, the machine has multiple homes. Each NIC is defined with its own IP address and subnet mask. Such a system is able to route data between one network and another. To enable IP routing on a multihomed computer, simply check the Enable IP Forwarding box on the Routing tab of the TCP/IP Properties dialog box (shown in Figure 6.4), which is accessed through the Network applet in the Control Panel.

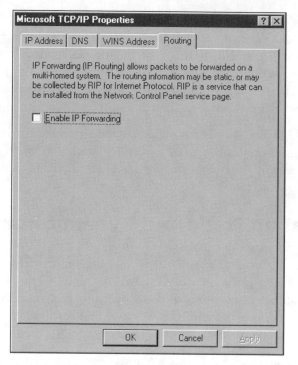

Figure 6.4 The Routing tab of the TCP/IP Properties dialog box.

Routing With Windows NT

Microsoft designed Windows NT Server 4 to act as a router to simplify the interconnection of multiple networks. Microsoft's MultiProtocol Router (MPR) is a service that can dynamically route TCP/IP traffic between different subnets as well as support IPX routing and DHCP Relay Agents. However, to use MPR, the server must have two or more NICs installed and must be configured in such a way that each NIC is part of a different subnet. In other words, a server must be multihomed to implement MPR.

MPR is comprised of:

➤ RIP For TCP/IP

➤ BOOTP Relay Agent For DHCP (also known as DHCP Relay Agent)

➤ RIP For IPX (which is not discussed in this book)

RIP is a protocol used to dynamically exchange routing information between routers. Once RIP is installed, NT will route these protocols and dynamically exchange routing information with other routers running the RIP protocol. Additionally, the BOOTP Relay Agent For DHCP will forward DHCP requests to DHCP servers located on other subnets over the NT router. Thus, a single DHCP server can support or service multiple subnets.

A router can exchange routing information with neighboring routers if RIP is enabled. Alterations in the network layout (such as a downed router) are broadcast by routers to neighboring routers. Routers also transmit descriptions of all known routing information by using periodic broadcasts. RIP routers share routing information dynamically.

Windows NT can be either a dynamic IP router or a static IP router. Dynamic routers share routing information with other routers to automatically build routing tables. Static routers employ manually configured routing tables.

Dynamic routing is enabled when you install RIP For IP. This is done through the Services tab of the Network applet in the Control Panel. Once it is installed, no further configuration is necessary. The service is started and the Enable IP Routing option in the Advanced TCP/IP Configuration dialog box is checked automatically. RIP For IP runs as a service. It can be started and stopped via the Control Panel Services icon.

Static routing eliminates the traffic associated with routing table updates, and can thus reduce network traffic loads. But static routing requires that all routing tables be maintained by hand, and can impose unwanted administrative burdens.

Follow these steps to enable static routing:

1. Go to the Control Panel and choose the Network icon.

2. Select the Services tab. If RIP For IP is installed on your computer, you must remove it before enabling static routing. To remove RIP For IP, choose it from the Network Services list in the Services tab and then click Remove. (If RIP For IP remains installed, dynamic routing will occur.)

3. Select the Protocols tab, highlight TCP/IP Protocol, and then click Properties.

4. Select the Routing tab, enable IP Forwarding by marking the checkbox, and then click OK.

Once the computer is rebooted, dynamic IP routing will be disabled. If you do not disable dynamic routing, the RIP update broadcasts will occur every 30 seconds. You can alter this interval through the following Registry value:

```
HKEY_LOCAL _MACHINE\SYSTEM\CurrentControlSet\Service\IpRip\
Parameters\UpdateFrequency
```

It can be set to an integer between 15 and 88,440 seconds.

Exam Prep Questions

Question 1

> A router is or can be which of the following? [Check all correct answers]
>
> ❑   a. A multihomed computer
>
> ❑   b. An information service
>
> ❑   c. A gateway
>
> ❑   d. A standalone device

A router is or can be a multihomed computer, a gateway, and a standalone device. Therefore, answers a, c, and d are correct. A router is not an information service. Therefore, answer b is incorrect.

Question 2

> If the address of the destination host is unknown, where is the data sent?
>
> ○   a. To the first network address in the routing table
>
> ○   b. To the router's cache
>
> ○   c. To the default gateway
>
> ○   d. To the RIP host

All data packets with unknown destination addresses are sent to the default gateway. Therefore, answer c is correct. The other answers are wrong (a and d) or imaginary (b).

Question 3

> Which items detailed in a routed packet are different after the packet reaches its destination than their original values at the source host? [Check all correct answers]
>
> ❑ a. Source HWA
>
> ❑ b. Source IP address
>
> ❑ c. Destination HWA
>
> ❑ d. Destination IP address

The source and destination hardware addresses (HWA) change each time a packet traverses a router or makes a hop. Therefore, answers a and c are correct. The source and destination IP addresses remain the same throughout the transmission of routed packets. Therefore, answers b and d are incorrect.

Question 4

> Which of the following are characteristics of dynamic routing? [Check all correct answers]
>
> ❑ a. Route tables manually maintained
>
> ❑ b. Routers share data
>
> ❑ c. Useful for small networks
>
> ❑ d. Requires RIP or OSPF

Dynamic routing enables routers to share data and requires RIP or OSPF. Therefore, answers b and d are correct. Static routing tables are manually maintained and are useful for small networks. Therefore, answers a and c are incorrect.

Question 5

Which of the following items are found in a static routing table?
[Check all correct answers]

- ❏ a. Interface IP address
- ❏ b. Source host IP address
- ❏ c. Hop metric
- ❏ d. Network address
- ❏ e. DHCP server IP address
- ❏ f. Netmask
- ❏ g. DNS server IP address
- ❏ h. Gateway address

A static routing table is comprised of five items: interface HWA, hop metric, network address, netmask, and gateway address. Therefore, answers c, d, f, and h are correct. The source host IP address, DHCP server IP address, and DNS server IP address are not listed in a static routing table. Therefore, answers a, b, e, and g are incorrect.

Question 6

More than one gateway can be defined. The primary or first default gateway is used unless it is offline or unreachable.

- ○ a. True
- ○ b. False

True, multiple gateways can be defined, but the primary or first gateway is the only one used for routing unless it is unavailable. Therefore, answer a is correct.

Question 7

> The ROUTE utility can be used to perform which functions on a routing table? [Check all correct answers]
>
> ❑ a. Add new routes
>
> ❑ b. Test a route
>
> ❑ c. Remove entries
>
> ❑ d. Display existing routes

The ROUTE utility can add new routes (with the *add* command), remove gateway entries (*with -f:* parameter), and display existing routes (with the *print* command). Therefore, answers a, c, and d are correct. The ROUTE utility cannot test a route; TRACERT is used for that function. Therefore, answer b is incorrect.

Question 8

> By default, newly defined routes added to the static routing table are persistent across system reboots.
>
> ○ a. True
>
> ○ b. False

False, routes are not persistent, by default, across system reboots; the *-p* parameter must be used to force a route to be persistent. Therefore, answer b is correct.

Question 9

> Why is the dynamic routing protocol RIP limited to 15 hops?
>
> ○ a. The routing table uses hex codes to store hop values.
>
> ○ b. To prevent infinite counting of looped paths.
>
> ○ c. To force large networks to be divided into smaller subnets.
>
> ○ d. No network system ever needs more than 15 hops.

RIP is limited to 15 hops to prevent infinite counting of looped paths. Therefore, answer b is correct. Routing tables do not use hex codes to store hop values; the 15-hop limitation encourages larger single networks, not several small ones; and many network systems use more than 15 hops (the Internet, for example). Therefore, answers a, c, and d are incorrect.

Question 10

A computer with more than one NIC that is configured so that it's active in more than one network is called what? [Choose the best answer]

- ○ a. Internetworked
- ○ b. Multihomed
- ○ c. An MPR host
- ○ d. A RIP server

A computer with several NICs is called multihomed. Therefore, answer b is correct. A multihomed computer does not have to be a router, but even if it is, the terms MPR host and RIP server are not correct. Therefore, answers c and d are incorrect. Internetworked means that the computer interconnects more than one network, making answer a technically correct but not specific enough to qualify as the right answer, especially in terms of Microsoft jargon. It is, however, close enough to permit this question to qualify for "trick" status.

Need To Know More?

Donald, Lisa and James Chellis: *MSCE: NT Server 4 in the Enterprise Study Guide*. Sybex Network Press, San Francisco, CA, 1997. ISBN 0-7821-1970-0. Chapter 13, "Internetwork Routing," gives brief but useful information regarding MPR. TCP/IP issues are discussed in Chapter 11.

Huitema, Christian: *Routing in the Internet*. Prentice-Hall, Englewood Cliffs, NJ, 1995. ISBN 0-13-132192-7.

Lammle, Todd, Monica Lammle, and James Chellis. *MSCE: TCP/IP Study Guide*. Sybex Network Press, San Francisco, CA, 1997. ISBN 0-7821-1969-7. Chapter 3, "Implementing IP Routing," contains information regarding routing with IP.

Perlman, Radia: *Interconnections*. Addison-Wesley Professional Computing Series, Reading, MA, 1992. ISBN 0-201-56332-0.

Search the TechNet CD (or its online version through www.microsoft.com) and the *Windows NT Server Resource Kit* CD using the keywords "routing," "RIP," "ROUTE," "TRACERT," "MPR," and "gateway."

IP Address Resolution

Terms you'll need to understand:

√   Address Resolution Protocol (ARP)

√   ARP cache

√   Proxy ARP

√   RARP

Techniques you'll need to master:

√   Performing local and remote address resolution

One of the tricks to working with TCP/IP is associating a MAC (hardware) address with an IP (logical) address. In this chapter, we discuss the TCP/IP Address Resolution Protocol (ARP) and how it functions in a TCP/IP network. ARP is very seldom mentioned in the exam, and when it is, it's usually as a way to throw you off. It's important, then, to know what ARP does so that you'll know when it's the wrong answer.

ARP: Explored And Explained

As discussed in Chapter 2, " Concepts And Planning: TCP/IP And Windows NT 4," the TCP/IP protocol suite does not take into account the Data Link or Physical layers of the OSI Model. For a packet to travel across the network, it must have a physical (MAC) destination address. The TCP/IP Address Resolution Protocol (ARP) is used to determine a destination computer's MAC address. ARP is defined in detail in RFC (Request For Comments) number 826.

This process is, in principle, very simple. When a computer has data to send, ARP sends a broadcast to the local network requesting the hardware address that goes with the destination IP address. If the destination host is on the local network, it responds to the ARP request. If the host is on a remote network, the default gateway returns its hardware address in response to the request and the packet will be sent there.

Once the sending computer knows the physical address associated with a particular IP address, it records the address in its "ARP cache," which is discussed in more detail in the section titled "The ARP Cache" later in this chapter. Then, if the sending computer needs to send another packet to the same IP address, the computer reads the address from the ARP cache rather than sending another request.

Local Address Resolution

The process for resolving addresses on the local network involves four steps. To illustrate the process, let's use the following example:

You're sitting at your desk and you want to Telnet to the Unix system in the Computer Control Center. The IP address for your computer is 187.34.234.200 with the subnet mask 255.255.255.0 (Class C), and the address for the Unix system is 187.34.234.10 with the same subnet mask. By using what you've already learned about IP addressing and subnet masks, you can determine that the Unix system is on the same subnetwork as your computer, so this is a local address resolution situation.

From your computer you type "Telnet 187.34.234.10". At this point, your computer checks its local ARP cache to see if it already has the physical address for the specified IP address. For argument's sake, we'll say it doesn't have the physical address for the system. So, ARP steps in.

ARP sends a broadcast message to the local network: "Would the owner of IP address 187.34.234.10 please respond with your MAC address?" This broadcast request has all the return information so that when the actual owner of the requested address (the Unix machine) responds, it is able to send the response directly to your computer.

The Unix box then sends its reply to the hardware address of your computer. When your computer gets this response, it adds the information to its ARP cache so that it doesn't have to go through this rigmarole again—or at least not in the near future. Once all this has taken place, the computers are ready to trade data.

Remote Address Resolution

Now let's take the same example and add a router to the mix. Let's assume that the IP address for the Unix system is actually 109.220.10.10, again with a Class C subnet mask. This means that the Unix system is on another subnet, and you must pass through a router with the local IP address 187.34.234.1. This changes the process a little, but not enough to worry too much about.

Okay, you're at your desk and you run "Telnet 109.220.110.10". Your computer realizes instantly that you're trying to reach a computer on a remote network. Its next step, then, is to see if it knows how to get to that particular remote network. For most computers, this is relatively straightforward, because they have only one destination for remote networks, the default gateway. Therefore, your computer, knowing that it has to use the default gateway to get to the network the Unix machine is on, checks the ARP cache for the MAC address of the default gateway; in this case, the router.

If your computer does not have the hardware address of the default gateway (187.34.234.1) in its ARP cache, it sends an ARP request for the hardware address of the router.

The router replies to your computer's ARP request with its hardware address. Now, this is where it gets a little strange. Your computer sends an ICMP (Internet Control Message Protocol) echo request to the Unix system through the router, which attempts to send it to the destination. At this point, the router begins its own ARP request/response session with each router in the path to the destination, until a router discovers that the destination computer is local. So, let's assume there are three routers between your computer and the Unix system, all of which have to resolve the physical address of the destination computer (in other words, the address is not in their ARP caches). The router nearest to you sends an ARP request to the next router in line, that router sends a request to the next router, and the third router sends a request to the computer itself.

Finally, the Unix system responds to its local router with its hardware address as well as to the ICMP request your computer sent. This process of remote address resolution is also called "proxy ARP," because the router is acting as a proxy for the requests.

 The most important difference to remember between local and remote address resolution is this: When you resolve a remote address, the hardware address of the default gateway is returned. When you resolve a local address, the hardware address of the computer itself is returned.

The ARP Cache

As you've seen, the ARP cache is a very important part of address resolution. It stores the IP-address-to-hardware-address information for hosts on the network. Every time your computer tries to communicate with another host, it checks its ARP cache for the physical address of the host. If it is unable to find the address, your computer initiates the ARP request process discussed earlier. Once the address is resolved, it updates its cache with the information received. An ARP cache might look like what's shown in Figure 7.1.

As you can imagine, computers cannot keep every entry in their ARP caches forever. By default, entries are valid for 10 minutes. After that, the entry is removed from the cache. In some implementations of TCP/IP, the counter is reset if the computers communicate within the 10-minute timeout.

Windows NT treats the ARP cache a bit differently. It removes entries from the table when it reaches capacity, even if they have not expired. NT removes the oldest entries, regardless of how often they have been used.

ARP.EXE

Microsoft includes the ARP.EXE utility for viewing and modifying the ARP cache with its Windows products. Figure 7.1 was captured using the ARP.EXE utility to display the ARP cache on a Windows 95 machine.

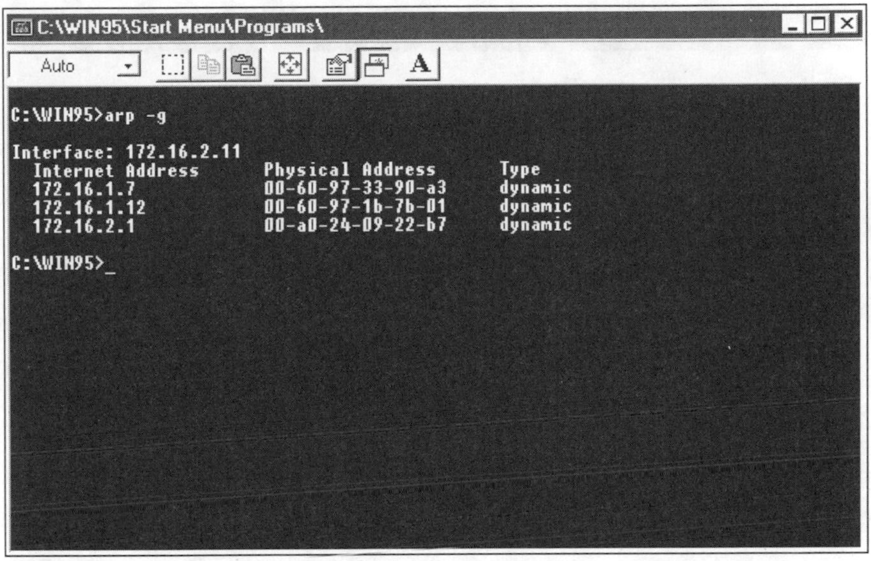

```
C:\WIN95\Start Menu\Programs\                              _ □ ×

  Auto    ▼   [ ]  🗈 🗈  🖽  🖆🗗  A

C:\WIN95>arp -g

Interface: 172.16.2.11
  Internet Address        Physical Address        Type
  172.16.1.7              00-60-97-33-90-a3       dynamic
  172.16.1.12             00-60-97-1b-7b-01       dynamic
  172.16.2.1              00-a0-24-09-22-b7       dynamic

C:\WIN95>_
```

Figure 7.1   The ARP cache displays IP and physical addresses for computers on the network.

Addresses can be manually added to the ARP cache by using ARP.EXE with the following switch: -s *IP address MAC address*. These are static entries that do not expire, but they will be removed when the computer is powered off or if a broadcast is received indicating that the entry is wrong. For example, if you add 199.200.100.11 10-CE-08-6C-23-1A to the ARP cache, and your computer receives a broadcast that the IP address for MAC address 10-CE-08-6C-23-1A is actually 199.200.100.100, the entry will be changed. If the entry is updated by a broadcast, its type is changed from static to dynamic and will be subject to the 10-minute rule. To remove a static ARP cache entry, use **ARP -d** *IP address MAC address*. The -a or -g switches can be used to display the entire ARP table or specific entries in the table by physical or IP address. The only caveat here is that -g does not work with Windows for Workgroups. Table 7.1 lists the switches available for ARP.EXE.

    It's important to know ARP.EXE and its switches for the exam. You might encounter questions that list the results of a particular ARP.EXE switch or ask how it can be used to troubleshoot problems.

Table 7.1   ARP switches and their descriptions.

Switch	Description
-a	Displays the current ARP cache entries.
-g	Displays the current ARP cache entries. (Not available in Windows for Workgroups.)
-N	Displays the ARP entries for a specific network interface.
-s	Adds a static entry to the ARP cache. The syntax is **ARP -s *IP Address MAC Address***.
-d	Removes a static entry from the ARP cache.

Reverse Address Resolution Protocol

As a point of reference, the Reverse Address Resolution Protocol (RARP) should be mentioned. Its function is the reverse of ARP. It provides an IP address when given a physical address. It's used mostly with diskless workstations that must get their IP address from a server. The workstation sends an RARP broadcast that is received by the RARP server. The RARP server then supplies the workstation's IP address.

It's important to note that, unlike ARP, RARP requires a server to provide the IP address to the workstation. For this reason, RARP is not widely used, and with the advent of DHCP, it's more a curiosity than a functional protocol.

Resolution Problems

The most often encountered problem with address resolution concerns incorrect subnet masks. This is a resolution problem because, when a computer is trying to decide whether the address is local or remote, it uses the subnet mask to make its determination. If it discovers a remote machine on the local network, it continuously sends broadcasts in an attempt to resolve the address. In the most extreme situation, incorrect subnet masking can result in a *broadcast storm*. A broadcast storm is a phenomenon which occurs when a network device malfunctions and floods the network with broadcast packets.

Exam Prep Questions

Question 1

> For local address resolution, what step does the sending computer take if it does not find the information in its cache?
>
> ○ a. Sends a request to the ARP server.
>
> ○ b. Sends a broadcast packet.
>
> ○ c. Sends a request to the router.
>
> ○ d. Checks its HOSTS file for the information.

The correct answer for this question is b. If the computer does not find the destination hardware address in its cache, it sends a broadcast packet to the network. Answer a is incorrect because there is no such creature as an ARP server. Answer c is incorrect because the question refers to a local address resolution and the router is queried only for remote resolutions. The HOSTS file does not contain address resolution information. Therefore, answer d is incorrect.

Question 2

> Which of the following commands will display the ARP cache for a Windows for Workgroups computer? [Check all correct answers]
>
> ❑ a. arp -a
>
> ❑ b. arp -r
>
> ❑ c. arp -s
>
> ❑ d. arp -g

The correct answer for this question is a. On most Windows machines, both -a and -g will display the ARP cache. However, remember that only -a works with Windows for Workgroups, making d incorrect. There is no -r switch, and -s is used to add a static entry to the cache. Therefore, both b and c are incorrect.

Question 3

What is the default time an entry will stay in the ARP cache?

- ○ a. 20 minutes
- ○ b. 5 minutes
- ○ c. 10 minutes
- ○ d. 15 minutes

The correct answer for this question is c. The default time an entry will stay in the ARP cache is 10 minutes.

Question 4

Under what circumstances is a static ARP cache entry changed or deleted? [Check all correct answers]

- ❏ a. When the computer is powered off
- ❏ b. When the **arp-a** command is issued for that entry
- ❏ c. When contradictory information is received via broadcast
- ❏ d. When the **arp -d** command is issued for that entry

The correct answers to this question are a, c, and d. A static ARP cache entry is changed or deleted when the computer is powered off, when contradictory information is received via broadcast, or when the -*d* switch is used. Remember that the arp -a command displays the cache, but has no effect on its contents. Therefore, answer b is incorrect.

Question 5

What type of address resolution takes place with proxy ARP?

- ○ a. Local address resolution
- ○ b. Kinetic address resolution
- ○ c. Router address resolution
- ○ d. Remote address resolution

The correct answer to this question is d. Proxy ARP is another term for remote address resolution, because the default gateway or router acts as a proxy agent for the local computer. Local address resolution does not involve a proxy of any kind. Therefore, answer a is incorrect. Kinetic address resolution sounds good, but does not exist. Router address resolution is also a fictional term. Therefore, answers b and c are incorrect as well.

Need to Know More?

 Lammle, Todd, Monica Lammle, and James Chellis. *MCSE: TCP/IP Study Guide.* Sybex Network Press, San Francisco, CA, 1997. ISBN 0-7821-1969-7. Chapter 4, "IP Address Resolution," discusses the IP address/name resolution process in detail.

Stevens, W. Richard. *TCP/IP Illustrated, Volume 1.* Addison Wesley Publishing Company, Reading, MA, 1994. ISBN 0-201-63346-9. Chapter 4, "ARP Address Resolution Protocol," contains detailed information on ARP and its inner workings.

Search the TechNet CD (or its online version through www.microsoft.com) using the keywords "ARP," "IP address," "Address Resolution Protocol," and related query items.

The *Windows NT Server Resource Kit* contains a lot of useful information about TCP/IP and related topics. Useful TCP/IP-related materials can be found throughout the "Networking Guide" volume of the *Resource Kit*.

Host Name
Resolution

· ·

Terms you'll need to understand:

√ Host name

√ HOSTS file

√ NetBIOS name

√ LMHOSTS file

√ Host name resolution

√ DNS (Domain Name Service)

√ NetBIOS name cache

√ FQDN (fully qualified domain name)

√ DNS domain versus NetBIOS (Windows NT) domain

Techniques you'll need to master:

√ Creating a valid host name for a Windows NT workstation or server

√ Configuring a host name and a DNS domain name for Windows NT

√ Determining the host name or FQDN of a host

√ Configuring and troubleshooting a typical HOSTS file

√ Configuring a Windows NT machine to use NetBIOS name resolution with host names

IP addressing can be a difficult process. This chapter discusses the various methods used to resolve IP host name resolution. This discussion includes a short history of host naming, host name configuration, and fully qualified domain names (FQDNs). In addition, we explore the Domain Name Service (DNS), HOSTS and LMHOSTS files, as well as NetBIOS naming.

Host Names: Explored And Explained

In Chapter 4, "IP Addressing," we discussed the need for each and every host on a TCP/IP network to be identified by a unique IP address. The IP address of a remote machine must be known by the local machine in order for communication to be established. However, IP addresses are relatively long, and they are hard for most of us to remember. Therefore, more user-friendly names, such as "Dilbert" and "PrintServ1," are used to identify other TCP/IP hosts. These names are easier to remember and have more meaning than, say, 128.98.212.12.

Although user-friendly names make it easier to remember and identify TCP/IP hosts, they must be resolved to an IP address before communication can be established between two hosts. This chapter explains acceptable host names, fully qualified domain names (which are created by combining a host name with a domain name), and the process used to resolve host names to IP addresses.

Host Names Defined

An IP address can be used in most Windows Sockets applications, such as PING, FTP, Telnet, and most Web browsers, to connect to other TCP/IP hosts. However, remembering the IP address of your favorite Web sites or the IP addresses of multiple FTP servers can be quite a chore; therefore, these TCP/IP hosts are assigned names or aliases that are easier to remember. For example, "Binky," "Dopey," "Server1," "TLP133," and "DRT-398" are all valid host names.

Host names are also convenient because they allow you to locate and identify a machine without regard for its physical location or its IP address. Recall that a machine's IP address corresponds to its physical location within the network. If the machine is moved from one network or subnet to another, the IP address will need to be changed for this machine to communicate properly using TCP/IP. Using a host name to identify this machine makes any IP address change transparent to the end user.

Certain restrictions exist on the types of host names that can be used. RFC 1123 states that a host name can contain up to 255 alphanumeric characters, including a–z, A–Z, 0–9, and a hyphen (-) or a period (.). Special characters such as !, %, and * (that is, exclamation point, percent sign, and asterisk, respectively) are not allowed by RFC standards. Additionally, a host name cannot contain all numeric characters and should not contain any underscores.

At one time, the host name was not allowed to begin with a numeric character, but this rule has been relaxed; therefore, names such as "411info.com" and "3com.com" are valid host names. RFC 1033 states that the use of the underscore is allowed, but this RFC is an FYI (for informational purposes only) and does not define an RFC standard. You should avoid using the underscore in the names of hosts on your network, because this can cause problems with name resolution on the Internet.

 For additional information on valid host names and DNS configurations, view RFC 1912, RFC 1035, RFC 1033 (information, not a standard) and RFC 1123. These files can be found at http://ds.InterNIC.net/rfc/rfc####.txt. Where "####" is the number of the RFC you need to view.

Configuring A Host Name

During the installation of TCP/IP on a Windows NT Workstation or Server, you must supply a valid and unique host name to identify the machine on the TCP/IP network. By default, Windows NT will use the NetBIOS name of the machine as the host name, replacing any invalid characters used in the NetBIOS name (such as an underscore "_") with a hyphen (-). You may change this default name to another name if you wish. However, to keep name resolution troubleshooting simple, it is recommended that you choose a name that is valid as a host name as well as a NetBIOS name. (NetBIOS names were introduced in Chapter 3, "Installation And Configuration," and will be discussed at length in Chapter 10, "NetBIOS Name Resolution.")

To configure the host name for a given Windows NT machine, you need to open the Network Control Panel at Start|Settings|Control Panel|Network and click the Protocols tab. Next, double-click the TCP/IP protocol icon to view the TCP/IP Properties sheets. Select the DNS tab and then enter a host name and domain name in the respective fields, near the top of the Properties sheet. The combination of the host name and the domain name creates a fully qualified domain name (FQDN).

Don't confuse a DNS domain with a Windows NT domain; these two types of domains are not related. A DNS domain is a logical grouping of TCP/IP hosts on an IP network and is joined with the host name to produce a fully qualified domain name. A Windows NT domain pertains to a group of Windows-based machines that all use the same PDCs and BDCs to provide security for the group.

Host Names And FQDNs

The FQDN should uniquely identify a host among all other hosts on the Internet. It can also allow the host name to be unique across large networks (such as the Internet) because the namespace for Internet domains is hierarchical. This means that each name is divided into several different parts rather than a single part like NetBIOS names (which utilize a flat namespace). The authority over each division and subdivision of the namespace can be delegated to a local group, which can then ensure that each branch and node of the namespace is unique within that group. Figure 8.1 shows an example of two possible branches of the DNS domain namespace and those responsible for maintaining each layer of the namespace.

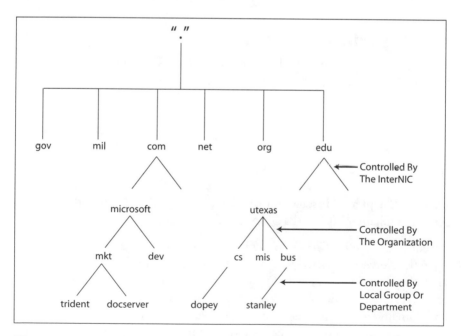

Figure 8.1 DNS domain name hierarchy and distributed responsibility.

The InterNIC currently supports the use of six commonly used, top-level domains (other than the abbreviations for foreign countries): .gov, .mil, .net, .com, .edu, and .org. Within each of the domains are subdomains that are usually named after the company or organization the subdomain name represents.

For example, Microsoft as well as other companies can be found within the commercial domain (.com); for instance, at microsoft.com or hp.com. The University of Texas and most other educational institutions can be found within the education domain (.edu); for example, at utexas.edu or tamu.edu.

The InterNIC has control over the names found in each of these top-level domains. You must choose a unique domain name, one that is not already being used in the top-level domain in which you would like your organization registered. Additionally, you must pay a registration fee for your domain name. This fee is used to defray the cost of maintaining the DNS servers at these top-level domains.

Once your domain has been registered, your organization has control over the namespace within your domain. Microsoft is free to create subdomains within the microsoft.com domain and delegate the control of those subdomains to local groups. It might, for example, have marketing.microsoft.com and finance.microsoft.com domains within the Microsoft domain. The marketing group and the finance group can each assign the same host name, "Fred," to their file servers and be sure that the FQDNs for each of the machines will be unique (for example, fred.marketing.microsoft.com and fred.finance .microsoft.com). Notice that FQDNs get more specific from right to left.

There are two Windows NT command-line utilities that can help you quickly determine the host name or FQDN of a particular host. The first, **HOSTNAME**, returns the host name configured for the machine you are using. The second, **IPCONFIG /ALL**, gives you the FQDN for the machine you are using. The first name in the FQDN—that is, the first word/label from the left and before the first dot or period (.)—is the name of the local host.

Host Names, Domain Names, And DNS (Domain Name Service)

Before communication can begin between any two IP hosts, the IP address of the remote host must be known by TCP/IP. The process of converting a user-friendly host name or domain name to an IP address is known as "name resolution." The HOSTS file is one means of resolving host names to IP addresses; it's simply a list of host names and their corresponding IP addresses. The HOSTS file works well when there are only a limited number of IP hosts on a given network. However, it would be quite difficult for users to maintain a list with the name of every TCP/IP host with which they connect to the Internet.

DNS, a distributed database of host- and domain-name-to-IP-address mappings, is used to provide name resolution services for TCP/IP client applications. DNS is able to overcome the need to maintain a single list of IP hosts by distributing the list among many different machines across the network. Each DNS server is responsible for maintaining a database of host- and domain-name-to-IP-address mappings for its local area of the network. A DNS server can be configured to contact other DNS servers when it cannot find a host- or domain-to-IP-address mapping in its local database.

Just as the host name is a logical identifier for a TCP/IP host, the DNS domain name logically identifies a group of TCP/IP hosts. These domain names usually correspond to a group of computers or hosts within an organization or company.

For example, your local TCP/IP client application might contact the DNS server to resolve the name "www.widgets.com" to an IP address. If your DNS server does not have an entry for the requested host, it contacts the DNS server responsible for the group of computers in the widgets.com domain. This second DNS server is likely owned by the widget.com company and maintains a list of all the computers and hosts within this domain.

How Host Name Resolution Works

As noted earlier, although host names are convenient to use and easier to remember, TCP/IP requires these names to be resolved to an IP address and eventually to a hardware address before a connection can be established with another host. Host name resolution is generally needed when a TCP/IP client utility needs to connect to a TCP/IP server. Telnet and FTP clients as well as the PING utility all require host name resolution. Figure 8.2 illustrates the default process of host name resolution on Microsoft Windows NT.

Be sure to understand that WinSock (Windows Sockets) applications such as PING, Telnet, and FTP can all use host names and therefore require host name resolution via the HOSTS file or a DNS server. Do not confuse these applications with Microsoft-based applications such as the **NET** command— **NET USE G: \\server1\share** is a NetBIOS command used to connect to a NetBIOS resource and therefore requires NetBIOS

> name resolution via WINS or LMHOSTS. For additional information on NetBIOS name resolution, see Chapter 10, "NetBIOS Name Resolution."

The first place TCP/IP checks to determine a host's IP address is its own host name cache. It compares the name of the host to which it would like to connect with its own host name configured in the TCP/IP properties. If the two names are the same, the computer simply establishes a TCP/IP connection with itself on the correct port.

If the two names do not match, it checks a local file named HOSTS for a host-name-to-IP-address mapping. This is a simple text file that is parsed (read) one line at a time from top to bottom. If no host-name-to-IP-address mapping is found, TCP/IP will contact a DNS server (if it has been configured to do so). (The DNS process is discussed in greater detail in the section entitled "DNS" later in this chapter.) If the DNS process is unsuccessful, the source host checks its local NetBIOS name cache.

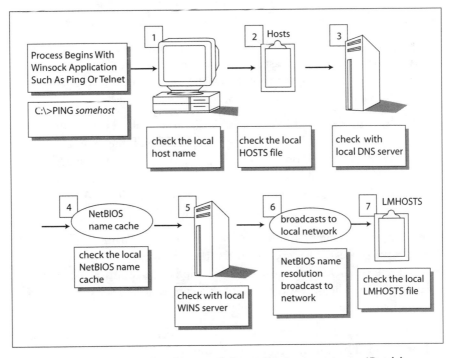

Figure 8.2 Steps involved in resolving a host name to an IP address.

All of the name resolution methods mentioned up to this point pertain only to host name resolution, because the type of name that is being resolved is in fact a "host" name, not a NetBIOS name. However, you can give your Windows NT Workstation or Server the same names for both the host and NetBIOS name. These two types of names, however, are very different from one another. The host name represents a particular IP host, whereas a NetBIOS name can represent a Windows NT Workstation or Server machine, a Windows NT domain, a service, or a network share.

If DNS is unable to resolve the host name to an IP address, Windows NT will check its local NetBIOS name cache for a name-to-IP-address mapping. The only reason it checks the cache of NetBIOS names is the assumption that the NetBIOS name and host name could be the same.

If the mapping is not found in the NetBIOS name cache, Windows NT can contact a WINS server, if it is configured to do so. The WINS server is similar to the DNS server in that it provides for the resolution of user-friendly names to IP addresses. However, a WINS server contains a database of NetBIOS names, rather than host names, and their corresponding IP addresses.

If no mapping is found in the WINS database, Windows NT will send out a NetBIOS name query broadcast to the local network to see if any of the local hosts will respond. If no host responds and the source host is configured to use the LMHOSTS file, the name resolution process continues.

Finally, if no other method of name resolution has resolved the host name to an IP address, Windows NT will parse the LMHOSTS file in an attempt to locate a valid name-to-address mapping for the host being sought. The LMHOSTS file is similar in purpose to the HOSTS file, mentioned previously. The LMHOSTS file is a file that resides on the local Windows NT machine and is used to map NetBIOS names to IP addresses.

If any one of these name resolution methods returns a name-to-IP-address mapping, the process will stop, even if the IP address that is returned is incorrect. If none of these name resolution methods can return a name-to-IP-address mapping, the only way to establish a connection to the remote host is by using its IP address.

In the remainder of this chapter, we will take a closer look at each of the previously mentioned host name resolution methods.

HOSTS File

The HOSTS file is a simple text file—originally used before the advent of DNS—to provide host name resolution on a machine-by-machine basis. TCP/IP reads this file one line at a time in an attempt to locate a host-name-to-IP-address mapping. The user of each machine can maintain this file, or it can be maintained in a central location and copied to the local machine each time the machine is booted. However, this file must be updated every time a host's IP address changes.

Each line of the HOSTS file contains an IP address on the left side, followed by at least one space and the corresponding host name(s) or FQDN(s) on the right. No one line of this file should ever have more than a single IP address on it, although multiple aliases are allowed per line. Additionally, if the HOSTS file is configured to be used for name resolution, it is read one line at a time from top to bottom each time a host name needs to be resolved. You should place frequently accessed host names near the top of the file to provide for quicker name resolution. Figure 8.3 shows an example of a HOSTS file from a Windows NT machine.

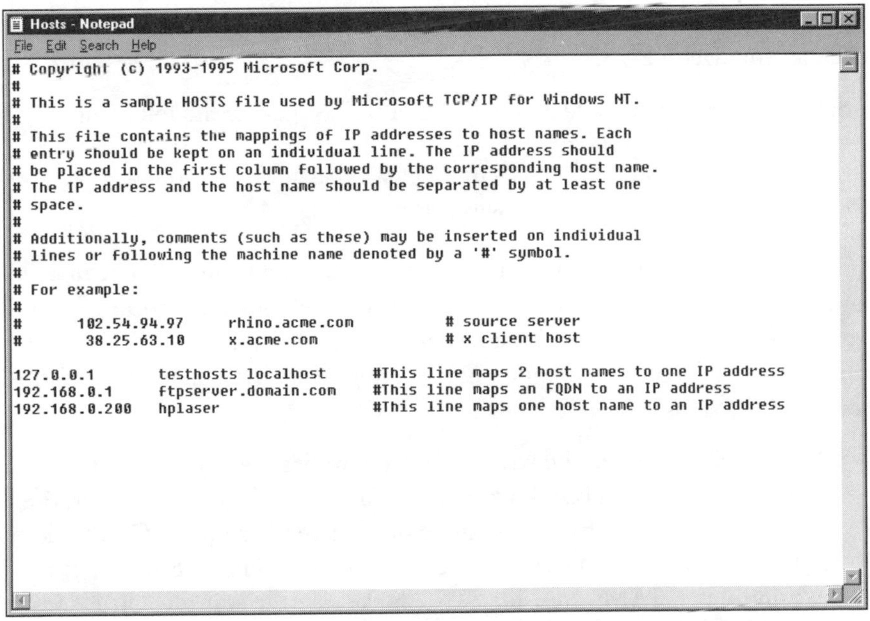


```
# Copyright (c) 1993-1995 Microsoft Corp.
#
# This is a sample HOSTS file used by Microsoft TCP/IP for Windows NT.
#
# This file contains the mappings of IP addresses to host names. Each
# entry should be kept on an individual line. The IP address should
# be placed in the first column followed by the corresponding host name.
# The IP address and the host name should be separated by at least one
# space.
#
# Additionally, comments (such as these) may be inserted on individual
# lines or following the machine name denoted by a '#' symbol.
#
# For example:
#
#      102.54.94.97     rhino.acme.com          # source server
#       38.25.63.10     x.acme.com              # x client host

127.0.0.1       testhosts localhost     #This line maps 2 host names to one IP address
192.168.0.1     ftpserver.domain.com    #This line maps an FQDN to an IP address
192.168.0.200   hplaser                 #This line maps one host name to an IP address
```

Figure 8.3 A sample HOSTS file from a Windows NT machine.

If you frequently connect to hosts that are mapped in the HOSTS file, you can optimize your machine by placing the most frequently accessed hosts near the top of the HOSTS file. This will speed up the name resolution process, because this file is read one line at a time from top to bottom.

The HOSTS file is located in the *systemroot*\system32\drivers\etc directory, and it can be edited with any standard text editor, such as Notepad. Be sure not to save the document with any of the default extensions that many programs add to a file. To save a file without any extensions when using Notepad, place double quotes around the name of the file (for example, "Hosts").

 In order for the HOSTS file to be properly accessed by Windows NT and TCP/IP, it must be in the correct directory. By default, the HOSTS file on Windows NT resides in the *systemroot*\system32\ drivers\etc directory.

If the HOSTS file is not in the correct directory or does not have the correct name, Windows NT will not be able to find it and use it for name resolution. To make sure that the HOSTS file is being used, you can modify or add an entry to the file and then use the **PING** command to see if the host name responds. Be sure to use a name that you know to be unique on your network, such as "mymachine123."

For example, you could add a line to the HOSTS file like the following:

```
192.168.0.1   mymachine123    #Use your IP address in place of the
                               one given
```

If you open a command window and issue the command **PING mymachine123** and you receive an echo response from the specified host, the HOSTS file is being used. If you do not receive a response after editing the HOSTS file, any number of things could be happening. The following lists some of these problems and the steps you can take to alleviate them:

➤ **The HOSTS file is in the wrong directory or has the wrong name.** Remember that the HOSTS file on a Windows NT host must be in the *systemroot*\system32\drivers\etc directory. There's a sample HOSTS file in this directory. If you use this to create your own HOSTS file, be sure to remove the .SAM extension. Also, make sure the editor you use does not add any other extension.

➤ **The HOSTS file contains more than one occurrence of a particular host name and the first one in the file has the wrong IP address.** If a HOSTS file is used and updated frequently, it can grow rather quickly. If a host that already exists in this file is added somewhere else in the file, the first occurrence of the host name will be used to resolve the IP address, whether or not the IP address is valid. For larger HOSTS files, be sure to use the Find command in your text editor to locate duplicate entries.

➤ **The HOSTS file entry contains a wrong IP address or is misspelled.** This can be one of the harder HOSTS file issues to troubleshoot. However, you can use the Find command in Notepad (or other text editor) to locate the offending entry and correct it.

 The most important thing to determine when troubleshooting connectivity issues is whether the problem stems from a physical connectivity problem between the source host and the destination host or is just a name resolution problem. The quickest way to determine this is to PING an IP address that is known to be valid instead of a host name or NetBIOS name. An echo reply will tell you that your connection to the network is still good and indicates a probable name resolution problem of some type.

DNS

If Windows NT is unable to find a name-to-IP-address mapping in the HOSTS file, it will contact a DNS server, as long as it has been configured to do so in the Network Control Panel|TCP/IP Properties sheet. If it has not been configured to contact a DNS server for name resolution, the process will skip to the next step in this section: checking the NetBIOS name cache.

Assuming that Windows NT has been configured to contact at least one DNS server, TCP/IP will send a request to the first DNS server in the list of DNS servers on the DNS properties sheet. This DNS server checks its local database for an entry matching the requested host name or domain name. If the DNS server has an entry for the requested host name, it sends the IP address to the host requesting the information and then the name resolution process stops.

If the DNS server does not have an entry for the specified host or domain name, it can contact another local DNS server or a remote DNS server, depending on the name or domain that needs to be resolved. Assuming that the second DNS server contacted has the requested information, it sends this information to the first DNS server and then that server returns the information to the host that originated the request. At this point, the name resolution process ends.

For example, let's assume that your company has registered the name "widgets.com," and your network administrator has created three subdomains within your primary domain. These subdomains are "marketing.widgets.com," "accounting.widgets.com," and "admin.widgets.com." You work in the marketing department and your workstation is configured with the host name "Fido." Therefore, the fully qualified domain name for your machine is "fido.marketing.widgets.com." Your machine has been configured to contact a DNS server if needed.

You want to browse some Web pages that reside on the server "budget" in the "admin" domain. You enter the address "http://budget.admin.widgets.com" in your Web browser. Windows NT first compares the name of the server with which you are trying to connect with its own host name. When it discovers they are different, it then tries to locate and parse the HOSTS file on the local machine. If TCP/IP on Windows NT does not find an entry in the HOSTS file that matches the host name or FQDN requested, it sends a request to the DNS server for name resolution. The DNS server finds an entry for the requested host name and returns the IP address for budget.admin.widgets.com to your machine.

Now, let's assume that you want to connect to the host ftp.customer.com, which is not within the widgets.com domain, and that your local DNS server does not have the entries for this host. In this case, your DNS server must contact another DNS server to resolve your request, and it could contact the DNS server for the customer.com domain and ask for help in the resolution process. Assuming this DNS server has the requested information, it returns the information to your local DNS server, which in turn passes the information to your machine. With the host name resolved, the resolution process ends.

If the DNS server returns the wrong IP address, the resolution process ends as well. Contact your local administrator or the administrator of the DNS server that resolved the name and ask him or her to update the DNS entry.

If the DNS server cannot resolve the IP address and gives a negative response, Windows NT checks the NetBIOS name cache. If the DNS server is unavailable (that is, no response of any kind is received), Windows NT continues to try to contact the DNS server at intervals of 5, 10, 20, 40, 5, 10, and 20 seconds. After a total elapsed time of 1 minute and 50 seconds, Windows NT will either generate an error or continue the name resolution process, depending upon the configuration of the machine.

NetBIOS Name Cache

If DNS is unable to resolve a given host address to an IP address, Windows NT checks its local NetBIOS name cache to see if it can find a match there. The NetBIOS name cache does not actually contain host names, but because host names and NetBIOS names can be the same, this cache might contain a valid IP address mapping. If a match is found, the name is resolved and the name resolution process stops. If no match is found in the NetBIOS name cache, Windows NT contacts a WINS server, if it has been configured to do so.

The only reason a name might be found in the NetBIOS name cache is because the name has been recently resolved or it has been loaded into the cache from the LMHOSTS file.

WINS Server

If no match is found in the NetBIOS name cache and Windows NT has been configured as a WINS client, it sends a directed request to WINS. The WINS server is much like the DNS server—it's responsible for resolving user-friendly names to IP addresses. However, the WINS server is a repository for NetBIOS names rather than DNS host names.

The WINS server checks its local database for a name-to-IP-address match and, if one is found, returns the requested IP address to the source host. If the WINS server does not respond, Windows NT tries to contact the WINS server up to a total of three times.

If WINS is able to resolve the name to an IP address, the name resolution process ends at this point. TCP/IP initiates a NetBIOS name resolution broadcast to the local network if the WINS server is not able to resolve the name to an IP address.

Broadcast To The Local Network

Resolving NetBIOS names by broadcasting is also known as "NetBIOS b-node resolution." The source host sends a b-node (or broadcast) name query to the local network. Each host on the local network processes this request to determine whether it is the intended recipient of the name query. If the receiving host is using the name the source host is seeking, the receiving host creates a response packet with its IP address and sends it to the source host, thus ending the name resolution process. If the source host does not receive a response from any machine on the local network after three attempts, TCP/IP on Windows NT then parses the LMHOSTS file.

NetBIOS names and services can be registered, maintained, and released by broadcast to the local network. However, the traffic generated by this process is very costly in terms of network bandwidth and the processor time used by each machine to process the broadcasts—which is one good reason why this method of name resolution comes so far down in the process.

LMHOSTS File

The LMHOSTS file is similar to the HOSTS file in that it's a static text file kept on and used by the local machine to resolve friendly (NetBIOS) names to IP addresses. This file is also kept in the *systemroot*\system32\drivers\etc directory on a Windows NT host machine. The LMHOSTS file must be maintained manually and can be edited by any standard text editor. We discuss the LMHOSTS file in greater detail in Chapter 10, "NetBIOS Name Resolution."

If a name matching the host name sought is found in the LMHOSTS file, the IP address is returned to the source host and the resolution process ends. If no match is found, an error is generated and the host name resolution process ends. At this point, you'll need to supply TCP/IP with the IP address of the host to which you would like to connect or determine what part of the name resolution process is not working correctly.

Exam Prep Questions

Question 1

> Which of the following is not a benefit of using host names to identify TCP/IP hosts?
>
> ○ a. Host names are easier to remember than IP addresses.
>
> ○ b. Alphanumeric host names can convey more meaning than plain numeric IP addresses.
>
> ○ c. Host names allow you to assign several IP addresses to the same machine.
>
> ○ d. The use of a host name to identify a machine allows the IP address and the location of the machine to be transparent to the end user.

The best answer for this question is c. Multiple host names or aliases can be assigned to the same TCP/IP host, but host names do not allow you to assign multiple IP addresses to a host. Answers a, b, and d are all benefits of using host names to identify TCP/IP hosts.

Question 2

> Which of the following set of characters is not allowed for use in a valid host name?
>
> ○ a. A–Z
>
> ○ b. 0–9
>
> ○ c. a–z
>
> ○ d. &, !, *, _

The correct answer is d. A valid host name can contain the characters A–Z, a–z, 0–9, and the hyphen (-) and dot (.). A valid host name cannot contain special characters such as the ampersand, the exclamation point, the asterisk, or the underscore.

Question 3

> Which of the following statements about configuring a host name
> on a Windows NT machine are true? [Check all correct answers]
>
> ❑ a. By default, the NetBIOS name of the machine is used as
> the host name.
>
> ❑ b. Any invalid characters in the NetBIOS name are con-
> verted to hyphens (-) in the host name.
>
> ❑ c. You must change the default host name (that is, the
> original NetBIOS name) to some name other than the
> name that is currently being used as the NetBIOS name.
>
> ❑ d. You can configure the host name and the DNS domain
> name in the DNS properties sheet of the TCP/IP
> properties.

The correct answers for this question are a, b, and d. By default, Windows NT uses the NetBIOS name as the host name for TCP/IP. Windows NT converts any nonvalid characters in the NetBIOS name to hyphens in the host name. If you want to change the host name to something other than the default, you can do so in the Network Control Panel|Protocols|TCP/IP Properties|DNS tab. Answer c is incorrect because it is not mandatory that you change the default host name.

Question 4

> Which of the following statements best describes a DNS domain?
>
> ○ a. A logical grouping of Windows hosts that all use the
> same security provider or PDC
>
> ○ b. A logical grouping of Windows hosts
>
> ○ c. A logical grouping of TCP/IP hosts
>
> ○ d. A logical grouping of TCP/IP hosts that corresponds to a
> particular organization and name, and usually a particular
> group of IP addresses

The correct answer for this question is d. A DNS domain implies a logical grouping of computers that share the same domain suffix. The computers and the namespace of a domain are usually controlled by one organization, or smaller groups within the organization. Because most organizations are assigned IP addresses in blocks, these domain names also loosely correspond to a set of IP addresses. Answer a is incorrect because it defines a Windows NT or NetBIOS domain based on a single security provider. Answer b is incorrect because it's simply a less-specific version of the previous answer. Answer c is a better answer than either a or b, but it is not as specific as answer d.

Question 5

Which of the following commands will not result in the HOSTS file being accessed?

○ a. PING

○ b. Telnet

○ c. FTP

○ d. NET VIEW

The correct answer for this question is d, because NET VIEW is one of the many NetBIOS network commands that can be used with Windows NT. This command results in a list of currently available NetBIOS resources, such as servers and network shares. PING, Telnet, FTP, and even Web browsers are all WinSock applications that will access the HOSTS file when they are given a host name, assuming that the host is properly configured to access this file.

Question 6

Which of the following statements are benefits provided by a DNS server? [Check all correct answers]

❑ a. A DNS server provides for centralized administration of host names and domain names.

❑ b. A DNS server allows for the dynamic registration and release of host names as TCP/IP hosts come up and go down on the network.

❑ c. A DNS server is relatively easy to install, configure, and administer.

❑ d. A DNS server uses a distributed database to maintain access to a large number of host names and domain names.

The correct answers for this question are a and d. DNS servers allow for the centralized administration of numerous host and domain names, eliminating the need for each user to maintain his or her own HOSTS file. DNS servers do use a distributed database to maintain access to extremely large numbers of host- and domain-name-to-IP-address mappings. Answers b and c are incorrect because DNS servers are fairly complicated to configure and must be maintained manually by an administrator. Microsoft's DNS does not currently support dynamic registration of host names and IP addresses.

Question 7

Using the default host name resolution order for Microsoft Windows NT, complete the following statement:

"After TCP/IP checks the local _____, the _____ is consulted. If it cannot resolve the host name, TCP/IP will next consult the _____."

○ a. host name; the LMHOSTS file; NetBIOS name cache

○ b. HOSTS file; local DNS server; NetBIOS name cache

○ c. DNS server; NetBIOS name cache; local host name

○ d. NetBIOS name cache; WINS server; local HOSTS file

The correct answer to this question is b. The configuration of a particular Windows NT machine can cause one or several of the default name resolution steps to be skipped. Therefore, several of the proposed answers appear to be correct at first glance. However, only b has three steps of the process in the correct order. Remember that host name resolution has the following order, by default:

Local host name>HOSTS file>DNS>NetBIOS name cache>WINS>Broadcast>LMHOSTS.

Answer a is incorrect because right after checking the local host name, TCP/IP checks the HOSTS file. Answer c is incorrect because, by default, TCP/IP tries the local Windows NT host name before it tries any other method of name resolution. Answer d is incorrect because, by default, the HOSTS file is consulted before any type of NetBIOS name resolution is attempted.

Question 8

Which of the following statements properly characterizes the HOSTS file? [Check all correct answers]

❏ a. The HOSTS file is a simple text file that can be edited with any ASCII text editor.

❏ b. The HOSTS file must be located in the *systemroot*\system32 directory.

❏ c. The HOSTS file only needs to be updated when a machine is moved to another network, not when it simply receives a new IP address.

❏ d. The HOSTS file can map IP addresses to simple host names or FQDNs.

The correct answers for this question are a and d. The HOSTS file is a simple text file that can be edited with any standard ASCII text editor. It can map an IP address to a single host name, a fully qualified domain name, or it can map a single IP address to multiple host names. Answer b is incorrect because the HOSTS file is, by default, located in the *systemroot*\system32\ drivers\etc directory. The HOSTS file for a machine is only updated when new hosts are added to a network, not when the computer is moved. Therefore, answer c is incorrect as well.

Need To Know More?

 Heywood, Drew. *Inside Windows NT Server 4.* New Riders Publishing, Indianapolis, IN, 1996. ISBN 1-56205-649-2. Chapter 9, "Using TCP/IP," contains information regarding the management of the HOSTS file, the use of the LMHOSTS file, the internal structure of the HOSTS file, host names, and name resolution.

Lammle, Todd, Monica Lammle, and James Chellis. *MCSE: TCP/IP Study Guide.* Sybex Network Press, San Francisco, CA, 1997. ISBN 0-7821-1969-7. Chapter 5, "Host Name Resolution," contains information about FQDN naming hierarchy, standard methods of host name resolution in a Windows NT environment, and host name resolution via DNS.

McLaren, Tim and Stephen Myers. *MCSE Study Guide: TCP/IP and Systems Management Server.* New Riders Publishing, Indianapolis, IN, 1996. ISBN 1-56205-588-7. Chapter 8, "Host Name Resolution," contains information regarding the proper configuration of the HOSTS file, Microsoft's method and order of host name resolution, and some common name resolution problems.

Microsoft Technical Information Network (TechNet). September, 97. PN99367. Contains numerous articles on host name resolution. Search for "host name resolution," "valid host name," "HOST," "LMHOSTS," and "NetBIOS name cache."

Domain Name System (DNS)

9

Terms you'll need to understand:

- √ DNS (Domain Name System)
- √ BIND (Berkeley Internet Name Domain)
- √ Domain Name Space
- √ Zone
- √ Master name server
- √ Primary name server
- √ Secondary name server
- √ Cache-only name server
- √ Recursive name query
- √ Iterative name query
- √ Inverse name query

Techniques you'll need to master:

- √ Installing DNS on Windows NT 4
- √ Configuring DNS zones
- √ Setting up DNS domains
- √ Creating DNS records
- √ Building in-addr.arpa domains
- √ Configuring DNS to use WINS

In this chapter, you'll learn how the Domain Name System (DNS) can be used to resolve computer name queries. We'll discuss how it is installed, give you some configuration tips, and explain some of the many DNS service options. You'll also learn how to integrate the Windows Internet Name Service (WINS) with DNS; a full explanation of WINS can be found in Chapter 12, "Windows Internet Name Service (WINS)."

DNS: Explored And Explained

The Domain Name System (DNS) is the foundation of name resolution on the Internet today. The Internet's domain system is a worldwide hierarchy administered by the InterNIC (Internet Network Information Center).

When the Internet was still ARPANet (Advanced Research Project Agency Network) and only a handful of computers were on the entire network, name resolution was not a problem; it could be handled by a single computer maintained at the Stanford Research Institute (SRI). The file that this computer maintained was called the HOSTS. This file simply listed IP addresses on the left and their corresponding computer names on the right. As the Internet grew, this single text file became an inefficient method for resolving computer names to IP addresses.

Eventually, the Domain Name System was conceived. DNS provides a similar but more efficient method of name resolution than that of the HOSTS file. DNS does resolve computer names to IP addresses via manually configured files, but DNS uses a hierarchical database of names that is maintained across multiple computers. The hierarchical and distributed nature of DNS makes the system more efficient and easier to maintain than a single, massive text file, like HOSTS.

> **TIP** Internet Request For Comments 882 and 883 outline the DNS. You can find these RFCs at http://ds.internic.net/rfc/rfc882.txt and http://ds.internic.net/rfc/rfc883.txt.

BIND

Berkeley Internet Name Domain (BIND) is a specification of the DNS that came from the University of California at Berkeley. This implementation of DNS was originally written for Berkeley's 4.3BSD Unix operating system. BIND is currently the most popular implementation of DNS in use; however,

BIND is not an official Internet specification and is not maintained as an RFC. Microsoft's DNS is based on the BIND implementation and is BIND-compatible.

Windows NT supports the BIND specification through its BIND boot file, which is located in the *systemroot*\system32\DNS directory. The boot file is not required by Windows NT or DNS, by default. DNS actually boots from settings configured in the Windows NT Registry. However, Windows NT will use the boot file during startup if you specify in the Registry for it to do so. To configure this option, you must edit the following Registry location: HKEY_LOCAL_MACHINE\SYSTEM\CurrentControlSet\Services\ DNS\Parameters.

To enable the boot file, simply delete the value that reads EnableRegistryBoot. After that, you should place the desired boot file in the *systemroot*\system32\ DNS directory. To learn more about creating or maintaining a boot file, search on "BIND boot file" in the Microsoft TechNet.

 Remember that the BIND boot file makes Windows NT BIND-compatible; however, BIND is not defined in an RFC.

The Domain Name Space

The term "Domain Name Space" refers to the structure and data that create the distributed Domain Name System used on the Internet. This hierarchy has many levels, and many different computers are responsible for maintaining each piece or level.

At the Root level of this hierarchy are the root name servers, which are maintained by the InterNIC. Most DNS servers are configured with the IP addresses of these root servers. The next level contains the Top level domains, including .com, .net, .org, .edu, and several other name suffixes that indicate country names or the types of domains that appear below them. For example, microsoft.com is the domain name for the commercial organization Microsoft, so it logically belongs under the .com (commercial) group. Because the University of Texas is an educational institution, it is listed under the .edu (education) domain. There are also identifiers for countries (you may have already seen .uk for the United Kingdom, .au for Australia, or one of the other country designators). Many U.S. government agencies are starting to use the .us domain to indicate the United States; however, this practice is not pervasive.

Below the Top and Root levels are a host (pardon the pun) of other domains. Take a look at Figure 9.1 to see a graphical representation of the Domain Name Space; this is just a small piece of the entire picture!

Table 9.1 describes some of the domain suffixes you see in Figure 9.1.

In this hierarchy, an individual computer is represented by a host name that can be several layers deep in the structure. For example, it could be an FTP server at Microsoft named ftp.microsoft.com, or it could be a production control machine in an Austin, Texas, division of an auto manufacturer, as in product.aus-tx.saturn.com. No matter how long the name, the host is the endpoint of the Domain Name Space hierarchical structure. This type of name is called a fully qualified domain name (FQDN), because it lists the full path through the hierarchy to the host.

Notice that an FQDN goes from the most-specific to the least-specific name. In the previous example, the "product" computer resides in Austin, Texas under the Saturn domain. You can identify that the computer resides in an Austin, Texas–based company named Saturn (which is a commercial organization). This information is normally read from the most-specific to most-general specification when reading from left to right. However, when you read the IP address for this computer, let's say 205.240.248.93, you actually read it from most general to most specific. For example, the address 205 belongs at

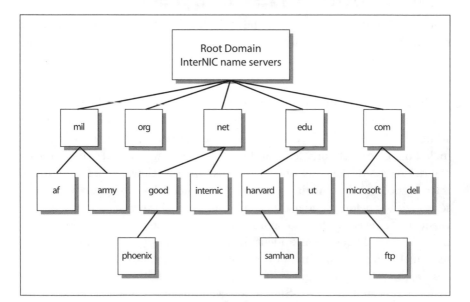

Figure 9.1 The Domain Name Space hierarchy.

Table 9.1 Common domain suffixes.	
Domain Suffix	**Type**
.com	Commercial organizations
.edu	Educational institutions
.gov	Government
.int	International organizations
.mil	Military operations
.net	Networking organizations
.org	Noncommercial organizations

the domain level, and 93 identifies a specific computer on that network. This fact will be important later when we discuss inverse name resolution.

Note: The name product.aus-tx.saturn.com is completely fictional and was created for this example only.

Name Resolution

DNS name resolution is similar to host name resolution in that user-friendly names are converted into IP addresses so that computers can communicate over TCP/IP. However, the DNS name resolution process is a bit more complex than scanning a simple text file. When using DNS, clients call a DNS server for name resolution. The DNS server attempts to provide name resolution services. The DNS server has the capability to collect additional information from other DNS servers in resolving the client's query.

In the DNS name resolution process, the client computer attempting to resolve a name is called the "resolver." A server that provides name resolution services is known as a "name server." The name server maintains a list of entries that map IP addresses to computer names; these are known as "resource records."

 The term "resolver" actually refers to the software running on the client computer that forwards name resolution requests to a name server.

Different Name Server Roles

A name server can take four different roles, and any given name server may have multiple roles. These roles are as follows:

➤ A primary name server is responsible for a piece of the Domain Name Space hierarchy known as a "zone." The information that creates a zone is maintained in a zone file. The zone file contains IP-to-host-name entries and other types of records, such as a record identifying the mail exchanger (email server). The primary name server is the name server that creates and maintains a given zone and is said to have *authority for that zone*. The primary name server also answers name resolution requests that come from clients.

➤ A secondary name server maintains a copy of the zone information that it receives from the primary server or another secondary server. This allows a secondary server to provide redundancy of the zone's name list as well as fault tolerance for the zone. For example, if the primary server experiences a critical hardware failure, the secondary server can continue resolving names because it has a copy of the list. A secondary name server reduces the load on the primary name server by answering name resolution requests from resolvers on the network.

➤ A master name server is any name server that provides a zone list to a secondary name server. The process of copying a zone list is called a "zone transfer." Secondary name servers are configured to call master servers to initiate a zone transfer.

➤ A caching-only name server does just what its name implies: it caches name resolutions. The sole purpose of a caching-only name server is to increase name resolution efficiency. This type of name server does not keep a permanent zone list. A caching-only server does resolve queries, often by using the help of other name servers. However, once a caching-only name server resolves a query, it caches that name resolution so that if another client asks for a name that has recently been resolved, the server can provide a name resolution immediately. Caching-only servers are useful when placed at the opposite ends of a slow WAN (wide area network) connection, because they can answer resolver requests but do not require zone transfers.

Name Server Resolution

Name servers are not limited to their own databases or name caches when attempting to resolve name queries; they can also call on other name servers. This enables the Domain Name Space hierarchy to work worldwide. For example, a name server in Australia can resolve a computer name of a host in North America by calling a name server (or several name servers, if necessary) in North America.

In the name resolution process, there are three types of name queries: recursive, iterative, and inverse.

Recursive Queries

Recursive queries are most commonly issued by resolvers. The client (resolver) wants an absolute name resolution, meaning that it needs a complete IP address returned from the name server. For example, if a resolver wants to resolve the IP address for the FTP server at the Microsoft site, it would essentially ask, "What IP address corresponds to ftp.microsoft.com?" If the name server can't give the client a complete answer, it has to answer with a "destination unknown" message.

Iterative Queries

Iterative queries are most often used between name servers to obtain partial name resolutions. For example, a name server might not know the entire IP address for ftp.microsoft.com, but it might know the IP address for the name server that handles microsoft.com. In this way, the name resolution occurs in pieces. The original name server must do the leg work (or bit work in this case) by calling the name server for microsoft.com. The client still gets an absolute answer from the name server; however, the original name server does not require the same from the other name servers it calls.

Inverse Queries

What happens when you know an IP address, but you want to find out what Internet name goes with it? DNS can also help resolvers with this type of a search; however, such searches require the creation of a special domain called "in-addr.arpa." The in-addr.arpa domain maintains a sort of reverse list of IP addresses to Internet names. One peculiar item about this domain (besides its name) is that IP addresses are listed in reverse order. As noted in an earlier example, the IP address 205.240.248.93 for the fictional product.austx.saturn.com would be listed as 93.248.240.205 to match the way the user-friendly name appears.

Name Resolution Steps

To further understand the DNS name resolution process, consider the following sample steps. This list shows you each step in the process used to resolve the FQDN ftp.microsoft.com after the client sends a recursive query to its name server:

1. The name server looks in its DNS cache and database for the name and IP address. If it does not find a matching entry, it queries the root name server(s).

2. The root-level name server should provide the location of a lower-level name server (for example, microsoft.com).

3. The original name server (from Step 1) can then contact the name server at microsoft.com and request the name of ftp.microsoft.com.

4. Once the original server has located the entire mapping for the domain name, it answers the resolver.

Caching And Time To Live (TTL)

When a name server resolves a name query, it places the name in a name cache. Entries in the name cache are given a specific time to live (TTL), which prevents a previously cached item from causing name resolution problems in the future. In other words, you wouldn't want your name server to give you the old IP address for ftp.microsoft.com; you would want the most recent mapping.

When the TTL expires, the cached item is removed. Resolvers can also place entries in their caches. Resolver software is configured to adhere to the TTL entries assigned by the name server. The resolver also removes the entry from its cache once the TTL has expired.

> If the IP addresses on your domain rarely change, configure a higher TTL in order to optimize your name resolution.

Installing And Configuring DNS

In Windows NT, DNS is run as a network service and is installed through the Services tab of the Network applet in the Control Panel, just as you do other network services. You simply click the Add button on the Services dialog box, select Microsoft DNS Server, and then click OK (see Figure 9.2). After that, you must insert a Windows NT Server 4 CD-ROM (or enter the path to the Windows NT Server installation files). Once the service has installed, reboot the computer.

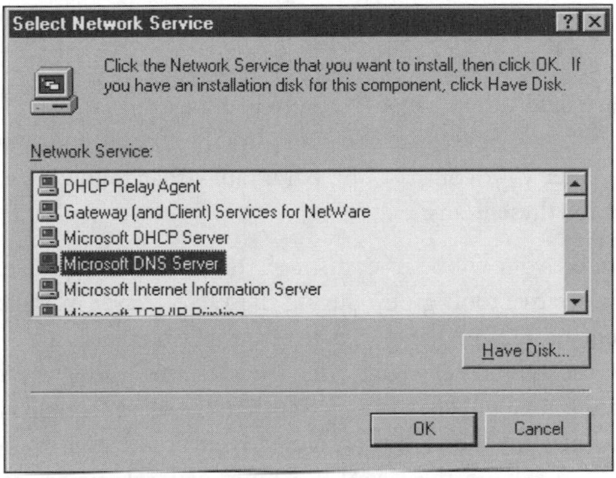

Figure 9.2   Installing the Microsoft DNS Server.

After you have installed the DNS service, it will appear in the Control Panel|Services utility. You should see that its status is "Started" and has a startup configuration of "Automatic" (see Figure 9.3).

Configuring Domain And Zones

Before you actually configure a name server, you should plan how your entire name structure is going to be configured internally. This assignment is far beyond the scope of this book and the Microsoft exam. You can learn quite a

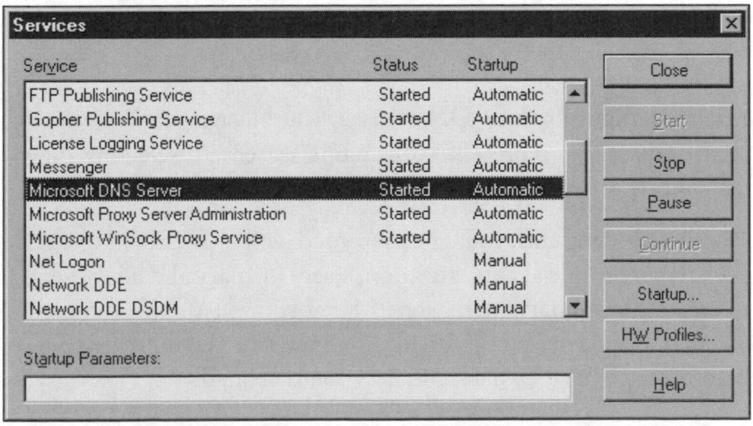

Figure 9.3   The Microsoft DNS Server service in the Services dialog box.

bit more about this topic in the Microsoft TechNet article "DNS and MS Windows NT 4.0."

Once you have determined what structure you are going to use for your piece of the Domain Name Space, you can configure the servers, zones, and domains that will be under your control. The paragraphs that follow explain the creation process for these items.

You can configure your DNS server through the DNS Manager, which is added to the Administrative tools group during the DNS Server installation. When you first open the DNS Manager, it is essentially a clean slate. To add your server, select the DNS menu and click New Server. Enter the name or IP address of your server and click OK. After that, the server should appear in the Server list. To view the hierarchy configured below the server, double-click the server object and expand the tree. By default, new servers are configured as caching-only name servers, so only a cache object should appear below a new name server.

When you double-click the cache object, it expands and provides you with a list of all the root name servers that are preconfigured with your name server in the right-hand window pane of the DNS Manager. This information comes from the CACHE.DNS file that is located in the *systemroot*\system32\DNS directory.

Once your DNS server is running, you might see entries appear and disappear from the cache. These items represent the name resolutions your server is making. When the TTL on the cached name expires, the entries disappear.

To continue configuring your DNS server, you must create a zone by right-clicking the object that represents your name server and selecting New Zone from the context menu (see Figure 9.4).

Immediately following this, you'll be presented with a Creating New Zone For dialog box. For your initial configuration, select Primary and click Next. If you want to create a secondary name server later, you must enter the zone name and the name of a master name server. DNS imports the master name server's records automatically when a secondary zone is created.

When you're creating a primary name server, you must next configure the zone information. Enter the domain name you're creating. For example, if your domain name is hudlogic.com, enter hudlogic.com in the Zone Name box. If you press the Tab key, the next part will be filled out for you. By default, the file

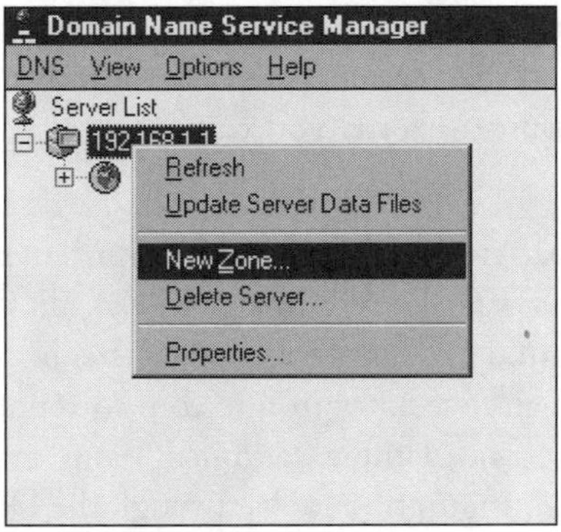

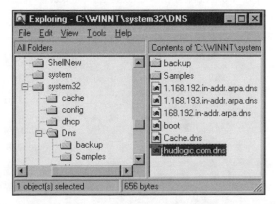

Figure 9.4   New Zone configuration.

name for your new domain is your domain name plus the extension .DNS. This actually creates an equivalent file in the *systemroot*\system32\DNS folder. Using the previous example, HUDLOGIC.COM.DNS should be entered into the Zone file box, which creates the file HUDLOGIC.COM.DNS in the C:\WINNT\system32\DNS folder (see Figure 9.5). To complete the new zone creation, click Next and then Finish.

Once you have configured all of the zones you need for this server, you can add subdomains. To do so, right-click the object that represents the zone and select New Domain from the context menu. Then, enter the name of the new subdomain in the dialog box and click OK. Should you require multiple levels of subdomains, repeat this process for each new object down the hierarchy.

You can enter "resource records" in each of the domains and subdomains you create. Resource records are the entries that map host names to IP addresses.

Figure 9.5   New zone and zone files in DNS Manager and the creation of those files as viewed through Explorer.

To create a resource record, right-click the domain or subdomain where you want to configure it and then select New Record from the context menu. The different types of resource records you can create in DNS are described in Table 9.2.

"A" records are the basic type of IP-address-to-host-name records you might expect to see in a HOSTS file. A CNAME is an alias for a given host. For example, if you wanted to be able to use the host names superman.kryptonite.com and manofsteel.kryptonite.com to represent the same server, you could make the second name a canonical name for the first. Figure 9.6 illustrates how such a configuration looks through the DNS Manager. You can see how these names resolve when PING is used from the command prompt.

In the following sections, the PTR, WINS, and WINS-R record types will be described with their related subjects. PTR records are used for reverse name resolution, which is discussed in the in-addr.arpa section that follows. The WINS and WINS-R records are discussed in the section titled "Integrating DNS With WINS." To learn more about the wide variety of record types that are available in DNS, consult the resources listed at the end of this chapter.

 If you want to configure an alias name for DNS records, you would use a canonical name record, or CNAME.

Table 9.2	Types of resource records.
Record Type	**Description**
SOA	The *start of authority* record is the first record in a zone database file. It defines the name server that is authoritative for the zone.
A	*A* records are host address records, which match an IP address to a host name.
NS	*Name server* records identify other name servers.
CNAME	*Canonical name* records are aliases for host names. These records allow you to associate more than one host name with an IP address.
MX	*Mail exchange* records identify mail routing servers.
PTR	*Pointer* records are used for IP-address-to-name resolution in reverse lookup zones (in-addr.arpa).
WINS	*WINS* records are used to identify Windows Internet Name Service (WINS) servers.
WINS-R	*WINS-R* records allow the DNS server to use WINS for inverse name resolution.

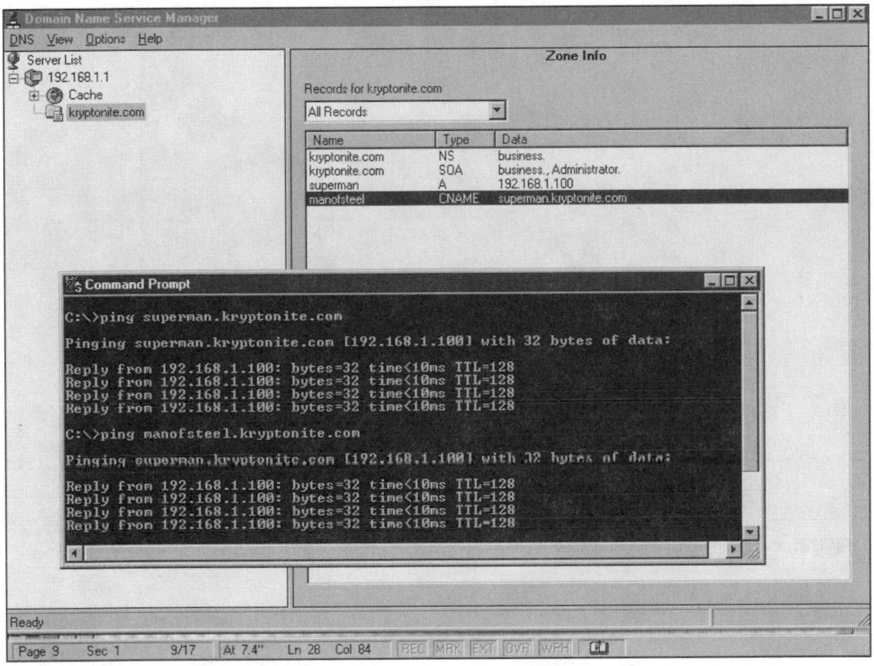

Figure 9.6   Canonical names in the DNS Manager and the results of PING after their creation.

in-addr.arpa

The in-addr.arpa domain is used for reverse name resolution. As previously mentioned, reverse name resolution occurs when you have an IP address and you (or the software you're using) need to determine the computer name for that IP address. To make this type of name resolution possible, you must create an in-addr.arpa domain by inverting the network portion of your IP address. For example, if you have the Class C address 192.168.1.0, you would invert the 192.168.1 part to get 1.168.192 and then add "in-addr.arpa" to the end of the number. This makes your in-addr.arpa domain 1.168.192.in-addr.arpa. All you need to do after that is create a new zone with that name.

> PTR records are pointers to the in-addr.arpa domain and are used for reverse name resolution.

Also, in-addr.arpa records can be created automatically when you create A records. The checkbox Create Associated PTR Record is checked, by default, when you enter a record (see Figure 9.7).

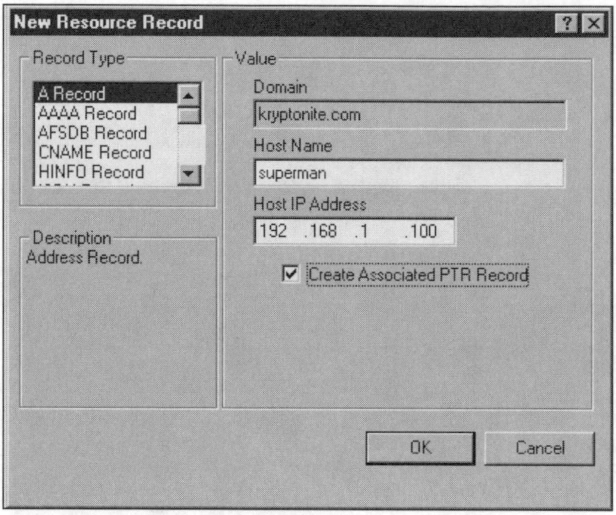

Figure 9.7 PTR record creation.

If for some reason the automatic PTR record creation fails—which usually happens only when you haven't created the in-addr.arpa domain—you can create the record manually. To do this, right-click the in-addr.arpa domain and select New Record. Next, select PTR Record and enter the host's IP address and computer name. This is illustrated in Figure 9.8.

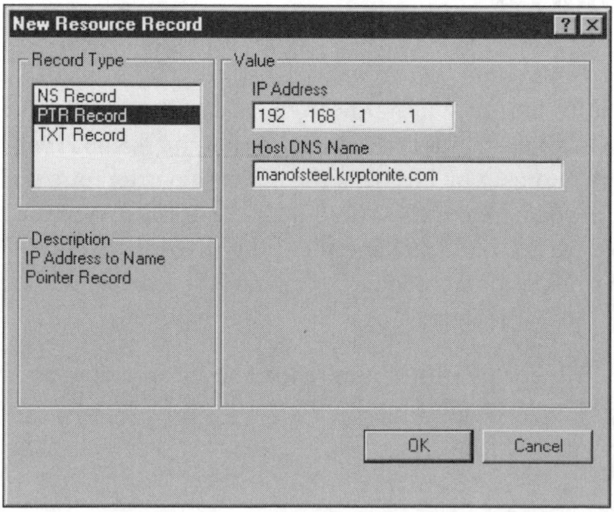

Figure 9.8 Manual PTR record creation in the in-addr.arpa domain.

Integrating DNS With WINS

Your DNS server can be configured to call a WINS server as well as other name servers to resolve names. The WINS server can help the DNS server with the last piece (the host name) of the FQDN. For example, if your name server is trying to resolve the name product.aus-tx.saturn.com, a WINS server might be able to help it out with the resolution of the "product" portion of the FQDN.

> **TIP**
>
> In Chapter 12, "Windows Internet Name Service (WINS)," you'll learn about the WINS name resolution process. For now, you only need to understand that WINS is another method for resolving computer names to IP addresses. In this section, you should concentrate on configuring the resource records for WINS. WINS will be used to resolve only the last part of a fully qualified domain name; this part is also known as the "host name."

To enable WINS Lookup on your DNS server, right-click the icon that represents your domain (for example, kryptonite.com) and select Properties. Click the WINS Lookup tab and check the Use WINS Resolution checkbox. Enter the IP addresses for the WINS servers you would like your DNS server to contact when resolving host names; this creates a WINS Record in your domain (see Figure 9.9).

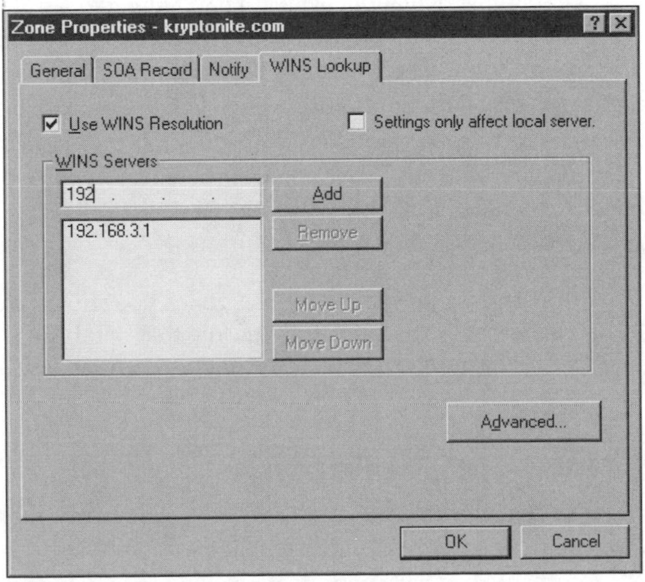

Figure 9.9   Creating a WINS Record.

When you configure a zone to perform WINS Lookup, you should ensure that any name server that is authoritative for that zone (in other words, maintains a zone name list) is also configured for WINS Lookup. Otherwise, name resolution on your domain may be inconsistent, which could be difficult to troubleshoot. In this location, you can also enable the TTL for WINS name resolutions by clicking the Advanced button on the WINS Lookup sheet.

 Be sure to remember the process for integrating DNS and WINS for the Microsoft exam.

WINS And Reverse Lookup

Even though WINS was not designed to provide reverse name resolution, DNS can be configured to call a WINS server for that purpose as well. To configure this, right-click the in-addr.arpa domain for your site and select Properties. Click the WINS Reverse Lookup tab and then check the Use WINS Reverse Lookup checkbox. In the DNS Host Domain dialog box, enter the name of your DNS domain (for example, kryptonite.com). The name you enter is appended to all WINS Lookups for this domain before it is returned to the resolver.

DNS Notify

The Microsoft DNS implementation includes DNS Notify, which allows master servers to inform secondary servers when changes have been made to the DNS database. The master name server prompts the secondary name servers to call for a zone transfer. To configure Notify, right-click the icon that represents your domain and select Properties. Click the Notify tab and then enter the IP addresses of secondary servers in your zone. If you check Only Allow Access From Secondaries Included On Notify List, the name list will be available only to those name servers on the Notify list.

 When configuring secondary DNS zones, you should place servers in the DNS Notify list to ensure that database changes are replicated from the master to secondary name servers.

DNS Round-Robin Feature

DNS can also be used for distributing loads on your network. For example, Microsoft has multiple physical computers that create its Web site; when you go to the Microsoft site, you have no way of knowing to which physical server you are actually going to connect. This is possible because DNS can resolve the same name to multiple IP addresses. If you enter the same computer name twice, giving each a separate IP address, DNS will rotate through these names. For instance, if you enter the name www.kryptonite.com twice and map it to two different IP addresses, DNS will answer queries for www.kryptonite.com with alternating IP addresses. Figure 9.10 illustrates this point, showing the DNS configuration in the background and the result of PING in the foreground. Notice that the name is resolved to IP address 192.168.1.100 the first time and 192.168.3.1 the next.

 When configuring DNS Round-Robin, remember to enter the same computer name multiple times, mapping it to a different IP address each time. After that, DNS automatically rotates through the name list.

Configuring DNS Clients (Resolvers)

Configuring Microsoft Windows NT clients for DNS is extremely easy: just access the TCP/IP properties sheet through the Protocols tab of the Network dialog box. Then, double-click the TCP/IP protocol to open its properties sheet and select the DNS tab (see Figure 9.11).

By default, your computer's host name is identical to the computer name you have in the Identification tab of the Network dialog box. You can also configure your computer's domain name (this is an Internet domain name, *not* a Windows NT domain name). In the DNS Service Search Order section, enter the IP addresses for the name servers you would like the client to contact when

```
Command Prompt

C:\>ping www.kryptonite.com

Pinging www.kryptonite.com [192.168.1.100] with 32 bytes of data:

Reply from 192.168.1.100: bytes=32 time<10ms TTL=128
Reply from 192.168.1.100: bytes=32 time<10ms TTL=128
Reply from 192.168.1.100: bytes=32 time<10ms TTL=128
Reply from 192.168.1.100: bytes=32 time<10ms TTL=128

C:\>ping www.kryptonite.com

Pinging www.kryptonite.com [192.168.3.1] with 32 bytes of data:

Reply from 192.168.3.1: bytes=32 time<10ms TTL=128
Reply from 192.168.3.1: bytes=32 time<10ms TTL=128
Reply from 192.168.3.1: bytes=32 time<10ms TTL=128
Reply from 192.168.3.1: bytes=32 time<10ms TTL=128

C:\>_
```

Figure 9.10   Round-Robin resolution.

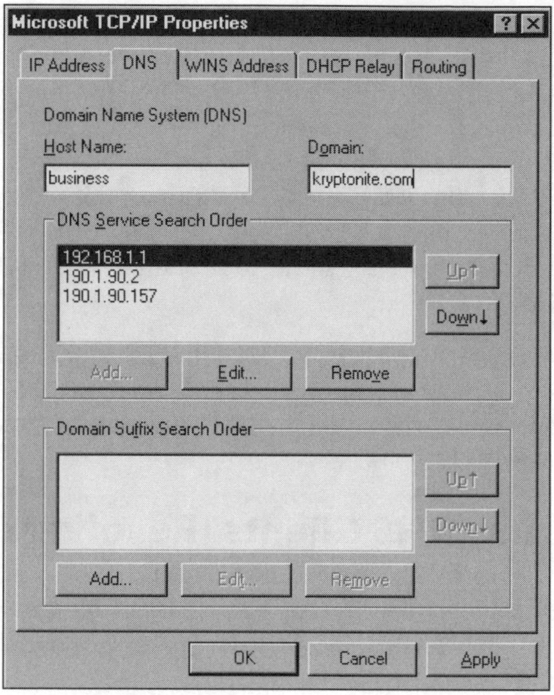

Microsoft TCP/IP Properties   [?][X]

IP Address | **DNS** | WINS Address | DHCP Relay | Routing

Domain Name System (DNS)

Host Name: Domain:

business   kryptonite.com

DNS Service Search Order

192.168.1.1
190.1.90.2
190.1.90.157

Up↑

Down↓

Add...   Edit...   Remove

Domain Suffix Search Order

Up↑

Down↓

Add...   Edit...   Remove

OK   Cancel   Apply

Figure 9.11 Configuring a DNS resolver.

attempting to resolve a computer name. Notice that you can also set the order in which these servers are called. In the Domain Suffix Search Order section, you can enter the order you want the top-level domains to be searched. For example, you can enter .com, .edu, and .mil in that order, indicating that the .com domain is to be searched prior to the .edu or .mil domains.

Troubleshooting DNS With NSLOOKUP

DNS servers are not automated; they do require manual upkeep and sometimes they have errors. Besides troubleshooting by directly modifying your DNS files or using the DNS Manager application to view and correct entries, you can employ the NSLOOKUP utility.

NSLOOKUP is a command-line utility that can be used to trouble-shoot the Domain Name Server database.

NSLOOKUP is a great utility to use to query a Domain Name Service server. It works even on Unix-based DNS implementations. You can run NSLOOKUP from the command line using the following syntax:

```
nslookup [[-option ...] [computer-to-find]] | - [server]
```

NSLOOKUP has two modes: interactive and noninteractive. If you are looking up only one record, you'll find that noninteractive mode is the most convenient. The commands in Figure 9.12 were run in noninteractive mode.

If you type a hyphen (-) instead of the *computer-to-find*, NSLOOKUP switches into interactive mode, in which case you can issue multiple name queries. If you are not sure what names you are looking for, try the interactive mode and enter multiple queries, one right after the other, until you find what you need. For more information on the Windows NT NSLOOKUP utility, check the WINNT.HLP file supplied with Windows NT 4. You can also enter the search term "NSLOOKUP" in the Microsoft TechNet to read more about it.

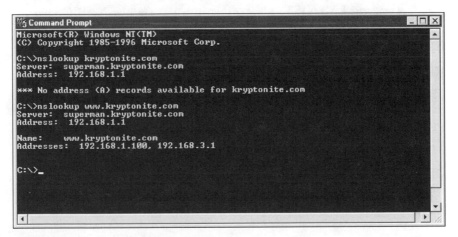

Figure 9.12   NSLOOKUP in action.

Exam Prep Questions

Question 1

> Which method of host name resolution uses a single static text file to resolve Internet names? [Check the best answer]
>
> ○ a. Domain Name System
>
> ○ b. Domain Name Space
>
> ○ c. HOSTS
>
> ○ d. LMHOSTS

The correct answer here is c. This question is actually testing your knowledge of the history of computer name resolution on the Internet. A tricky part to this question is listing the LMHOSTS file, which is a static name resolution file. However, the LMHOSTS file is primarily used to resolve NetBIOS names, not host names. Therefore, d is incorrect. Domain Name System and Domain Name Space both refer to a distributed name resolution system and not a single text file. Therefore, a and b are incorrect.

Question 2

> Which RFC explains the BIND specification?
>
> ○ a. RFC 882
>
> ○ b. RFC 883
>
> ○ c. RFC 1542
>
> ○ d. None

The correct answer for this question is d. The Berkeley Internet Name Domain (BIND) is not specified in an RFC. BIND is a prevalent method for the implementation of DNS, but it's not an official Internet standard. All the other answers are obviously decoys: RFC 882 and 883 define the Domain Name System, and RFC 1542 specifies BOOTP and DHCP.

Question 3

Which of the following files contain DNS resource records for name resolution? [Check all correct answers]

❑ a. CACHE.DNS

❑ b. 12.122.205.IN-ADDR.ARPA.DNS

❑ c. Boot file

❑ d. HUDLOGIC.COM.DNS

The correct answers for this question are a, b, and d. The CACHE.DNS file is used to point your name server to the root servers at the InterNIC that are used for name resolution. The file 12.122.205.IN-ADDR.DNS indicates that this file is for the Class C address 205.122.12.0 and is used for inverse name queries. HUDLOGIC.COM.DNS is a file that would hold resource records for name resolution on the HUDLOGIC.COM domain. The boot file contains only information that is used when starting DNS. On Microsoft DNS servers, the boot file is not enabled, by default. Therefore, answer c is incorrect. All the other files listed in this question are used for name resolution.

Question 4

How do you enable DNS to allow it to call a WINS server in order to resolve a host name?

○ a. Add an entry in the WINS database pointing to the DNS server.

○ b. Check Enable DNS For Windows Resolution on the client computer.

○ c. Add a WINS resource record to the zone and enable WINS resolution.

○ d. In the name server properties, configure WINS Lookup.

The correct answer is c. You should have been able to eliminate answers a and b quickly. You do not configure WINS to call DNS, you configure DNS to call WINS. Therefore, answer a is incorrect. The second item does not allow DNS to call WINS, it enables a WINS client to resolve FQDNs. The last two options are a little tricky. In DNS, you do configure WINS Lookup, but it is not located in the name server properties; it's actually in the properties for the zone; therefore, answer d is incorrect. **In the WINS Lookup tab, you must check the Use WINS Resolution checkbox and then enter the IP address of the WINS server. When you okay these changes, a WINS record is added to the zone.**

Question 5

Which types of names can WINS resolve for DNS?

○ a. Host

○ b. FQDN

○ c. Domain

○ d. Root

The correct answer is a. Probably the only trick here is knowing that even though DNS resolves FQDNs, it sends only the host portion of the name to the WINS server. Domain names and root names would not be handled by the WINS server, because they are outside the scope of WINS.

Question 6

Which type of query is used by a name server to navigate the Domain Name Space hierarchy to answer a name query from a resolver?

○ a. Recursive

○ b. Iterative

○ c. Inverse

○ d. WINS

The correct answer for this question is a. Recursive queries are used by the resolver to obtain an absolute answer from the server. Iterative queries are used to obtain partial name resolutions; therefore, answer b is incorrect. Inverse queries are used to resolve IP addresses into their user-friendly counterparts; therefore, answer c is incorrect. WINS is used to resolve the host portion of an FQDN; therefore, answer d is also incorrect.

Question 7

Your company has configured seven different Internet-style domains for your network. You are responsible for the Southwestern domain. Which of the following could you implement to distribute the name resolution load of your domain? [Check all correct answers]

❏ a. DNS Round-Robin

❏ b. Secondary zone

❏ c. Primary name server

❏ d. Caching-only server

The correct answers to this question are b and d. DNS Round-Robin does not allow you to distribute the name resolution load. Instead, this is a method for DNS to distribute the load of client requests to your network servers by resolving names to alternating addresses. A primary name server will not help because it would handle name resolution for another domain rather than the one you are presently working on. **The options you have are to configure a secondary zone or add a caching-only name server to your existing zone.**

Question 8

Which record type allows the DNS server to call WINS for inverse name resolution?

○ a. A

○ b. CNAME

○ c. WINS

○ d. WINS-R

The correct answer is d. The only record that allows DNS to call WINS for reverse (inverse) name resolution is the WINS-R record. CNAME records are alias records; A records are used for straight name resolution; and WINS records point to WINS servers for regular name resolution services.

Need To Know More?

Albitz, Paul and Cricket Liu. *DNS and BIND*. O'Reilly & Associates, Inc. Sebastopol, CA, 1997. ISBN 1-56592-236. The entire book is dedicated to the subject of the Domain Name System. Focus is placed on the Berkeley Internet Name Domain (BIND) implementation.

Heywood, Drew. *Networking with Microsoft TCP/IP*. New Riders Publishing, Indianapolis, IN, 1996. ISBN 1-56205-520-8. Chapter 12, "Managing DNS," contains some useful information on configuring DNS, the boot file, and the cache file.

Lammle, Todd, Monica Lammle, and James Chellis. *MCSE: TCP/IP Study Guide*. Sybex Network Press, San Francisco, CA, 1997. ISBN 0-7821-1969-7. Chapter 5, "Host Name Resolution," contains information about the FQDN naming hierarchy, standard methods of host name resolution in a Windows NT environment, and host name resolution via DNS.

Search the TechNet CD (or its online version at www.microsoft.com) using the following keywords: "DNS," "Domain Name System," "CACHE.DNS," and "DNS zone."

The *Windows NT Server Resource Kit* contains a lot of useful information about TCP/IP and related topics. You should search for the article titled "DNS and Windows NT 4.0" by Scott B. Suhy and Glenn Wood.

Internet Request For Comments 882 and 883 outline the DNS. You can find these RFCs at http://ds.internic.net/rfc/rfc882.txt and http://ds.internic.net/rfc/rfc883.txt.

NetBIOS Name Resolution

. . . .

Terms you'll need to understand:

√ NetBIOS name

√ LMHOSTS file

√ Name registration

√ Name discovery

√ Name release

√ B-node broadcast

√ WINS

√ Node types

√ Browsing

Techniques you'll need to master:

√ Identifying the different methods of NetBIOS name resolution

√ Identifying the types of applications and services that use NetBIOS names

√ Understanding how the process of NetBIOS name registration, discovery, and release works

√ Determining the default methods of name resolution used by Windows NT

√ Determining the difference between NetBIOS name resolution and browsing

√ Troubleshooting browsing and NetBIOS name resolution problems

In this chapter, we discuss NetBIOS names and how they are used in the Windows networking process. NetBIOS names are similar in function to host names, because they provide user-friendly names by which Windows-based machines can be identified on a network. However, NetBIOS names are used to identify more than just an IP host. Windows-based hosts use NetBIOS to register and advertise not only their names, but also network-based file and print services and other Windows-based services.

NetBIOS Names: Explored And Explained

In Chapter 8, "Host Name Resolution," we introduced the concept of identifying and contacting a host by using its host name rather than its IP address. A host name is usually more user-friendly and easier to remember than an IP address. This user-friendly name also provides a logical identifier for each host that does not need to be changed should the host's IP address change for some reason (for example, it is moved to another subnet).

 In order to understand NetBIOS names, it helps to compare them to host names, and vice versa. Throughout the rest of this chapter, we'll compare NetBIOS names to host names and explain the differences in functionality between the two. A good knowledge of the similarities and differences of each will be very helpful during the exam.

NetBIOS Names Defined

Each Windows NT host (as well as other Windows-based hosts) receives a NetBIOS name during the installation of the operating system. This name is used to uniquely identify the machine on the network. However, the NetBIOS name is not used itself to identify a host; it is used by NetBIOS applications and processes to establish communication with other NetBIOS applications on remote hosts.

A NetBIOS name consists of 15 alphanumeric characters. If a NetBIOS name does not contain 15 characters, Windows will add the necessary number of null characters to fill the name out to the required 15 characters. A sixteenth character (called a node), which is not usually visible, is added to each NetBIOS name. This final character is a hexadecimal value that indicates the type of name, service, or group that the NetBIOS name represents.

For example, a Windows NT workstation named HORTON has a number of shared directories available for others to access: FUNNIES, DOCS, and

MEMOS. When this machine boots up, it announces to the local network (or to a WINS server if it is configured to access one) the NetBIOS name it intends to use, the workgroup or domain with which it wishes to be associated, and the services that it has to provide. The machine name and any of the server services all register the NetBIOS name HORTON, but each uses a different hexadecimal value for the sixteenth character.

The following output of the **NBTSTAT-N** command shows what the NetBIOS name table for HORTON might look like. We'll discuss this and other utilities throughout this chapter.

```
Node IpAddress: [192.168.0.1] Scope Id: [null]
NetBIOS Local Name Table
Name          Type            Status
HORTON        <00> UNIQUE     Registered
CORP          <00> GROUP      Registered
JAMES         <03> UNIQUE     Registered
HORTON        <20> UNIQUE     Registered
CORP          <1E> GROUP      Registered
```

The first line of the table gives the NetBIOS name HORTON with the hexadecimal node value <00> and says that this name is unique. The hex value <00> means that this NetBIOS name is the name of the computer and is registered by the workstation service of the named computer. CORP, the second NetBIOS name in the list, is the name of the domain with which this host is associated. The NetBIOS name JAMES is designated by the hexadecimal node value <03> and indicates the logon ID of the user currently logged into the workstation named HORTON. Finally, the NetBIOS name HORTON with the hexadecimal node value <20> indicates that this name is associated with the server service running on HORTON.

To see how these NetBIOS names would be used, assume that you are going to map a drive from your machine to a shared directory on HORTON. You open Windows NT Explorer, choose Map Network Drive, and enter G: as the drive letter and \\HORTON\memos as the network resource. (The format *computername**sharename* is known as UNC or Universal Naming Convention.)

Your computer will need to establish a connection to the server service on HORTON in order to access the shared resources. Using b-node broadcast resolution (discussed in greater detail in the section titled "B-Node Broadcast"), your workstation can send a request to HORTON asking that its NetBIOS name be resolved to an IP address and also to confirm that the server service is running on HORTON.

Now that you understand the basics of NetBIOS names and how they are used, let's take a closer look at how NetBIOS names are registered on the network and then resolved.

Registration, Discovery, And Release Of NetBIOS Names

A NetBIOS name is registered on the network each time a host boots—unlike a host name, which is resolved by either a static HOSTS file or DNS database. A host's NetBIOS name can be registered either on the local network by broadcast or with a WINS server to provide access to all other hosts on the entire network.

If a host is not configured to access a WINS server (NetBIOS Name Server), it broadcasts the NetBIOS name that it intends to use on the local network. This broadcast is known as a NetBIOS name registration request. All hosts on the local network process this name request packet to determine if they are already using the name being requested. If one of the hosts is already using this name, it sends a negative name registration response. This prevents TCP/IP from initializing on the booting machine and generates an error stating that the requested name is already in use. If the name is not in use and no other host challenges the use of the requested name, the requesting host continues the TCP/IP initialization and boot process.

The use of a WINS server on the network cuts down on the need for network broadcasts but works much the same way as broadcast resolution. Instead of sending a broadcast to the local network, a WINS client sends its name registration request directly to the WINS server. If the WINS server does not already have the name registered by another machine, it allows the requesting host to use the specified NetBIOS name. If the WINS server finds the requested name already registered in the WINS database, it sends a message to the host currently using the NetBIOS name and lets it know that it should defend the use of its name. If this host is currently up and running, it defends the use of its name, and the initializing host generates a NetBIOS initialization error. If the host does not defend its name, the host that initiated the name registration request is allowed to use the name.

The NetBIOS name discovery (read "resolution") process can occur by broadcast (b-node) or point-to-point (WINS) as well. To resolve a NetBIOS name to an IP address, a host first checks its local NetBIOS name cache. This area of memory on the local host contains recently resolved NetBIOS names and their corresponding IP addresses. If the host does not find a mapping in the name cache and it is not configured to use WINS, it initiates a NetBIOS name discovery broadcast on the local network. Only machines on the local network receive and process this resolution request, unless the routers on the network have been configured to forward packets on UDP ports 137 and 138. If a machine on the local network is using the requested name, it responds to the request with its IP address.

 A b-node broadcast is limited to the hosts on the local network segment unless your routers are configured to forward packets on UDP ports 137 and 138 to other networks. You should be very careful when deciding whether or not to use UDP ports 137 and 138 on your routers, because their use decreases the available bandwidth of the network.

If the requesting host is configured to access a WINS server, it sends the name discovery request directly to the WINS server before attempting a broadcast to the local network. The WINS server checks its database for the requested name and sends a response directly to the host needing the NetBIOS name resolved. If the WINS server cannot resolve the address, the host requiring the name resolution sends a broadcast to the local network segment. If no response is received, the host consults its local LMHOSTS file (that is, assuming it has been configured to do so).

Finally, during a proper shutdown, a NetBIOS host "releases" its NetBIOS name. This means that it informs the WINS server or other hosts on the local network segment that it's no longer using the specified name and any other hosts that request the use of the name will not be challenged.

A WINS-enabled client usually contacts the WINS server during the shutdown process and releases its NetBIOS name. The WINS server marks the name as "released" in the database. Should another machine request the name after that point, the WINS server allows the name to be reassigned to another IP address. Should a machine be shut down improperly, its name might not be removed from the database. However, if a new host requests the name for another IP address, the WINS server will ask the host at the current IP address to defend its name. If no host responds at the original IP address, the name is reassigned to the new IP address. This can happen when a laptop user moves from subnet to subnet.

Clients that are not WINS-enabled send a release broadcast to the local network. This allows other hosts on the local segment to remove NetBIOS name mappings from their name cache for the specified machine.

NetBIOS Name Resolution

A NetBIOS name can be resolved to an IP address via four means: the local NetBIOS name cache, WINS, b-node broadcasts, and the LMHOSTS file. If none of these is able to resolve the NetBIOS name, the HOSTS file and DNS can be consulted as well.

A good mnemonic for remembering the order in which NetBIOS names are resolved is "Can We Buy Large Hard Drives," which breaks down as follows:

1. NetBIOS name cache

2. WINS

3. B-node broadcast

4. LMHOSTS file

5. HOSTS file

6. DNS

The NetBIOS Name Cache

The NetBIOS name cache is an area of memory on the local host that contains recently resolved NetBIOS names and their corresponding IP addresses. Each entry in this cache has a TTL (time to live) associated with it. The more frequently a name in the cache is accessed, the longer it remains in the cache. This is the first place Windows NT looks for NetBIOS name resolution.

The name cache also contains entries from the LMHOSTS file. Entries in the LMHOSTS file that are followed by the **#PRE** tag are preloaded into the NetBIOS name cache during initialization. Preloaded entries do not have a typical TTL associated with them. They remain in the cache until the cache is purged with the **NBTSTAT -R** command or until the machine is turned off. If there's a machine on your network that you access frequently with NetBIOS applications and services, it's wise to give this machine a permanent entry in the NetBIOS name cache.

The **NBTSTAT** command, seen here

```
NBTSTAT [-a RemoteName] [-A IP address] [-c] [-n]
        [-r] [-R] [-s] [S] [interval] ]
```

allows you to view and manipulate the NetBIOS name cache of your local machine as well as the name tables on other machines. Table 10.1 explains NBTSTAT command's associated options.

Table 10.1   The NBTSTAT command's associated options.

Option	Description
-a (adapter status)	Lists the remote machine's name table given its name.
-A (Adapter status)	Lists the remote machine's name table given its IP address.
-c (cache)	Lists the remote name cache, including the IP addresses.
-n (names)	Lists local NetBIOS names.
-r (resolved)	Lists names resolved by broadcast and via WINS.
-R (Reload)	Purges and reloads the remote cache name table.
-S (Sessions)	Lists sessions table with the destination IP addresses.
-s (sessions)	Lists sessions table, converting destination IP addresses to host names via the HOSTS file.
RemoteName	Remote host machine name.
IP address	Dotted-decimal representation of the IP address.
interval	Redisplays selected statistics, pausing interval seconds between each display. Press Ctrl+C to stop redisplaying statistics.

WINS

If a host is unable to resolve a NetBIOS name using the local NetBIOS name cache and it has been configured with the address of at least one WINS server, it sends a resolution request directly to the WINS server.

The WINS server then checks its database for the IP address of the requested NetBIOS name. If one exists, the server sends the resolved address to the requesting machine, and the requesting host adds the mapping to its local NetBIOS name cache. If the WINS server does not have a mapping, it lets the requesting host know, and the requesting host moves to the next step in the NetBIOS name resolution process.

B-Node Broadcast

The local host initiates a b-node broadcast to the local network if the WINS server is unable to provide NetBIOS name resolution. Each NetBIOS host on the local network segment processes the broadcast request by comparing the name requested with its own NetBIOS name. When a host finds that it is using the same name as that requested for resolution, it responds to the requesting machine with its IP address.

This step of the NetBIOS name resolution process usually occurs *after* attempting to resolve the name from the name cache or the WINS server, because network broadcasts are very costly in terms of network bandwidth and processor cycles on each of the machines that must process the broadcasts. For this reason, these broadcasts are generally limited to the local network segment by routers. Most routers will not forward NetBIOS name registrations, resolution, or release broadcasts. In order for a router to forward such packets to other networks, it must be configured to forward packets received on UDP ports 137 and 138.

You can use the **NBTSTAT -r** command to see how many NetBIOS names have been resolved by broadcast and how many have been resolved by WINS. Do not confuse the lowercase -r with the uppercase -R. The former stands for names resolved, whereas the latter stands for cache reload.

 Become familiar with the different functions of the **NBTSTAT** command. A good knowledge of this command and its options is required on the exam.

LMHOSTS

If no other form of NetBIOS name resolution successfully resolves the NetBIOS name, the requesting host checks for the appropriate entry in its local LMHOSTS file (assuming it has been configured to do so).

LMHOSTS is a standard text file, much like the HOSTS file, that is used to resolve names to IP addresses. The LMHOSTS file should be located in the *systemroot*\system32\drivers\etc directory; a sample file, LMHOSTS.SAM, can be found in this location. The LMHOSTS file contains IP addresses on the left side of the file, followed by at least one space and a NetBIOS name. These entries can have additional meanings assigned to them by use of special "tags." The following is an example of an entry from the LMHOSTS file:

```
192.168.0.1    BONGO    #PRE #DOM:RESOURCE
```

This is a NetBIOS-name-to-IP-address mapping for the host named BONGO. The **#PRE** tag that follows this entry indicates that this entry should be loaded and remain persistent in the NetBIOS name cache. The **#DOM** tag that follows indicates that BONGO is a domain controller for the RESOURCE domain.

Table 10.2 provides a list of valid tags for use in the LMHOSTS file and their meanings.

Table 10.2	Valid tags for use in the LMHOSTS file.
Tag	**Description**
#	Indicates that a remark follows.
#PRE	Indicates that the preceding entry should be preloaded into the name cache.
#DOM:_domainname_	Denotes a domain controller and can be used by the local machine to validate logon requests and to exchange master browser lists with the domain master browser.
#INCLUDE	Used to include the location of LMHOSTS files on other hosts on the network. This can be used to include a centrally maintained LMHOSTS file in the path of the local machine.
#BEGIN_ALTERNATE	Used to group together multiple **#INCLUDE** statements.
#END_ALTERNATE	Used to designate the end of a block inclusion.
#MH	Associates one NetBIOS name with multiple IP addresses; used for multihomed hosts.
#SG	Allows for the creation of special groups. It creates groups in a way similar to the **#DOM** tag.

The LMHOSTS file is parsed from top to bottom. Each line of the file is read until the correct NetBIOS name is found or the end of the file is reached. Because of the way the file is read, it's best to have as few lines as possible in the file. The fewer lines of text to be read, the faster the name resolution process will occur.

For this reason, you shouldn't use the LMHOSTS.SAM file "as is" when creating an LMHOSTS file for production use. This file, as you'll see in a moment, has a large number of explanatory comments. Each of these comment lines must be read before a NetBIOS name can be resolved.

You should also place any entries that have the **#PRE** designator near the end of the LMHOSTS file, because these entries are given a persistent mapping in the NetBIOS name cache during the initialization process; there's no need to read these entries from the LMHOSTS file again. By placing them near the end of the file, all other entries are read before the unneeded **#PRE** entries are read again.

The following is an excerpt from the LMHOSTS.SAM file:

```
# Copyright (c) 1993-1995 Microsoft Corp.
#
```

```
# This is a sample LMHOSTS file used by the Microsoft TCP/IP for
# Windows NT.
#
# This file contains the mappings of IP addresses to NT computer
# names (NetBIOS) names. Each entry should be kept on an
# individual line. The IP address should be placed in the first
# column followed by the corresponding computer name. The
# address and the computer name should be separated by at least
# one space or tab. The "#" character is generally used to
# denote the start of a comment (see the exceptions below).


#
# This file is compatible with Microsoft LAN Manager 2.x
# TCP/IP lmhosts files and offers the following extensions:
#
#       #PRE
#       #DOM:<domain>
#       #INCLUDE <filename>
#       #BEGIN_ALTERNATE
#       #END_ALTERNATE

<Lines deleted from original file>


#
# The #BEGIN_ and #END_ALTERNATE keywords allow multiple
# #INCLUDE statements to be grouped together. Any single
# successful include will cause the group to succeed.

<Lines deleted from original file>

# 102.54.94.123 popular  #PRE #source server
# 102.54.94.117 localsrv #PRE #needed for the include
#
# #BEGIN_ALTERNATE
# #INCLUDE \\localsrv\public\lmhosts
# #INCLUDE \\rhino\public\lmhosts
# #END_ALTERNATE

<Lines deleted from original file>

# Note that the whole file is parsed including comments on each
# lookup, so keeping the number of comments to a minimum will
# improve performance. Therefore it is not advisable to simply
# add lmhosts file entries onto the end of this file.
```

You can add your own entries, such as the domain controller for your network, the address of a high-end workstation that you connect with frequently, and the location of a central LMHOSTS file that resides on the network, to the end of this file or in a completely new file. Here's an example:

```
128.131.98.225 PDC1 #DOM:ACCOUNTS
#This designates a domain controller
128.131.98.91 WORKSTATION1 #PRE
#This loads the address into the name cache upon boot
#BEGIN_ALTERNATE
        #INCLUDE \\SERVER8\public\LMHOSTS
        #INCLUDE \\SERVER9\public\LMHOSTS
#END_ALTERNATE
```

HOSTS File And DNS

If a NetBIOS name is not resolved by any of the native NetBIOS name resolution methods, TCP/IP on Windows NT can examine the HOSTS file and contact a DNS server if it is configured to do so. This form of resolution works only if the NetBIOS name is the same as the host name for the specified machine.

NetBIOS Over TCP/IP Node Types

Microsoft's implementation of TCP/IP uses all the previously mentioned name resolution methods to resolve NetBIOS names and generally performs these steps in the order they were presented in this chapter. However, the steps can take place in an order different from the one given, or not at all, depending on the configuration of each Windows machine.

In the next sections, we discuss the different combinations of name resolution methods allowed when using Microsoft TCP/IP.

B-Node

B-node resolution relies completely on local broadcasts for name registration, discovery, and release. If a host cannot be found in the NetBIOS name cache or reached by local broadcast, the NetBIOS name cannot be resolved. This method requires virtually no configuration to work correctly, but it creates a great deal of traffic on the network.

Enhanced B-Node

This is the default node configuration for Windows machines that are *not* configured to access a WINS server for NetBIOS name services. This modified version of the b-node allows Windows machines to consult the local LMHOSTS file should broadcast resolution fail.

P-Node

P-node name services rely completely on point-to-point communication for NetBIOS name services. If the NetBIOS name cannot be found in the cache, this method of resolution requires the client to contact a NetBIOS Name Server (such as a WINS server) directly. This method of resolution greatly reduces the amount of broadcast traffic that a network must process, but it does not allow any fault tolerance should the WINS server fail or go offline.

M-Node

M-node, or mixed node, resolution is just a combination of b-node and p-node resolution. The name cache is checked first. If the name is not found in the name cache, the host sends a b-node broadcast to the local network, and if that fails to resolve the desired NetBIOS name, the host sends a directed request to the WINS (or NetBIOS) name server.

This method of resolution allows for redundancy, but it does not reduce the amount of local network broadcasts. An m-node machine will always broadcast before attempting point-to-point resolution.

H-Node

By default, a Windows or Windows NT machine that is configured to access a WINS server uses hybrid-node (h-node) configuration. H-node name resolution uses both broadcast and point-to-point resolution (as does m-node), but in the reverse order.

An h-node machine first checks the NetBIOS name cache. If the name cannot be resolved from the name cache, the host contacts the WINS server with a directed name resolution request. If the WINS server is unable to resolve the NetBIOS name, the machine broadcasts up to three name discovery requests to the local network. If the NetBIOS name is still unresolved, the machine can be configured to access the LMHOSTS and/or HOSTS file, as well as a DNS server.

This method of name resolution is preferred because the WINS server, which is contacted before the use of broadcasts, usually has the requested information. This significantly reduces the number of network broadcasts required on each segment of the network. If, for some reason, the WINS server is unavailable or it cannot resolve the given name, the host can still use local broadcasts and the LMHOSTS file to resolve the NetBIOS name.

Using NetBIOS Over TCP/IP To Browse Across Routers

Windows NT 4 allows for browsing of network resources. Browsing is the ability to view the presence of and use NetBIOS network resources without having previous knowledge of their existence or location.

Browsing is possible because NetBIOS is used to distribute browse lists for each network to a special machine known as a master browser. A browse list is a list of available NetBIOS network resources for a particular network segment. Each segment of the network has a master browser or local backup browser that maintains the browse list for that segment. These backup browsers exchange browse list information with the domain master browser at regular intervals. The Primary Domain Controller (PDC) for the network is always the Domain Master Browser. This machine is responsible for combining all the partial lists received from each network segment into one master browse list. It then redistributes the master browse list to a backup browser for each local network segment. In this way, each local master browser or backup browser has a list of all currently available NetBIOS network resources for the entire network.

Each local master browser or backup browser is determined through a process called an election. Election can be forced at different times on the network. The winner of the election depends on the version and operating system of the machines running. The machine running the latest version of software is generally the winner, because these machines have a more current knowledge of the other operating systems that might be found on the network. For example, Windows NT Workstation 4 supersedes a Windows 95 machine, and a Windows NT Server running 3.51 software would lose to a Windows NT Server running 4.0 software.

The previous example presumes the ability to transmit information across routers. In Windows networking environments, several ways exist to get around the restriction of NetBIOS name services to each local segment. WINS, the LMHOSTS file, and specially configured routers can all provide means for NetBIOS name services in a routed domain environment.

WINS allows each NetBIOS host on a routed network to register and resolve names through point-to-point, directed requests. Each machine registers itself with the WINS server during TCP/IP initialization, and each host or browse master can contact the WINS server directly. Because these requests are directed to a particular IP address, the presence of routers is inconsequential.

The LMHOSTS file can be used by the master browser (domain controller) of each subnet to contact the domain master browser. The domain master browser then distributes a master browse list to each local master browser. This directed exchange of browse list information makes the presence of routers irrelevant.

Finally, in a small router environment that contains a limited number of NetBIOS hosts, the routers can be configured to forward NetBIOS name service packets. This, in effect, puts all the hosts on the same local network as far as NetBIOS services are concerned. In larger environments, however, this can have a detrimental effect on network performance.

Troubleshooting NetBIOS Naming Problems

The first step in troubleshooting a NetBIOS name resolution problem is to ensure that the problem is name resolution. In other words, make sure the problem is not a browsing issue.

Just because a machine or resource cannot be found in a local browse list—such as Network Neighborhood—does not mean that the host is unavailable or that a name resolution problem exists. The problem may simply be that a backup browser on one of the local network segments is down temporarily, causing the master browse list for the entire network to be outdated.

When a computer comes online, it announces itself. Initially, it announces itself once a minute, with the interval decreasing to once every 12 minutes. This repeated announcement is used by the master browser to determine if a resource is still available. The master browser maintains the list of resources for any machine for three missed announcements, to accommodate performance dips and communication bottlenecks. Thus, after a machine has been up and running for a reasonable time, then goes offline, its resources can remain in the master browser's list for up to 36 minutes. Backup browsers poll the master browser every 15 minutes to request an updated version of the browse list. Therefore, a failed resource can remain in the backup browser's list for up to 51 minutes.

The quickest way to determine the nature of the problem is to connect to the desired resource using the UNC of the resource rather than Network Neighborhood. For example, try connecting to \\TOTO\kansas instead of using Network Neighborhood to locate the needed resource.

If you are still unable to connect to the resource, try PINGing the IP address of the machine to which you want to connect, to be sure that it is still up and running. If the machine responds, you must determine what part of the name resolution process is failing.

If your machine is configured to use a WINS server and not the LMHOSTS file, and it's trying to resolve the name of a machine on another network segment, try PINGing the address of the WINS server. If the WINS server has become unavailable for some reason, you must enable another method of name resolution, such as the LMHOSTS file.

If you're using the LMHOSTS file, you should be aware of a number of common errors related to the use of this file. The name of the NetBIOS host to which you're trying to connect may not be in the LMHOSTS file, or the IP address of the machine to which you wish to connect may have changed.

There may be more than one occurrence of a NetBIOS-name-to-IP-address mapping in the LMHOSTS file. Remember that the first matching name found is used, regardless of whether or not the IP address is correct. Use the Find command in your text editor to eliminate duplicate NetBIOS name entries in the LMHOSTS file.

Finally, make sure that the LMHOSTS file has the correct name and extension and that it is located in the correct directory. Many text editors commonly add the .TXT extension to each file they save. This causes problems when Windows NT is trying to find the file LMHOSTS and the needed file is named LMHOSTS.TXT. Similarly, the name of the file must be LMHOSTS, not LMHOST.

Exam Prep Questions

Question 1

You have just received a new Windows NT Workstation and you
seem to be having trouble mapping a drive to another Windows
NT host that resides on a remote network. Your network does not
currently have a WINS server providing NetBIOS name resolution. Which of the following files should you modify to enable
Windows NT to correctly resolve the name of the Windows host
to which you are trying to connect?

O a. HOSTS

O b. LMHOSTS

O c. HOST

O d. LMHOST

The correct answer for this question is b. The LMHOSTS file is the file you
should modify to enable Windows NT to correctly resolve the name of the
Windows host to which you are trying to connect. Remember that both the
HOSTS file and the LMHOSTS file can contain multiple friendly-name-to-
IP-address mappings. Therefore, the names of each of these files take the plu-
ral form, not the singular form.

Question 2

Which of the following applications is not a NetBIOS application
or command? [Check all correct answers]

❑ a. net use \\server2\share1

❑ b. Windows NT FTP client

❑ c. Windows NT Telnet client

❑ d. Windows NT Explorer

The correct answers for this question are b and c. FTP and Telnet are Windows Sockets applications. The NET command and Windows NT Explorer,
on the other hand, were designed to provide access to other Windows-based
platforms, such as Windows NT Workstation, Server, and Windows 95. Therefore, these applications are NetBIOS-based. Just remember that TCP/IP-based

applications that were originally designed to provide interconnectivity to all types of TCP/IP host are generally based on the Sockets API; these are programs such as PING, FTP, Telnet, and Gopher. Windows applications that allow the use of TCP/IP, such as Windows Explorer, User Manager, and the NET command, were designed to provide Windows-based connectivity and are therefore NetBIOS applications. This is flagged as a trick question because careful reading is required to choose the applications that are *not* NetBIOS-oriented.

Question 3

Mary has just taken over the desktop support for a different department of her company. She would like to ensure that each workstation within her department has an updated LMHOSTS file and make sure that each file is in the correct location on the local machine. If Mary adds a new, preloaded (**#PRE**) NetBIOS name to each LMHOSTS file that she edits, which of the following commands will enable her to test whether or not the file is located in the correct directory and is being used for resolution.

- ○ a. NETSTAT -r, followed by NBTSTAT -d
- ○ b. NBTSTAT -r, followed by NBTSTAT -c
- ○ c. NETSTAT -R, followed by NBTSTAT -d
- ○ d. NBTSTAT -R, followed by NBTSTAT -c

The correct answer for this question is d. NBTSTAT (a NetBIOS utility) allows you to purge the NetBIOS name cache and reload it with entries from the LMHOSTS file, with the use of the *-R* option. Once the name cache has been successfully purged and reloaded from the LMHOSTS file, you can use the *NBTSTAT -c* (cache) option to view the new contents of the NetBIOS name cache. The presence of the newly added preloaded (*#PRE*) NetBIOS name in the NetBIOS name cache indicates that the LMHOSTS file was found in the correct directory and is being used for NetBIOS name resolution.

The NETSTAT -r command does not provide NetBIOS information. It is used to display the contents of the local routing table (similar output as the ROUTE print command). The lowercase -r option shows a list of statistics relating to registered and resolved NetBIOS names as well as the method used to resolve the name (either WINS or broadcast). There isn't a documented -d option for the NBTSTAT utility. Therefore, any answers containing these options are wrong.

Question 4

You have just taken a job with a company that would like to convert its current network operating system to Windows NT. The company has four subnets on its TCP/IP network, each of which will have its own Backup Domain Controller (BDC), except for the subnet on which the PDC will reside. The company would like to allow browsing across the entire network without needing to implement WINS. How should you modify the LMHOSTS file so that this is possible?

○ a. Create an entry in the LMHOSTS file on the PDC for each of the BDCs and use **#DOM**.

○ b. Create an entry in the LMHOSTS file on each BDC for the PDC and use **#DOM**.

○ c. Create a HOSTS file for each subnet of the network and place these files on each client.

○ d. This is not possible.

The correct answer for this question is b. By default, a BDC is elected as the master browser for a subnet, assuming no PDC is present on that subnet. By adding an IP-address-to-NetBIOS-name mapping in the LMHOSTS file (and using the *#DOM* tag to indicate that the machine is a domain controller), each of the BDC/master browsers can be configured to contact the PDC (which is the Domain Master Browser) and send a local browse list of the available machines. The PDC then combines the browse lists obtained from each subnet into a master list and delivers the master list to each of the BDCs for use on the local subnet. This allows each subnet to be aware of the machines available for browsing on each of the other subnets within the company.

Question 5

Which of the following statements are potential problems that can occur when using the LMHOSTS file?[Check all correct answers]

❑ a. The LMHOSTS file is not in the root directory of system drive.

❑ b. The LMHOSTS file has been saved with an incorrect name or extension.

❑ c. The entry in question has been misspelled or entered incorrectly.

❑ d. Two different entries exist for the same NetBIOS name, and the one that occurs first in the list is incorrect.

The correct answers for this question are b, c, and d. Answer b is correct because while editing the LMHOSTS file, it is possible to save the file with the wrong name—for example, as LMHOST—or to save it with an extension like .SAM or .TXT. The correct name for this file is LMHOSTS. Typos and spelling mistakes are quite common when editing text files such as the LMHOSTS file. Therefore, answer c is correct. Answer d is correct because the LMHOSTS file is parsed from top to bottom, a line at a time. When a matching entry is found, the NetBIOS name resolution process stops, whether or not another entry in the file exists. This problem occurs most often in environments where large LMHOSTS files must be maintained. Answer a is incorrect because the LMHOSTS file is supposed to reside in the *systemroot*\system32 \drivers\etc directory, not the root of the drive that contains the system files.

Question 6

> Curtis works for a local state agency that does not use WINS for NetBIOS name resolution. Instead, each client on the network copies a master LMHOSTS file from a central server during the logon process. After having a number of problems with the current PDC (MIS4) of the HR domain, Curtis decides to promote one of the BDCs (Payroll2) to PDC status and take the former PDC offline. What change must Curtis make to the master LMHOSTS file in order for each client to be able to contact the new PDC?
>
> ○ a. 128.131.24.122 #PRE Payroll2 #DOMAIN: HR
>
> ○ b. 128.131.24.122 HR: #DOM #PRE
>
> ○ c. 128.131.24.122 Payroll2 #PRE #DOM: HR
>
> ○ d. 128.131.24.122 Payroll2 #DOM

The correct answer to this question is c. The master LMHOSTS file needs to have an IP-address-to-NetBIOS-name mapping for the machine that is to be the new PDC. This entry in the LMHOSTS file, however, is a special one. It must also include the *#DOM* tag to indicate that the specified machine is also the primary domain controller. The *#PRE* tag is optional—it ensures that the IP address of the PDC resides in the NetBIOS name cache at all times. Answer a is incorrect because the name of the host must come immediately after the IP address. Answer b is incorrect because the name of the host is not given, and the domain name comes after the **#DOM** tag, not before it. Answer d is not correct (although it's close—the "trick") because it does not specify the name of the domain for which this host is now the PDC.

Question 7

The following are the first four steps of the NetBIOS name resolution process:

1. b-node broadcast

2. WINS

3. NetBIOS name cache

4. LMHOSTS

Which of the following options places these steps in the correct (default or hybrid node) order?

- ○ a. 3, 2, 1, 4
- ○ b. 3, 1, 4, 2
- ○ c. 2, 3, 1, 4
- ○ d. 1, 2, 3, 4

The correct answer to this question is a. By default, a Windows NT machine that is configured to contact at least a primary WINS server uses h-node resolution. The hybrid form of resolution first checks the NetBIOS name cache and then the WINS server. If WINS cannot resolve the requested name, the sending host initiates a broadcast to the local network in order to locate a machine that responds to the name being resolved. If no response is received, the sending host then checks for the presence of an entry in the local LMHOSTS file (assuming that it has been configured to do so).

Need To Know More?

 Heywood, Drew. *Networking with Microsoft TCP/IP.* New Riders Publishing, Indianapolis, IN, 1996. ISBN 1-56205-520-8. Chapter 11, "Managing WINS," contains information regarding client configuration for the use of the LMHOSTS file and node types.

 Lammle, Todd, Monica Lammle, and James Chellis. *MCSE: TCP/IP Study Guide.* Sybex Network Press, San Francisco, CA, 1997. ISBN 0-7821-1969-7. Chapter 6, "Host Name Resolution," contains relevant information about NetBIOS naming, node types, and resolution using the LMHOSTS file.

McLaren, Tim and Stephen Myers. *MCSE Study Guide: TCP/IP and Systems Management Server.* New Riders Publishing, Indianapolis, IN, 1996. ISBN 1-56205-588-7. Chapter 9, "NetBIOS Name Resolution," contains information regarding NetBIOS applications and protocols, NetBIOS over TCP/IP (NBT), and the NBTSTAT utility.

Search the TechNet CD (or its online version at www.microsoft.com) using the following keywords: "NetBIOS name resolution," "NetBIOS names," "LMHOSTS and 4.0," "NetBIOS name cache," and "WINS."

Dynamic Host Configuration Protocol (DHCP)

11

Terms you'll need to understand:

√ Lease

√ DHCP relay

√ Scope

√ Reserved client

Techniques you'll need to master:

√ Understanding the initial DHCP lease process

√ Understanding the lease renewal process

√ Understanding how DHCP relay is used in an internetwork

The Dynamic Host Configuration Protocol (DHCP) was designed to fill an obvious void in TCP/IP networking: centralized IP address management. DHCP is an extension of the Bootstrap Protocol (BOOTP), which previously handled dynamic IP address assignment. In this chapter, we'll discuss DHCP's role in host configuration and network management, as well as how it applies to the all-important exam.

DHCP: Explored And Explained

DHCP was designed by the IETF (Internet Engineering Task Force) to provide a robust method of dynamic IP address allocation that would ease the initial configuration of client computers while reducing the required administration overhead. DHCP is fully defined in RFCs 1533, 1534, 1541, and 1542; it provides automatic configuration for an IP address and a subnet mask and can also provide a default gateway address, DNS server address(es), or WINS address.

The central controlling point for DHCP is the DHCP server, which services the requests of the clients and ensures that no duplicate IP addresses exist on the network. The number of DHCP servers that can be placed on a network is unlimited; however, if more than one server is used, a separate list of addresses should be provided to each server. If the lists are the same or overlap, the potential for duplicate addresses seriously undermines the usefulness of DHCP.

On the surface, DHCP may seem like the simplest solution for client configuration; however, it does have some drawbacks. Table 11.1 highlights the pros and cons of implementing DHCP.

Table 11.1 DHCP pros and cons.

Pros	Cons
Easy to implement.	Difficult to track who has which address.
Centralized configuration means fewer errors.	Extremely difficult to implement across firewalls.
Machines can be moved.	Users with new machines may manually configure their systems, picking an address that has been dynamically assigned.
Included with most Microsoft operating systems.	Not *all* operating systems are supported.

DHCP: Obtain And Renew Your Lease

When a client utilizes DHCP for its configuration, it obtains a lease from the server that allows it to use the IP address for a specific amount of time, similar to leasing an apartment. When you sign a lease for an apartment, the lease specifies that you'll be able to use the apartment for a period of time. When it gets close to the end of your lease, you can either renew the lease or tell the landlord that you'll be moving out at the end of the lease. A client's DHCP lease works much the same way. As the lease gets closer to expiration, the client has the option to renew, which we'll discuss in a minute. The actual lease acquisition process consists of four steps.

In the first step, called the "lease request," the client sends a broadcast message to the network. Because the client does not know its own address or that of the server, the source address of the packet is 0.0.0.0 and the destination is 255.255.255.255. This type of packet is called the "DHCP discover message," and it contains the NetBIOS name for the client system, which is used in the second step. If no DHCP server responds, the client repeats the broadcast three times, at 9-, 13-, and 16-second intervals. If there's still no response, the client sends the broadcast every 5 minutes until it is answered. If there's never an answer, TCP/IP is not fully initialized on the client, and no communication takes place.

The second step is the "lease offer," in which all DHCP servers that have valid addressing information respond to the broadcast from the client. Their offer packets include the IP address and subnet mask the client will use, the lease period (in hours), and the servers' IP addresses. When a server makes an offer, it temporarily reserves the address so that it doesn't send it in another offer, avoiding sending duplicate addresses to different clients.

The next step is "lease selection," which is a bit of a misnomer because the client will take the first offer it receives, after which the client then broadcasts an acceptance message. This broadcast doesn't have source IP address information, but it does have the destination address of the DHCP server whose offer it is accepting. Any other DHCP servers who have made offers revoke their offers at this time.

The final step is the "lease acknowledgment." If all has proceeded according to plan, the server assigns an IP address and sends a DHCPACK (acknowledgment) message to the client, at which point the client integrates the new IP information. However, sometimes a DHCPNACK (a negative acknowledgment) message is sent—for example, when a client requests its old IP address but that address has been reassigned.

So now that you've got a lease on this information, what do you do with it? And, more importantly, what do you do when your lease runs out? Well, it's not as bad as you might think. Because the client doesn't really want to lose its configuration, it sends a DHCP lease request to the DHCP server that assigned the address when the client's DHCP lease is 50 percent complete. If the DHCP server is available and no reason exists to deny the request, the server will send a lease acknowledgment, updating the configuration and resetting the lease time. However, if for any reason the server is unable to fulfill the request, it sends a message stating that the lease has not been renewed. Never fear: The client still has 50 percent of its lease duration to try again—which is exactly what it does when 87.5 percent of the lease duration has expired. Unlike the conversation at 50 percent, any DHCP server can respond to this DHCP request. However, if the client does not receive a DHCPACK from a server, it starts the whole lease process over from the beginning.

As you might imagine, sometimes a lease is terminated. However, at the most logical time, when the computer is powered down, the lease is not terminated because the computer will attempt to renew the lease with the same address when it is powered up again. If a client is off and the lease time expires, the lease is terminated and the DHCP server has the option of using that IP address. A lease can also be terminated manually by the user by typing the **IPCONFIG /RELEASE** command, which will be discussed later, in the section titled "The IPCONFIG Utility."

Planning And Implementing DHCP On Your Network

As we discussed in the beginning of the chapter, using DHCP does have some drawbacks. Here are some further considerations to keep in mind once you have decided to utilize DHCP:

➤ **How many clients will use DHCP?** This is an important question in dealing with server configurations and performance. Microsoft recommends having at least two DHCP servers, configured to back each other up. This way, if one fails, all network communication does not come to a crashing halt.

➤ **What are the client operating systems?** Almost all Microsoft operating systems support DHCP, including Windows NT 3.5x and higher, Windows 95, Windows for Workgroups (with TCP/IP-32), LAN Manager 2.2 (DOS but not OS/2), and the Microsoft Network Client 3.0 for DOS.

➤ **Will they utilize DHCP to receive default gateway, DNS, or WINS server information?** Before installing DHCP on a network, you should know whether other information will be provided by the DHCP server.

➤ **How many subnets are involved?** If every client that will use DHCP is on one subnet, server configuration is easy; however, if multiple subnets are involved, routers come into play.

➤ **Are there routers involved, and if so, are they able to forward BOOTP broadcasts?** If the routers do not have the capability to forward BOOTP broadcasts, you'll have to place a DHCP server on each subnet.

> *Note: Remember that DHCP is based on BOOTP. Routers are not specifically configured for DHCP but rather for the BOOTP protocol it's based on.*

Installing

Any Windows NT Server that is not itself a DHCP client can be a DHCP server. Installation of the DHCP service is remarkably easy, and it follows the same procedure as the installation of all other NT Server components. From the Network applet, select the Services tab and click the Add button. A list of available services will be displayed, as shown in Figure 11.1. Select the Microsoft DHCP server service and click OK.

You will be prompted to enter the path to the Windows NT Server files. Enter the path and click Continue. Windows NT then copies the appropriate files. A window appears to inform you that any adapters that were previously using DHCP will require static IP addresses (as shown in Figure 11.2). Click OK.

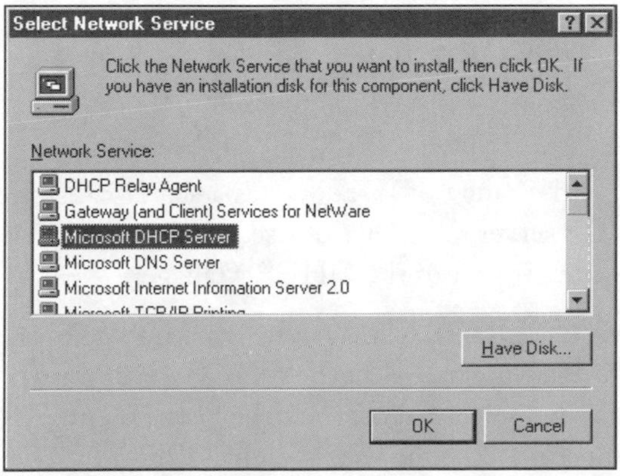

Figure 11.1 Select Microsoft DHCP Server from the list of available services.

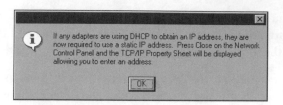

Figure 11.2 Only non-DHCP configured servers can operate as DHCP servers.

Click the Close button on the Network applet to finish copying the files. You must restart the computer for the DHCP service to start; click Yes to restart the computer immediately. After the computer has been rebooted, DHCP must be configured with a scope before it can service requests. The remaining configuration requirements are discussed throughout the rest of this chapter.

DHCP Relay

If your network contains routers between the DHCP server and DHCP clients, the routers must be able to forward the DHCP (BOOTP) broadcast packets. This is referred to as DHCP relay, and it's a very important consideration for installation.

 The DHCP relay process is a perfect candidate for Microsoft to ask a question about on the exam. Remember that a router must be configured to forward BOOTP broadcasts for DHCP relay to work.

Not surprisingly, a Windows NT 4 computer can act as a DHCP Relay Agent. To enable this function, select the DHCP Relay tab in the TCP/IP Properties section of the Network applet (shown in Figure 11.3) and insert the IP address(es) of the DHCP server(s).

Scope

A DHCP scope is the range of IP addresses a server can assign. At the very minimum, a DHCP server must have one scope. Figure 11.4 shows the Create Scope window, which is part of the DHCP Manager.

To create a scope, start DHCP Manager, which is under Administrative Tools (Common) in the Start menu. Select the DHCP server for which you want to create a scope and then select Create from the Scope menu. After entering the information in the Create Scope window, click OK. You'll be asked whether you would like to activate the scope; select Yes. At this point, the scope will be displayed with a yellow light bulb, indicating that it has been activated.

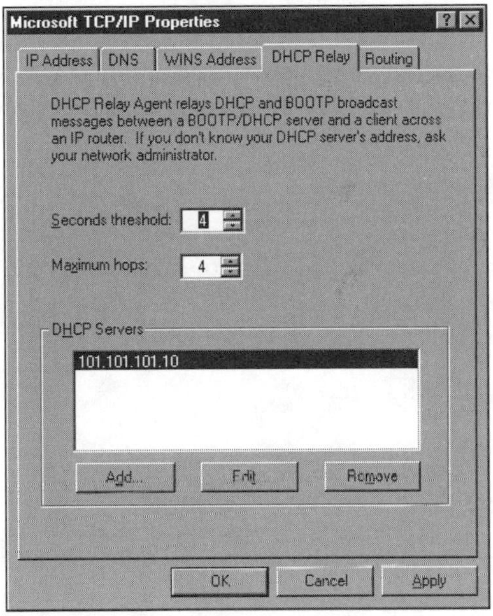

Figure 11.3   The DHCP Relay configuration screen.

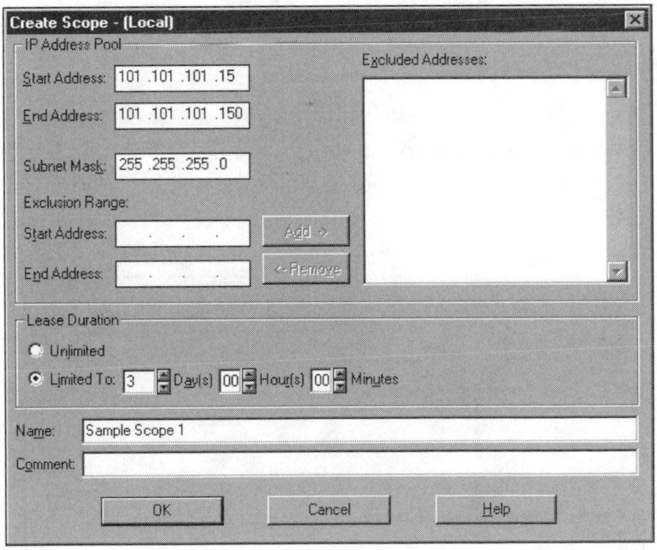

Figure 11.4   The Create Scope window in the DHCP Manager.

Scope Options

Each scope created has a number of available options that are accessed via the DHCP Options menu in the DHCP Manager, as shown in Figure 11.5.

These options define configuration settings that are assigned when a client is configured using DHCP. For example, to configure the DNS server settings for a particular scope, select 006 DNS Servers from the list and then click the Add button to activate the option. Click the Value button to display the bottom section of the screen (see Figure 11.6). The important scope options supported by Microsoft clients you should remember are:

➤ **003** Router (Default Gateway)

➤ **006** DNS

➤ **044** WINS/NBNS

➤ **046** WINS/NBT Node Type

➤ **047** NetBIOS Scope ID

To enter the DNS server addresses, click the Edit Array button. This activates the window shown in Figure 11.7.

Global Options

The global options available to a DHCP server are the same as the options available for a scope; however, these options are, as their name implies, *global*. Every client, no matter what scope, will be given these configurations. You should note that scope options take precedence over global options.

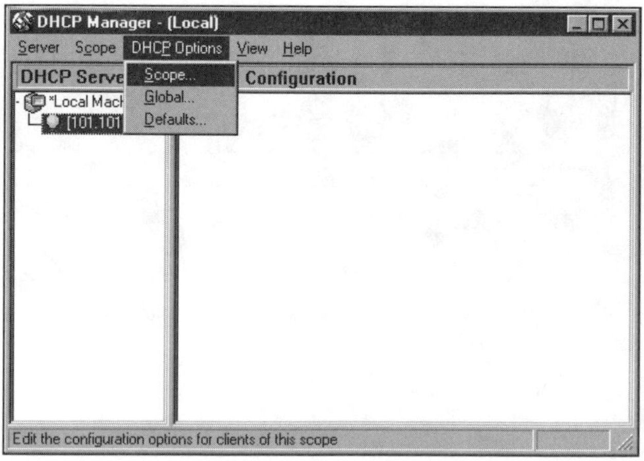

Figure 11.5 DHCP scope options are accessed via the DHCP Manager.

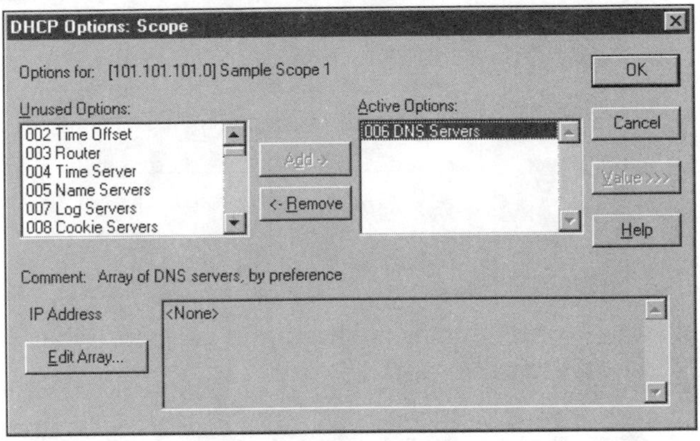

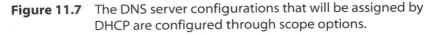

Figure 11.6 DHCP scope options.

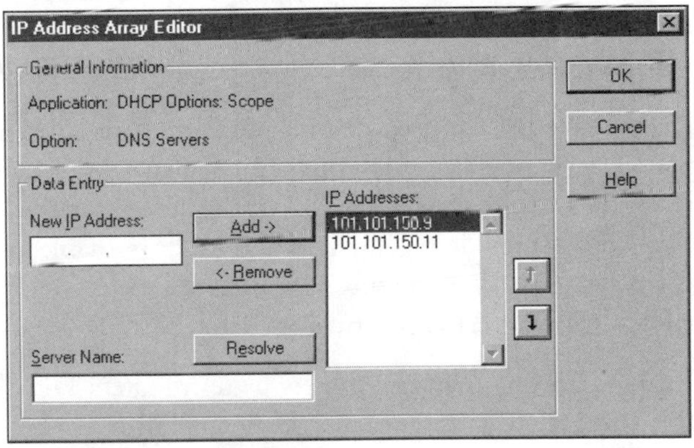

Figure 11.7 The DNS server configurations that will be assigned by
                 DHCP are configured through scope options.

Client Reservations

Sometimes a particular address will need to be reserved for a client, such as
when the client will be operating through a firewall. When a client reservation
is in place, that client is always assigned the same IP address whenever it
requests an IP address. Figure 11.8 shows the Add Reserved Clients window,
which is accessed through DHCP Manager by highlighting the scope and
selecting Add Reservations from the Scope menu.

The Unique Identifier field is what makes client reservations work. It must be
configured with the MAC address of the NIC for the client. Configuring this
option incorrectly will cause the reservation to fail, so be careful when you
enter the address. If in doubt, use the **IPCONFIG /ALL** command on the
client to determine its address. If more than one DHCP server exists, they all
should have the same reservation information.

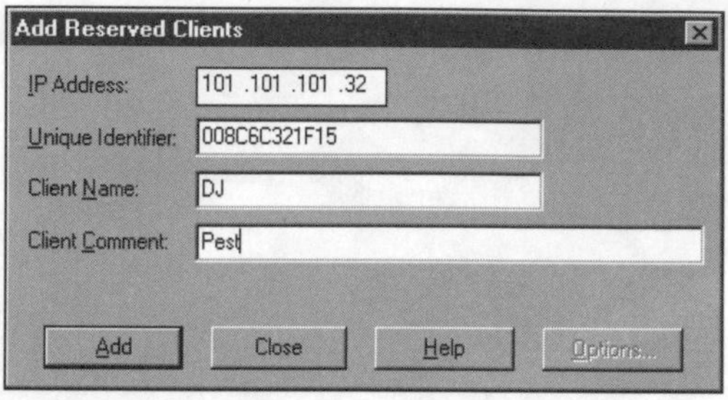

Figure 11.8   Client reservations are assigned to ensure that a client always has the same address.

The IPCONFIG Utility

The IPCONFIG utility can be run on any Microsoft client, providing valuable information and the mechanism for manually renewing or releasing a DHCP lease. Figure 11.9 shows the default output for IPCONFIG.

However, you can make IPCONFIG display much more detailed information by using the /**ALL** switch. This switch not only displays the default information for each adapter, but also the host name for the computer, the DNS server address(es), the NetBIOS node type, whether DHCP is enabled on an interface, and the hardware address for the interface. An example of the output generated by **IPCONFIG /ALL** is shown in Figure 11.10.

IPCONFIG can be used to manually renew or terminate a DHCP lease. By using **IPCONFIG /RENEW**, you can make the client try to renew its lease with the server. This is especially handy in the event that a server goes down.

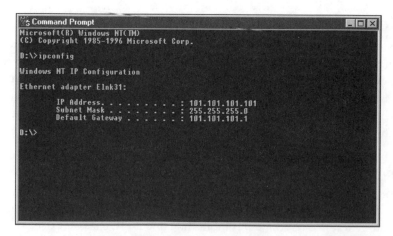

Figure 11.9   By default, IPCONFIG displays only the IP address, subnet mask, and default gateway for a particular adapter.

```
DOS Prompt                                              _ □ ×

D:\>ipconfig /all

Windows NT IP Configuration

        Host Name . . . . . . . . . : scorpio
        DNS Servers . . . . . . . . :
        Node Type . . . . . . . . . : Broadcast
        NetBIOS Scope ID. . . . . . :
        IP Routing Enabled. . . . . : No
        WINS Proxy Enabled. . . . . : No
        NetBIOS Resolution Uses DNS : No

Ethernet adapter Elnk31:

        Description . . . . . . . . : ELNK3 Ethernet Adapter.
        Physical Address. . . . . . : 00-A0-24-09-22-06
        DHCP Enabled. . . . . . . . : No
        IP Address. . . . . . . . . : 101.101.101.101
        Subnet Mask . . . . . . . . : 255.255.255.0
        Default Gateway . . . . . . : 101.101.101.1

D:\>_
```

Figure 11.10   Output generated by **IPCONFIG /ALL**.

As mentioned earlier, a client does not automatically terminate its lease when it is powered down. The IPCONFIG utility allows you to terminate a DHCP lease by using the **/RELEASE** switch. This is most often used when a computer is about to be moved to a new subnet. When **IPCONFIG /RELEASE** is used, the address is immediately available to other computers. When the client is started on the new subnet, it will request a new address.

Administering The DHCP Database

The DHCP database is managed the same way most databases are managed in Windows NT. You are able to back up, restore, and compact the DHCP database manually. You need to maintain your database as insurance against a catastrophic DHCP database collapse or hard drive failure.

By default, the DHCP server services back up the database after 60 minutes of inactivity. The files are placed in the *systemroot*\system32\dhcp\backup\jet directory and the contents of the \HKEY_LOCAL_MACHINE\SYSTEM\CurrentControlSet\Services\DHCPServer\Configuration subkey are saved to the *systemroot*\system32\dhcp\backup directory as DHCPCFG. The backup interval and backup path can be changed by adjusting the Registry setting in \HKEY_LOCAL_MACHINE\SYSTEM\CurrentControlSet\Services\DHCP Server\parameters.

One of the best aspects of the DHCP server service is its capability to automatically recover from a corrupt DHCP database—that is, if a backup exists. You can also manually restore the DHCP database two ways:

➤ Set the Restore Flag option in \HKEY_LOCAL_MACHINE\ SYSTEM\ CurrentControlSet\Services\DHCPServer\parameters to 1 and restart the machine. This reverts to the backup of the database.

➤ Copy the contents of *systemroot*\system32\dhcp\backup\jet to the *systemroot*\system32\dhcp directory and restart the machine.

As is the case with most Windows NT databases, the JETPACK utility can be used to compact the DHCP database. You must stop the DHCP server service before running JETPACK. To use JETPACK to compact the DHCP database, follow these steps:

1. From a command prompt, change to the *systemroot*\system32\dhcp directory.

2. Run JETPACK DHCP.MDB *temp*.MDB. The *temp* name can be anything because it will soon be renamed.

3. JETPACK automatically renames the *temp*.MDB to DHCP.MDB.

4. Restart the DHCP server service through Service Manager.

Exam Prep Questions

Question 1

> Which of the following are benefits of using DHCP? [Check all correct answers]
>
> ❑ a. Dynamic NetBIOS name registration
>
> ❑ b. Dynamic IP configuration
>
> ❑ c. Less chance of human error
>
> ❑ d. Centralized IP name resolution

The correct answers for this question are b and c. One of the major reasons for choosing DHCP is its capability to dynamically configure hosts (hence its name). Because configuration is centralized at the server, there's a smaller chance someone will make a mistake. DHCP does not concern itself with NetBIOS name registration, even though WINS server addresses can be assigned by DHCP. Therefore, answer a is incorrect. Centralized IP name resolution is done by DNS, not DHCP. Therefore, answer d is also incorrect.

Question 2

> What is the order of the DHCP lease process?
>
> ○ a. Request, Acknowledgment, Offer, Selection
>
> ○ b. Request, Offer, Selection, Acknowledgment
>
> ○ c. Request, Offer, Election, Selection
>
> ○ d. Request, Election, Selection, Acknowledgment

The correct answer for this question is b: Request, Offer, Selection, Acknowledgment. If you remember the process, this makes sense. Answer a is out of order and is therefore incorrect. There's no Election process in DHCP. Therefore, answers c and d are incorrect.

Question 3

> A DHCP-enabled client is moved from Subnet A to Subnet B. After the move, the user complains that he is no longer able to use TCP/IP. What is the possible cause for this problem?
>
> ○ a. The client did not terminate its lease before the computer was moved.
>
> ○ b. DHCP cannot support multiple subnets.
>
> ○ c. The client's WINS configuration is incorrect.
>
> ○ d. The router between Subnet A and Subnet B is not able to forward BOOTP broadcasts.

The best answer for this question is d. Remember that a router must support BOOTP broadcasts if the DHCP server and client are to be on separate subnets. Regardless of whether or not the client terminated its lease, the lease process will begin again when the computer is booted on the new subnet. Therefore, answer a is incorrect. As shown by the correct answer, DHCP does, in fact, support multiple subnets. Therefore, answer b is incorrect. The WINS configuration deals only with NetBIOS name resolution, not the basic operations of TCP/IP. Therefore, answer c is incorrect.

Question 4

> Which of the following are functions of IPCONFIG? [Check all correct answers]
>
> ❏ a. Renew DHCP lease
>
> ❏ b. View WINS configuration
>
> ❏ c. Release DHCP lease
>
> ❏ d. Request DHCP lease

The answers to this question are a, b, and c. By using */RENEW* and */RELEASE*, you are able to control your DHCP lease. WINS information is viewed when the */ALL* command is used. However, you are not able to initialize the DHCP lease process by requesting a lease. Therefore, answer d is incorrect.

Question 5

Which of the following utilities can be used to administer the DHCP database?

○ a. IPCONFIG

○ b. JETPACK

○ c. DHCP Manager

○ d. Network applet

The correct answer to this question is b. JETPACK is used to compress the DHCP database. IPCONFIG is used to view configuration information and to renew or terminate a DHCP lease, but it cannot administer the database. The DHCP Manager can be used to modify the database, but administration generally refers to backup, restoring, and compression, rather than management (therein lies the "trick"). The Network applet is used to install DHCP, but that's where its usefulness ends.

Need To Know More?

Lammle, Todd, Monica Lammle, and James Chellis. *MCSE: TCP/IP Study Guide*. Sybex Network Press, San Francisco, CA, 1997. ISBN 0-7821-1969-7. Chapter 7, "DHCP: Dynamic Host Configuration Protocol," contains detailed information on the DHCP service.

Parker, Timothy. *TCP/IP Unleashed*. Sams Publishing, Indianapolis, IN, 1996. ISBN 0-672-30603-4. Chapter 31, "DHCP and WINS," contains extensive information on DHCP and its configuration.

Microsoft TechNet. September, 97. PN99367. The section on DHCP is extensive and can answer any questions you might have.

The *Windows NT Server Resource Kit* contains a lot of useful information about TCP/IP and related topics. You can search the TechNet (either CD or online version at www.microsoft.com) or CD version using the keyword "DHCP."

Windows Internet Name Service (WINS)

12

Terms you'll need to understand:

√ Static entry

√ Push partner

√ Pull partner

√ NetBIOS Name Server

√ WINS Proxy Agent

Techniques you'll need to master:

√ Installing WINS

√ Configuring WINS clients

√ Configuring push/pull partners

√ Adding static entries to the database

√ Compacting the WINS database

In this chapter, you'll learn how to install WINS. You'll also learn about configuration options for clients and for servers, how to configure WINS servers for redundancy, and how to integrate non-WINS clients in a WINS environment. You'll also learn how to administer and maintain the WINS server database.

WINS: Explored And Explained

Windows Internet Name Service (WINS) is the NetBIOS Name Server (NBNS) provided with the Windows NT 4 Server product. WINS differs from the name resolution techniques we have previously discussed (DNS, HOSTS, LMHOSTS) in that it is a dynamic, or automatic, name resolution service. The WINS server actually collects computer names and IP addresses from clients on the network. When a WINS client wants to know the IP address of another computer on the network, it simply calls the WINS server to request the name resolution.

The most obvious benefit of using WINS is that it reduces broadcast traffic on the network. Without WINS, the name resolution and registration activities on a Microsoft network would be conducted by broadcasts, as described in the following list:

➤ When a computer first comes up, it announces itself by broadcasting its NetBIOS name. If no machine has that name already, the computer claims the NetBIOS name and is allowed to communicate on the network.

➤ If a computer is attempting to establish NetBIOS communications with another computer—for instance, by transmitting a **net send** command to dispatch a message to a destination machine—it broadcasts a message with the destination's NetBIOS name, requesting the IP address of that machine. When a response is received, communications are established and the message is sent.

➤ When a computer is shut down properly, it broadcasts a message releasing the NetBIOS name.

How Does WINS Work?

The WINS process is simple to understand when broken down into three parts: name registration, name discovery, and name release. This is illustrated in the list and graphic (Figure 12.1) that follow:

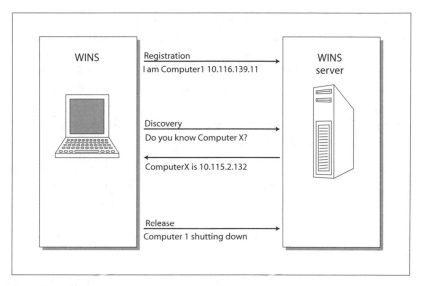

Figure 12.1   The WINS communication process.

➤ **NetBIOS Name Registration** When a WINS client initializes, it sends a directed message to a WINS server requesting registration of its name and IP address. The client name is given a fixed amount of time, or time-to-live (TTL), and the name is registered with the WINS server. When part of the TTL expires, the client attempts to renew the TTL for its NetBIOS name.

➤ **NetBIOS Name Discovery** When a WINS client attempts to establish communications with a destination computer, it sends a directed message to the WINS server requesting name resolution services. The WINS server replies with the IP address of the destination host.

➤ **Name Release** When the client is shut down properly, the client sends a directed message to the WINS server releasing its NetBIOS name. The name is marked in the database of the WINS server, reflecting that the TTL for that record is zero. Once released, the name is available for use by another computer.

Planning And Implementing A WINS Environment

When planning to deploy WINS for your network, you should consider several things:

➤ **Can all computers use WINS?** Most systems that can communicate on a Microsoft network running Microsoft products can be configured to use

WINS. If you have computers on your network that do not support WINS, you can configure static entries in the WINS server database for those clients. This enables the WINS clients to resolve the computer names of the non-WINS clients. However, the non-WINS clients cannot use the WINS database for name resolution. You must provide an alternate name resolution method for the non-WINS clients, such as a HOSTS file, DNS name server, or a WINS Proxy Agent. WINS Proxy Agents are explained later in the section entitled "WINS Proxy Agents."

➤ **How many WINS servers are needed?** WINS servers can provide about 1,500 name registrations and 4,500 name resolutions per minute; a conservative estimate for a network is a WINS server and backup WINS server pair for every 1,000 clients. If one WINS server goes down, your clients might notice a slight degradation in performance, but the name resolution process will still proceed.

➤ **Will the network be spanning a large distance using WAN (wide area network) technologies such as T1 or ATM communications?** If your network is connected using WAN technologies, you should consider putting a WINS server at the remote location. This enables NetBIOS name resolution services to be handled locally, rather than across the WAN.

Installing And Configuring A WINS Server

Only Windows NT Servers can be WINS servers. Installing the WINS service is similar to installing any other network service on Windows NT (see Figure 12.2). To configure your Windows NT Server as a WINS server, follow these steps:

1. Right-click the Network Neighborhood and choose Properties. This opens the Network dialog box.

2. Click the Services tab and then click the Add button.

3. Select Windows Internet Name Service from the list of services. Enter the path to the Windows NT Server source files and then click OK.

4. Click the Close button.

5. Reboot your computer when prompted.

After the system is restarted, a WINS Manager will be added to the Administrative tools and WINS is ready for use. No further configuration is needed to make WINS operational, but further configuration should be considered in order to make the WINS deployment successful.

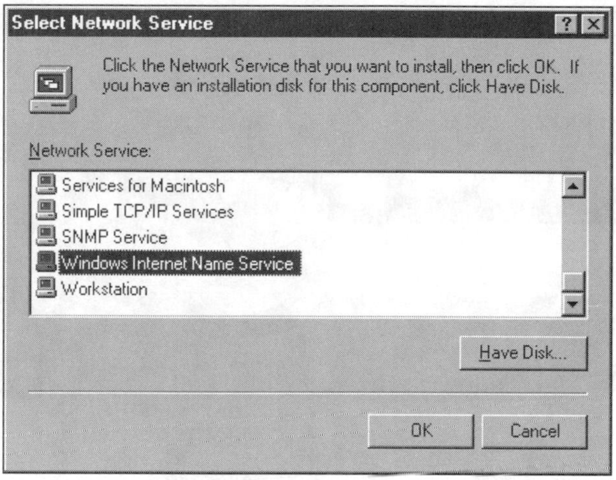

Figure 12.2   Installing a WINS server.

Administering WINS

The WINS Manager can be used to configure your WINS database. To open the WINS Manager, select Start|Programs|Administrative Tools (Common)|WINS Manager.

When the WINS Manager first opens, you should see your WINS server and related statistics. Like the DHCP Manager, the WINS Manager can be used to remotely support several servers. To add WINS servers to the WINS Manager, click Server and then select Add WINS Server. Enter the name or IP address of the WINS server you would like to add when prompted and click OK. The WINS server will appear in the list. To remove a WINS server from the list, select the server in the WINS Manager window and then select Server|Delete WINS Server; then confirm the deletion by clicking OK.

WINS Database

To look at the WINS database, select Mappings|Show Database. The Show Database dialog box (see Figure 12.3) displays the current server entries and gives you several view options for searching the database. In the Mappings window, you can see which entries are active and which are static, as well as the expiration date for each entry. On the far right of the Mappings window, you can see a column labeled Version ID. The Version ID number is used by a replication partner to identify which changes to the database are the most recent. Should you ever want to re-create the entire WINS database, click the Delete Owner button to purge the entire database.

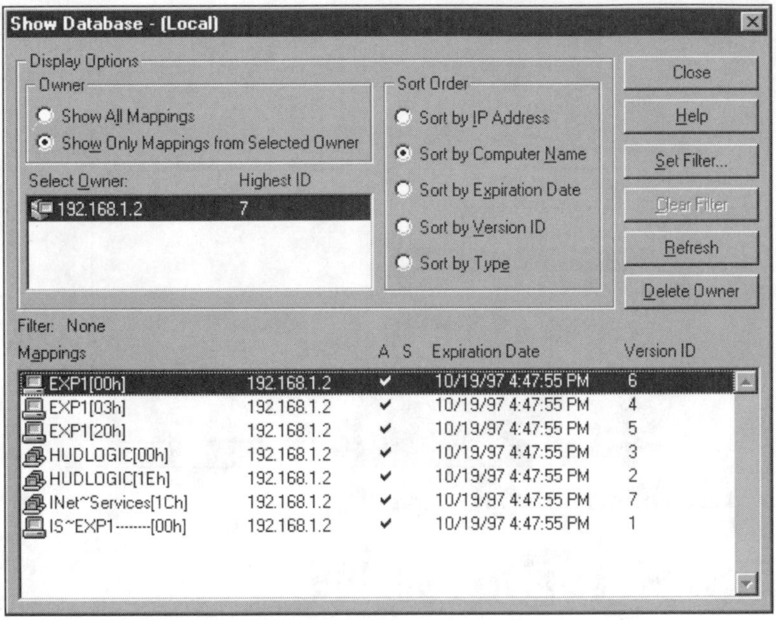

Figure 12.3 Viewing the WINS database.

Scavenging

The Mappings menu contains the Initiate Scavenging selection, which is a method of cleaning up entries in the WINS database. Scavenging causes the entries in the database to be checked against their owners. Entries that have expired or that have no owner will be removed from the database. Scavenging is done automatically by the WINS server. To configure the WINS server maintenance intervals (see Figure 12.4), click the Server menu and

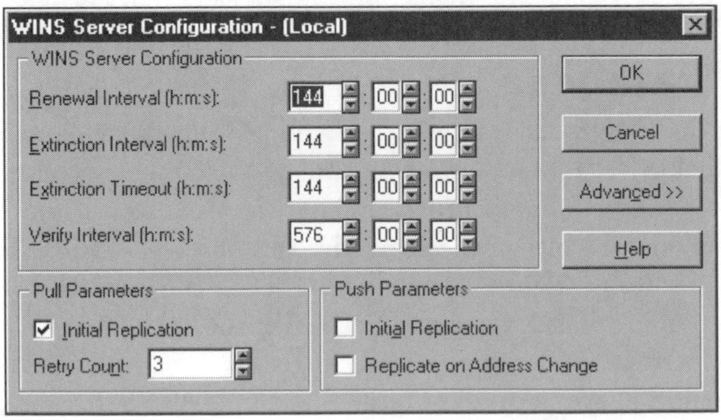

Figure 12.4 WINS configuration.

select Configuration. The following list describes the configurable intervals for the WINS server:

➤ **Renewal Interval** This is the maximum length of time the NetBIOS name is considered registered. In Windows NT Server 4, the default is 144 hours (or six days). After that, the client is expected to reregister its name with the WINS server; otherwise, the name will be considered released.

➤ **Extinction Interval** A released name is maintained in the database so that it does not have to be reentered if a WINS client attempts to reregister that name. By default, once an entry has been released for six days, it is considered extinct, which means that it will soon be removed from the WINS database altogether. You can configure the extinction interval in hours, minutes, and seconds.

➤ **Extinction Timeout** The extinction timeout controls how long entries are extinct before being removed from the database. An additional six days are given to extinct names by default before they are removed entirely from the database.

➤ **Verify Interval** The verify interval determines how long the WINS server allows entries from another WINS database (replication partner) to remain active in its database before those entries must be verified.

➤ **Pull Parameters/Push Parameters** These are used to configure intervals for WINS replication partners. (WINS replication partners are explained in the next section.)

Click the Help button to learn more about any of the settings.

WINS Replication Partners

WINS servers are typically paired for redundancy so that if one WINS server were to fail, name resolution could still proceed, reducing the impact on users. WINS servers can be configured to update each other's name resolution database, allowing all WINS servers to have identical databases.

A WINS server configured to "push" sends its database changes to its partner. This push occurs after a fixed number of changes have been made to the WINS database. A WINS server configured to "pull" requests database changes from its partner on a fixed interval. A WINS server can be configured as a push partner, a pull partner, or both, in order to synchronize its database with another WINS server (see Figure 12.5).

Replication Partners - [Local]

WINS Server   Push Pull

    192.168.1.1   ✓   ✓   OK
    192.168.1.2
                                                             Cancel

                                                             Help

                                                             Add...

                                                             Delete
WINS Servers To List
☑ Push Partners   ☑ Pull Partners   ☑ Other   Replicate Now

Replication Options   Send Replication Trigger Now
☑ Push Partner   Configure...   Push   Pull

☑ Pull Partner   Configure...   ☐ Push with Propagation

Figure 12.5 WINS Replication Partners dialog box.

Microsoft recommends that you configure pull partners on either side of a slow WAN link. This enables you to control when database changes are replicated over the link. Push partners are recommended only for fast LAN connections.

You have several configuration options in the Replication Partners dialog box. One of the options is to Push With Propagation. Configuring this option on your WINS server means that when your server sends a push of its database to its partner, the partner is prompted to push the changes to all of its partners. You can learn more about this and other options by clicking the Help button on the Replication Partners dialog box.

Database Backup

The WINS database uses the Microsoft Access engine. Like the DHCP database, the WINS database can be backed up using the WINS Manager. Backups of the resolved names and their TTLs should be done periodically so that the database can be restored in the event it becomes corrupted. Database backups must be started manually, but after you do a manual backup, subsequent backups occur automatically every 24 hours. To initiate a WINS database backup, follow these steps:

1. Open the WINS Manager.

2. On the Mappings menu, select Backup Database.

3. Select the directory location where you want the backup to reside.

4. Select Incremental Backup to back up only the changes that have occurred since the last backup. Otherwise, a full backup of the database is performed.

5. Click OK.

The database is automatically restored if corruption is detected. You can also force the database to be restored by selecting Restore Database from the WINS Manager Mappings menu.

Compact With JETPACK

The Microsoft Windows NT Server 4 software is designed to automatically compact the WINS database; however, you can also compact it manually. The database should be compacted when it grows larger than 30 MB. To determine the size of the WINS database, view the properties for the WINS.MDB file in the *systemroot*\system32\wins directory.

To compact the database manually, use the JETPACK utility. The syntax is as follows:

```
jetpack wins.mdb temp_name.mdb
```

When you use the JETPACK utility, you should change to the *systemroot*\system32\wins directory. Be sure to stop the WINS service before compacting the database. Restart the WINS service once compacting is complete.

Configuring WINS Clients

After the WINS servers are in place, the clients have to be configured to use them. This can be done at the client computer or centrally from a DHCP server.

At the Windows 95 or NT client, right-click the Network Neighborhood icon. In the Network dialog box, click the Protocols tab and then double-click the TCP/IP protocol, which opens the TCP/IP Properties dialog box. Select the WINS Address tab (shown in Figure 12.6). In the Primary WINS Server field, type the IP address of the WINS server. If two servers are available, add an entry in the Secondary WINS Server field.

If the network is configured for DHCP, open the DHCP Manager and configure the WINS server information in either the Default, Global, or Scope

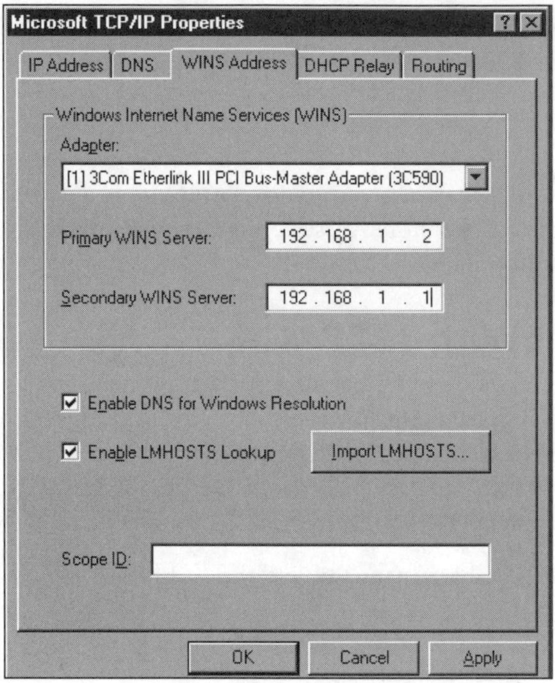

Figure 12.6 Setting a client computer to use WINS.

information (see Figure 12.7). WINS can be configured in any of these areas, depending on the network design. The optional information is 044-NBNS and 046-Node type. After DHCP is configured to use WINS, DHCP clients will become WINS clients after they terminate and renew their IP addresses.

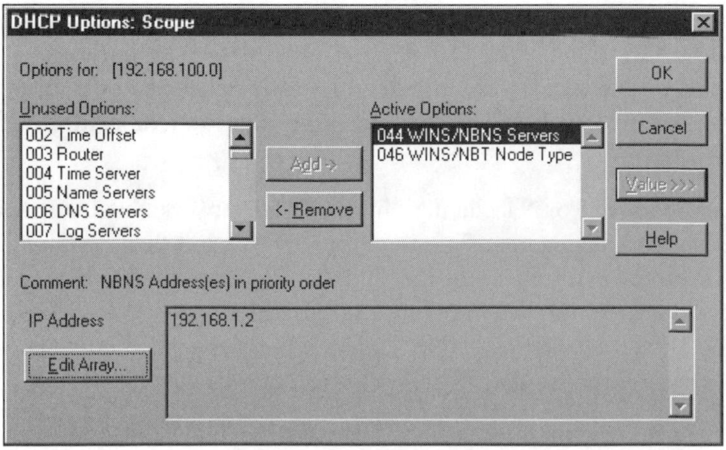

Figure 12.7 Configuring WINS via DHCP.

WINS Proxy Agents

Windows NT computers can be configured as WINS Proxy Agents, which allows the computer to forward the name resolution broadcasts of non-WINS clients to a WINS server. In effect, a WINS Proxy Agent is a method for allowing non-WINS clients to use a WINS server. The following list outlines this process:

1. The non-WINS client broadcasts for name resolution on the local segment.

2. The WINS Proxy Agent picks up that name resolution broadcast.

3. The WINS Proxy Agent forwards the name resolution broadcast to the WINS server.

4. The WINS server responds to the WINS Proxy Agent with a name resolution.

5. The WINS Proxy Agent forwards the reply from the WINS server to the non-WINS client.

WINS Proxy Agents are required only on subnets that do not have a WINS server. If a non-WINS client broadcasts a name resolution request on a segment that has a WINS server, the WINS server will reply with a resolution (see Figure 12.8). If your routers allow broadcasts to pass through (that is,

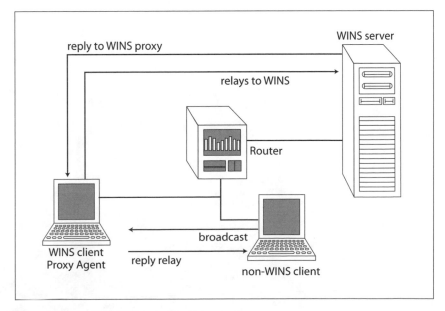

Figure 12.8   WINS Proxy process.

UDP ports 137 and 138 are enabled), WINS Proxy Agents are not required. However, enabling your routers to forward these broadcasts is not recommended because it increases network broadcast traffic.

Any computer running Microsoft Windows NT 4 that is configured as a WINS client can be configured as a WINS Proxy Agent. To configure a WINS Proxy Agent, open the following Windows NT Registry subkey:

```
HKEY_Local_Machine\System\CurrentControlSet
\Services\NetBT\Parameters
```

Next, set the **EnableProxy** value to 1. When you are finished, close the Registry Editor and restart your system to enable the WINS Proxy service.

 You should not enable more than two WINS Proxy Agents per subnet. Enabling more than two WINS Proxy Agents could increase network traffic beyond acceptable limits; each WINS Proxy Agent repeats all name resolution broadcasts it receives.

Exam Prep Questions

Question 1

> Which of the following are benefits of using WINS? [Check all
> correct answers]
>
> ❏ a. Dynamic NetBIOS name registration
>
> ❏ b. Dynamic IP configuration
>
> ❏ c. Reduction in broadcast traffic
>
> ❏ d. Increase in network throughput capacity

The correct answers for this question are a and c. WINS provides dynamic (automatic) name registration, release, and discovery services. In addition, WINS does reduce broadcast traffic on the network because WINS clients use the WINS server for name resolution instead of broadcasting. However, it is DHCP that provides dynamic IP configuration, not WINS. Therefore, answer b is incorrect. Answer d is incorrect because this usually requires a hardware upgrade and has nothing to do with WINS or name resolution.

Question 2

> Which utility is used to back up the WINS database?
>
> ○ a. JETPACK
>
> ○ b. WINS Manager
>
> ○ c. DHCP Manager
>
> ○ d. Server Manager

The correct answer for this question is b, WINS Manager. JETPACK is not used to back up the database but rather to compact it. Therefore, answer a is incorrect. The DHCP Manager can configure DHCP clients for WINS, but it cannot be used to back up the WINS database. Therefore, answer c is incorrect. The Server Manager is used to control servers on your network, but it does not have the capability to back up the WINS database. Therefore, answer d is incorrect.

Question 3

You manage a network of 1,500 Microsoft clients, all configured
to use DHCP. You have been asked to implement WINS on your
network for NetBIOS name resolution. What is the easiest way to
configure these client computers to use WINS?

○ a. Configure the DHCP server with options 44 WINS/NBNS
and 46 WINS/NBT.

○ b. Configure the DHCP server with option 44 WINS/NBNS
only.

○ c. Configure the DHCP server with option 46 WINS/NBT
only.

○ d. Configure each client with the address of the WINS
server manually.

The best answer for this question is a. There are 1,500 computers, so you don't
want to run around and configure the clients manually if you are using DHCP.
You cannot add option 44 without option 46 on the DHCP server.

Question 4

You have been asked to configure WINS name resolution for all of
the computers on your network. There are two WINS servers on
your network that reside on the same subnet. Your routers are not
configured to forward NetBIOS name broadcasts. If you have six
total subnets on your entire IP network, with a mixture of WINS
and non-WINS clients, how many WINS Proxy servers must you
configure to complete the objective, and where?

○ a. Six: one on each subnet.

○ b. Five: one on each subnet that does not have a WINS
server.

○ c. One WINS Proxy Agent.

○ d. Two WINS Proxy Agents on the same subnet as the
WINS servers.

The answer to this question is b. You must configure one WINS Proxy Agent on every subnet that does not have a WINS server. You don't need a WINS Proxy Agent on the subnet that has both WINS servers. Therefore, answer a is incorrect. The other answers would not provide complete name resolution for the network because the non-WINS clients are spread throughout your network.

Question 5

You have been asked to provide dynamic name resolution for your entire network. Your network is configured as shown in the following graphic. What is the minimum number of WINS Proxy Agents you require and where would you put them?

○ a. None

○ b. Two, one for segment H and one for segment B.

○ c. Seven, one for each segment except segment A.

○ d. One for segment H

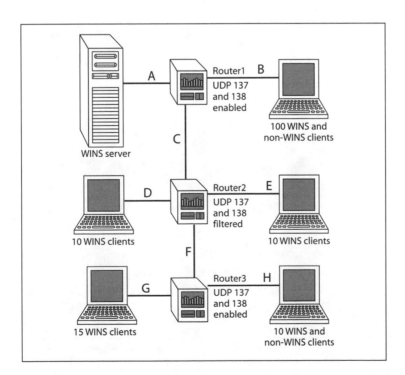

The correct answer to this question is d; only segment H requires a WINS Proxy Agent. If you thought a was the correct answer, look again at Router2. Router2 is going to filter broadcasts from the non-WINS clients on segment H before they reach the WINS server on segment A. Segment B does not require a WINS Proxy Agent because Router1 will forward broadcasts to segment A. Only subnets B and H contain non-WINS clients, so only those subnets should be considered candidates for a WINS Proxy Agent.

Need To Know More?

 Lammle, Todd, Monica Lammle, and James Chellis. *MCSE: TCP/IP Study Guide*. Sybex Network Press, San Francisco, CA, 1997. ISBN 0-7821-1969-7. Look for explanations on name registration, renewal, and termination in Chapter 8, "WINS: Windows Internet Name Service." Also check out WINS database replication in this chapter.

McLaren, Tim and Stephen Myers. *MCSE Study Guide: TCP/IP and Systems Management Server*. New Riders Publishing, Indianapolis, IN, 1996. ISBN 1-56205-588-7. Chapter 11, "Windows Internet Name Service," contains information regarding WINS server requirements, database scavenging, and configuring a WINS Proxy Agent.

Microsoft TechNet. September, 97. PN99367. Contains numerous articles on IP addressing and subnet masks. Search for "WINS," "Windows Internet Name Service," "NetBIOS Name Server," and "WINS replication partners."

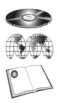 The *Windows NT Server Resource Kit* contains a lot of useful information about TCP/IP and related topics. You can search the TechNet (either CD or online version at www.microsoft.com) or CD version using the keywords "WINS," "WINS replication," and "WINS database."

Connectivity

Terms you'll need to understand:

√ NETSTAT

√ NBTSTAT

√ Telnet

√ FTP

√ LPR

√ LPQ

√ REXEC

√ RCP

√ RSH

√ IIS

√ Daemon

Techniques you'll need to master:

√ Using the utilities provided by Microsoft to monitor IP statistics

√ Understanding the functions of each of the switches for each of the utilities

As discussed throughout this book, TCP/IP has a number of attractive reasons for implementation, not the least of which is its cross-platform compatibility. In this chapter, we'll look at the Microsoft TCP/IP implementation. We'll discuss some of the utilities that are available, Microsoft's Internet Information Server (IIS), and printing with TCP/IP.

Microsoft IP Utilities

Along with standard TCP/IP utilities, such as FTP and PING, Microsoft includes two programs that can be used to monitor the state of TCP/IP on a system. These programs, NETSTAT and NBTSTAT, can provide valuable information, especially when troubleshooting.

NETSTAT

The NETSTAT utility displays protocol (TCP, IP, ICMP, or UDP) statistics and IP connection information. It can be used to display the routing table for the computer as well as per-port statistics. The syntax for the **NETSTAT** command is:

```
netstat [-a] [-e] [-n] [-s] [-p protocol] [-r] [interval]
```

Figure 13.1 is an example of the output received by using the **NETSTAT -a** command.

Table 13.1 outlines the switches that can be used in conjunction with NETSTAT and their descriptions.

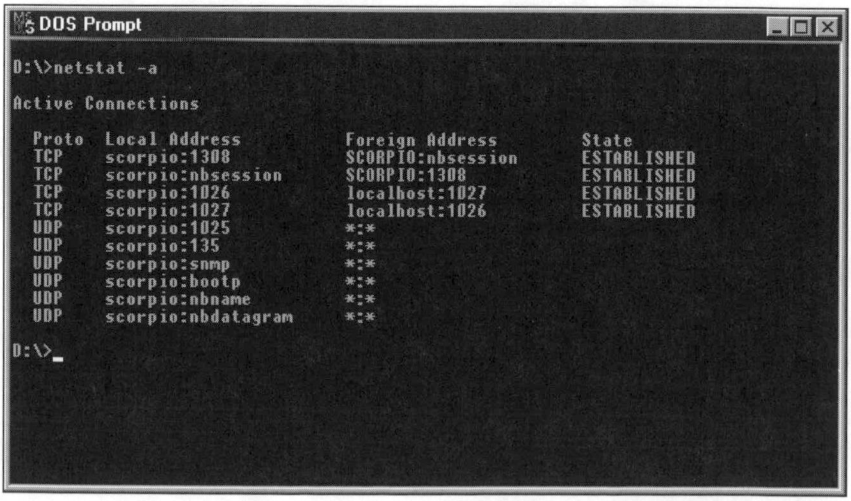

Figure 13.1 **NETSTAT -a** displays all connection information.

Table 13.1	Microsoft's NETSTAT utility.
Switch	**Description**
-a	Displays all connections and ports on which the computer is listening.
-e	Displays Ethernet information.
-n	Displays the information in numerical form rather than attempting to resolve names.
-s	Displays detailed per-protocol statistics. Can be used with **-p** for detailed statistics for a specific protocol.
-p *protocol*	Displays connections for the protocol. **-p** alone can be used to display TCP or UDP, whereas using **-p** in conjunction with **-s** can also display ICMP or IP.
-r	Displays the routing table for the computer.
interval	Used to display current information every *interval* seconds. Use Ctrl+C to terminate.

NBTSTAT

NBTSTAT provides statistical information specifically for NetBIOS over TCP/IP (NBT). Figure 13.2 is an example of the output generated by the **NBTSTAT** command using the **-n** switch, which displays the local NetBIOS name table.

Table 13.2 shows the parameters that can be used with the NBTSTAT utility. One major difference between NETSTAT and NBTSTAT is that whereas

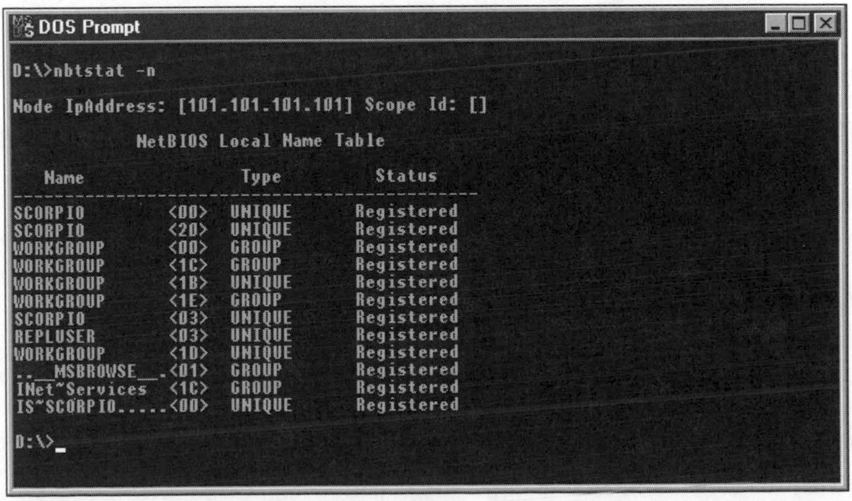

Figure 13.2 NBTSTAT is used to display local NetBIOS name table entries.

Table 13.2	Microsoft's NBTSTAT utility.
Switch	**Description**
-a *remotename*	Displays a remote computer's NetBIOS name table using the computer name for the lookup.
-A *IPaddress*	Displays a remote computer's NetBIOS name table using the computer's IP address for the lookup.
-c	Displays the contents of the local NetBIOS name cache, giving the IP address of each name.
-n	Displays the local NetBIOS name table.
-r	Displays the number of names resolved and registered via broadcast or WINS.
-R	Purges the NetBIOS name cache and reloads the LMHOSTS file.
-s	Displays sessions currently in use on the computer and the state of those sessions. Displays the information using resolved names rather than IP addresses.
-S	Displays sessions currently in use on the computer and the state of those sessions. Displays the remote computer information using IP addresses.
interval	Used to display current information every *interval* seconds. Use Ctrl+C to terminate.

NETSTAT can be used with no switches, NBTSTAT must have at least one parameter to function.

Others, Briefly

The other utilities listed in this section are similar to programs that are part of most TCP/IP implementations. They are used for remote terminal emulation (Telnet), remote program execution (REXEC), remote file copy (RCP), and remote command execution through the shell (RSH). In each case, a server must be running the appropriate "daemon" for each of these commands to work. A daemon is a program that runs constantly, listening for and fulfilling requests for a particular service. For example, if a Unix computer is running the Telnet daemon, Windows 95 users are able to access the system. Without the daemon running, there is no access. Windows NT provides only the client applications for these commands, not the server process.

Telnet

Telnet is a very useful remote terminal emulation application that has its own protocol for transport, defined in RFC 854. The protocol operates at the

Application layer of the TCP/IP Model. Telnet was designed to work between any host and any terminal. It provides VT-100, VT-52, and TTY emulation and is most often used for cross-platform access. For example, rather than have a direct connection from a PC to a router, the administrator can use Telnet to act as a terminal on the router. This way, the manager is able to manage the router from his or her desk. Another example of Telnet is realized when a Windows NT user requires control of a VMS computer. The user can use Telnet to open a terminal session on the VMS computer, eliminating the need for a direct connection to the system.

To connect to a remote system using Telnet, type "Telnet *destination IP Address*". When a connection has been made to the system, you'll be prompted to enter a user name and password. If, when you type the **Telnet** command, no destination is specified, the Telnet program window will open. Select Remote System from the Connect menu to access a remote host, as shown in Figure 13.3.

REXEC (Remote Execution)

The REXEC utility can run a process on a remote computer running an REXEC server service. REXEC is password protected and will execute the process only after receiving a valid password. The system will prompt you for a password after it verifies the user name. The syntax for the **REXEC** command is:

```
REXEC host [-l username] [-n] command
```

Table 13.3 outlines the parameters used with REXEC.

RCP (Remote Copy)

The RCP utility is similar to FTP in that it copies files from one TCP/IP-enabled computer to another. The difference is that RCP does not require user validation. The designated user name must exist in the Unix file RHOSTS.

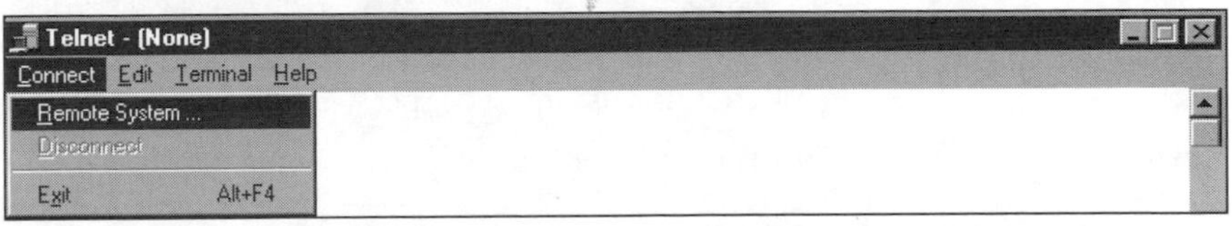

Figure 13.3   To connect using Telnet, select Remote System from the Connect menu.

Table 13.3   REXEC parameters.

Switch	Description
host	The host name or IP address of the computer on which the process is to be run.
-l *username*	The user name to be used on the remote computer.
-n	Specifies that the input for REXEC is to be redirected to NULL.
command	The command to be issued on the remote computer.

When the daemon is started, it reads the file and accepts the users defined within. The syntax for RCP is:

```
RCP [-a | -b] [-h] [-r] [host][.user:]source
[host][.user:] path\destination
```

Table 13.4 outlines the parameters used with RCP.

RSH (Remote Shell)

RSH is similar to REXEC in that it allows a user to issue a command on a remote system. However, RSH does not require the user to log into that system. Like RCP, RSH uses the RHOSTS file for security. One of the most

Table 13.4   RCP parameters.

Switch	Description
-a	Specifies that the file(s) is to be transferred in ASCII mode. This is the default transfer mode.
-b	Specifies that the file(s) is to be transferred in binary mode.
-h	Transfers sources files marked with the **hidden** attribute.
-r	Recursively copies all subdirectories from the source to the destination. Both the source and destination must be directories.
host	Specifies the local or remote host. If the host is specified as an IP address, a user must be specified.
.user:	Specifies a user name to use other than the current user name.
source	Specifies the files to copy.
path\destination	Specifies the path, relative to the logon directory, on the remote host.

common uses for RSH is executing program compilers on Unix systems. The syntax for **RSH** is:

```
RSH host [-1 username] [-n] command
```

Table 13.5 outlines the parameters used with RSH.

Internet Information Server Services

The Microsoft Internet Information Server (IIS) has an entirely separate set of classes and tests. For now, you should know how IIS is installed and what each of the services does. IIS is included with Windows NT Server 4. A scaled-down version, called Peer Web Services, is included with Windows NT Workstation 4. There is also a version called Personal Web Server for Windows 95. For our purposes, we'll concentrate on IIS.

You might think that, like every other service, IIS is installed from the Network applet; if so, you would be wrong. After the operating system is installed, an icon is created on the desktop to run the IIS installation. However, if you're like most people, you deleted that icon immediately after installing NT. In that case, you should know that the IIS installation program is located in the \processor\INETSRV directory and is called INETSTP.EXE

The first screen presented is the standard program installation screen. Click OK to bring up the second setup screen (see Figure 13.4), which lets you choose which elements of IIS to install. The standard IIS Manager runs as an application on the Windows NT computer; an HTML version is available as well—Internet Service Manager (HTML). After selecting which programs to install, click OK.

Table 13.5	RSH parameters.
Switch	**Description**
host	The host name or IP address of the computer on which the process is to be run.
-l *username*	The user name to be used on the remote computer.
-n	Specifies that the input for RSH is to be redirected to NULL.
command	The command to be issued on the remote computer.

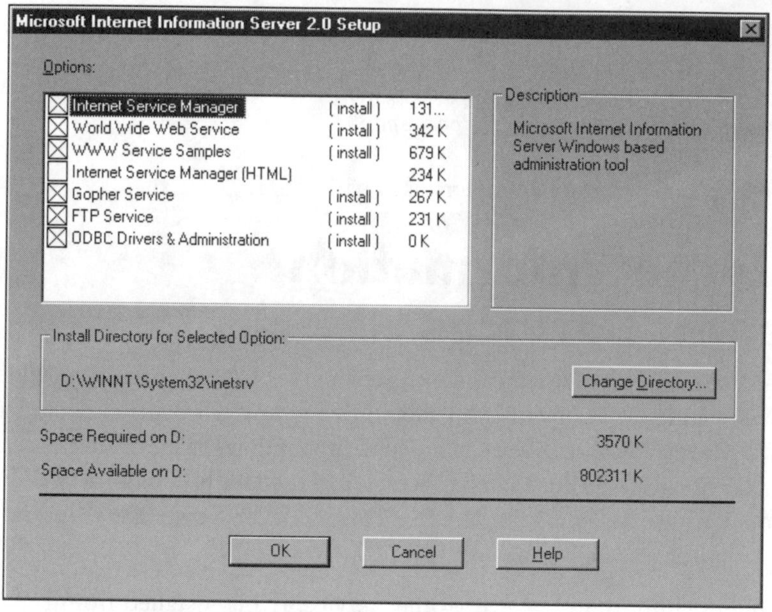

Figure 13.4   Microsoft Internet Information Server installation
options.

The next screen provides options for the publishing directories for each service, as shown in Figure 13.5. After choosing the directories, click OK. This
begins the IIS installation process.

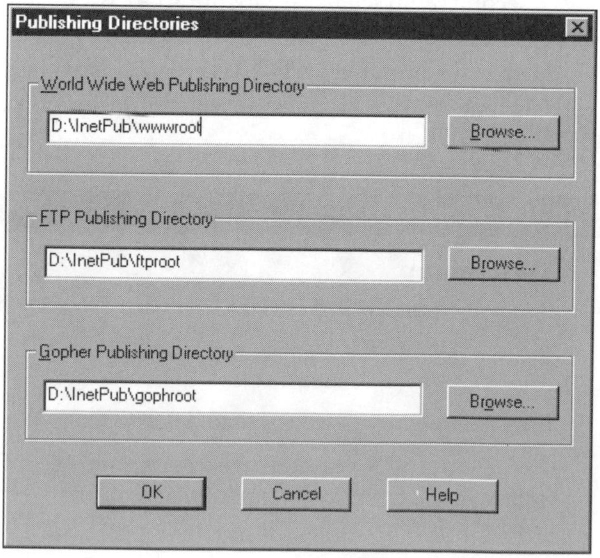

Figure 13.5   Each service has its own publishing directory.

If the installation program does not find a domain name for the computer, it prompts you to enter one to ensure that Gopher operates properly. Click OK. When prompted, select which ODBC drivers to install and click OK. Once the installation is complete, click OK.

Each of the services is controlled through the IIS Manager, shown in Figure 13.6, which is accessed from the Programs section of the Start menu. To configure a particular service, double-click on the service. You can also select the service and choose Service Properties from the Properties menu.

FTP

The FTP Service in IIS allows the Windows NT Server to operate as an FTP server. Figure 13.7 shows the Service tab of the FTP Service Properties applet. Through this tab, the most significant changes can be made to the FTP Service.

Here are some of the key settings that can be configured through the FTP Service Properties applet:

➤ **TCP Port (Service tab)** The port number TCP/IP uses to control the file transfer. *Not* a good idea to mess with this one.

➤ **Connection Timeout (Service tab)** The length of time a connection can remain idle before the system disconnects.

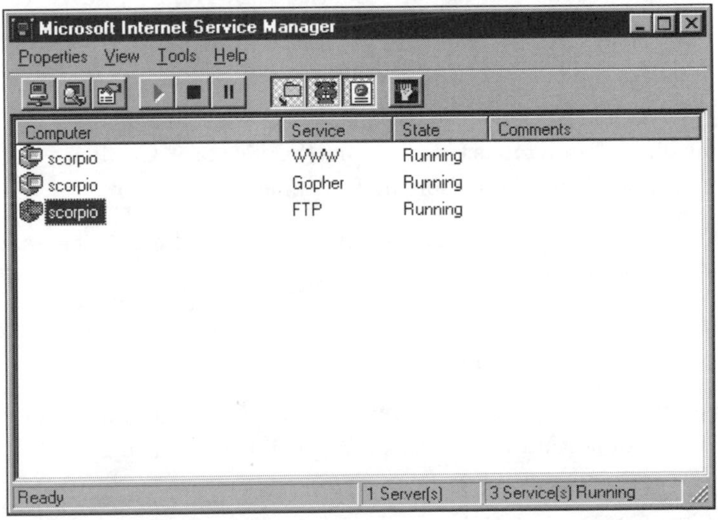

Figure 13.6   The Internet Service Manager is used to monitor and configure IIS services.

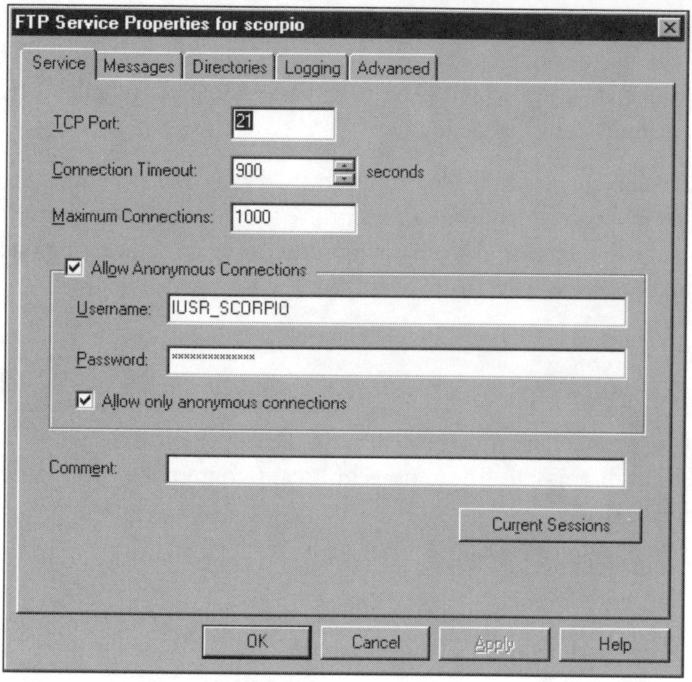

Figure 13.7 The FTP Service Properties applet is used to configure the FTP Service.

➤ **Allow Anonymous Connections (Service tab)** The FTP server can be configured to allow anonymous connections along with regular connections. The Username and Password fields define the configuration a user will use if he or she connects anonymously.

➤ **Allow Only Anonymous Connections (Service tab)** Configures the FTP server to only allow anonymous connections.

➤ **Messages tab** Separate messages can be established for Welcome, Exit, and Maximum Connections.

➤ **Directories tab** Defines the directories the users have access to when they use FTP to access the server.

➤ **Logging tab** A log file can be created and configured using this tab. This log can automatically be sent to an SQL/ODBC database.

➤ **Advanced tab** The settings on this tab can be used to grant or deny access to a single computer or range of computer addresses.

Gopher

Gopher is a menu-based program that allows you to browse for information without having to know exactly where the material is located. It allows you to search lists of resources and then helps send the material to you. It also integrates programs such as FTP and Telnet into the menus for easy navigation between resources. Historically, Gopher has been widely used to view information on servers. However, since the growth of the World Wide Web, many Gopher servers have died a rather quick and painless death.

The Gopher Service properties are identical to the FTP Service properties with one exception: Gopher provides a Service Administrator name and email address that furnish the Gopher user contact information.

WWW

The World Wide Web (WWW) Service provides HTML pages to users. Servers that use HTTP to transfer these pages make up the largest part of what we call the Internet. WWW can easily provide pages for an intranet or the Internet. Figure 13.8 shows the Service tab of the WWW Service Properties applet.

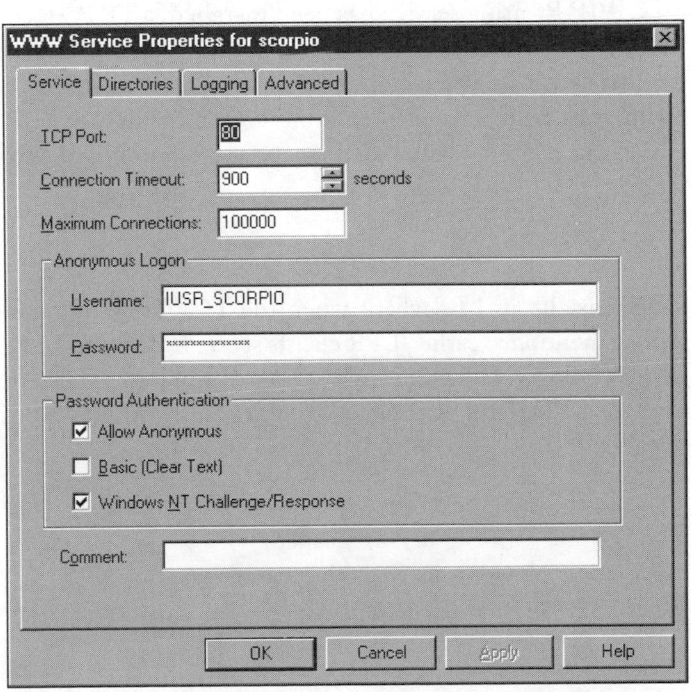

Figure 13.8   The Service tab of the WWW Service Properties applet.

Notice that, again, the configuration options for this service are almost identical to the FTP and Gopher services. However, the WWW Service can host multiple virtual domains, whereas FTP can only host a single domain name; the WWW Service also provides the following Password Authentication options:

➤ Allow Anonymous

➤ Basic (Clear Text)

➤ Windows NT Challenge/Response

TCP/IP Printing

Three utilities are included with both Windows NT 4 Workstation and Server that provide printing functions between NT and Unix computers. To use these utilities, you need to load the Microsoft TCP/IP Printing service through the Services tab of the Network applet.

Installing An NT TCP/IP Printer (LPDSVC)

Once the TCP/IP Printing service has been installed, a TCP/IP computer, such as a Unix system, can print to a Windows NT printer. This service is also referred to as LPD, which stands for line printer daemon. The LPD receives print jobs from line printer remote (LPR) clients. LPR clients are usually Unix systems, but LPR software is included with most TCP/IP stacks.

LPR

Windows NT installs an LPR client when the TCP/IP Printing service is installed. As we mentioned earlier, LPR clients send print jobs to LPD servers. In this case, a Windows NT system is able to send print jobs to Unix (or other) systems running LPD. **LPR** is executed from a command prompt using the following syntax:

```
LPR -S server -P printer [-C class]
[-J job] [-o option] [-x] [-d] filename
```

Table 13.6 outlines the parameters used with LPR.

LPQ

The LPQ utility is used to display the status of a remote print queue. For example, after a job is sent using LPR, you can use the **LPQ** command to

Table 13.6	LPR parameters.
Switch	**Description**
-S *server*	The host name or IP address of the computer providing the LPD service.
-P *printer*	The name of the print queue on the server.
-C *class*	The job classification to print on the banner page.
-J *job*	The job name to print on the banner page.
-o *option*	Defines the type of file being sent. The default is ASCII. Use **-o l** for binary (postscript) files.
-x	Specifies compatibility with SunOS 4.1.x and earlier.
-d	Specifies that the data file is to be sent first.
filename	The name of the local file to be printed.

determine whether the job has been processed or is waiting to print. LPQ is also executed from the command prompt using the syntax:

```
LPQ -S server -P printer -l
```

Table 13.7 outlines the parameters used with LPQ.

Table 13.7	LPQ parameters.
Switch	**Description**
-S *server*	The host name or IP address of the computer providing the LPD service.
-P *printer*	The name of the print queue on the server.
-l	Specifies verbose output.

Exam Prep Questions

Question 1

> Which of the following commands can be used to execute a
> command on a remote system? [Check all correct answers]
>
> ❑ a. RCP
>
> ❑ b. RSH
>
> ❑ c. REXEC
>
> ❑ d. RPD

The correct answers for this question are b and c. Both *RSH* (remote shell)
and *REXEC* (remote execute) can run a command on a remote system. However, remember that a password is required for REXEC. RCP will copy files,
but nothing more. Therefore, answer a is incorrect. RPD is a bogus acronym.
Therefore, answer d is incorrect.

Question 2

> Which of the following will display the NetBIOS names that have
> been resolved via broadcast or WINS?
>
> ○ a. **NETSTAT -R**
>
> ○ b. **NBTSTAT -R**
>
> ○ c. **NETSTAT -r**
>
> ○ d. **NBTSTAT -r**

Trick! question

The correct answer for this question is d, *NBTSTAT -r*. Remember that *-R*
and *-r* have different meanings when using NBTSTAT, but not when using
NETSTAT. NBTSTAT -R clears the cache and reloads the LMHOSTS file,
whereas **NETSTAT** -R or -r displays the TCP/IP routing table.

Question 3

Which of the following utilities is used to monitor printing on a
remote Unix system?

○   a. LPD

○   b. LPQ

○   c. LPR

○   d. LPS

The answer to this question is b. Remember that LPQ is used to check the
print queue on a remote system. LPD is the daemon that enables printing
from remote systems. Therefore, answer a is incorrect. LPR sends the job to a
remote printer. Therefore, answer c is incorrect. And, finally, LPS is an acronym for Lilly's Publishing Service (a fictional service), not for TCP/IP printing. Therefore, answer d is incorrect.

Question 4

Which of the following are services of IIS? [Check all that apply]

❑   a. FTP

❑   b. LPD

❑   c. NETSTAT

❑   d. Gopher

The answers to this question are a and d. IIS includes FTP, Gopher, and
WWW services. LPD is loaded with the TCP/IP Printing Service. Therefore,
answer b is incorrect. NETSTAT is included with the NT operating system.
Therefore, answer c is incorrect.

Question 5

Which of the following utilities provide file transfer capabilities in a TCP/IP environment? [Check all that apply]

❑ a. FTP

❑ b. RCP

❑ c. Telnet

❑ d. RSH

The correct answers to this question are a and b. FTP provides full file transfer with security via user names and passwords, whereas RCP copies files to a remote system using user names assigned in the RHOSTS file. Telnet is a terminal emulation application, but it does not provide file transfer. Therefore, answer c is incorrect. RSH is able to execute a command on a remote system, but it's not able to transfer files. Therefore, answer d is incorrect.

Need To Know More?

Lammle, Todd, Monica Lammle, and James Chellis. *MCSE: TCP/IP Study Guide*. Sybex Network Press, San Francisco, CA, 1997. ISBN 0-7821-1969-7. Chapter 10, "Connectivity in Heterogeneous Environments," contains detailed information about the issues discussed in this chapter.

The *Windows NT Server Resource Kit* contains a lot of useful information about TCP/IP and related topics. You can search the TechNet (either CD or online version at www.microsoft.com) or CD versions using the keywords "NETSTAT," "NBTSTAT," "IIS," "LPR," and "LPD."

14

Implementing The SNMP Service

Terms you'll need to understand:

√ Request For Comments (RFCs)

√ Get

√ Set

√ Traps

√ Trap destinations

√ Management Information Base (MIB)

√ Community names

√ Agents

√ Managers

√ Management console

Techniques you'll need to master:

√ Identifying communities of agents and managers

√ Planning for the implementation of SNMP

√ Understanding how the process of traps and authentication are related

√ Knowing how the use of MIBs allows SNMP backward compatibility and universality

√ Determining differences between a get and a set request

√ Troubleshooting SNMP problems

Windows NT includes an SNMP service that allows central management of NT-based computers. This subject is addressed on the TCP/IP exam and may also be included on other exams, such as NT Server 4 and NT Server 4 in the Enterprise. This isn't a very difficult subject to master for the exams, but you should be aware that in reality, SNMP is a rapidly evolving technology. In the first sections of this chapter, we'll explore SNMP, discuss Management Information Bases (MIBs) in depth, and move on to Microsoft's implementation of SNMP. After that, we will review installation and configuration of Microsoft's SNMP and end with a look at SNMP in action. You are advised to complete the sample exam questions at the end of the chapter for maximum benefit.

SNMP: Explored And Explained

Simple Network Management Protocol (SNMP) is the descriptive name for a simple set of protocols developed to assist in network management. When networks became more prevalent in the 1970s, they were usually small and very rarely connected. But as they grew and became more complex and interconnected, a standard set of network monitoring and management protocols became desperately needed. Thus, SNMP was introduced in the 1980s as a quick Band-Aid measure until more extensive and comprehensive tools could be developed. SNMP was originally intended only as a stopgap measure to address communications problems between different types of networks, but nothing better has come along, and SNMP version 2 is still in widespread use today, with SNMP version 3 on the horizon.

Request For Comments

Networking protocols are addressed by the Internet Engineering Task Force (IETF) as a series of Requests For Comments (RFCs). RFCs are a group of documents describing TCP/IP standards and the internal workings of the Internet. SNMP is no exception; its development is governed in large part by RFCs 1155 through 1158, and 1213, although there are many, many more. RFCs are managed by the IESG (Internet Engineering Steering Group). Other groups you may need to be aware of include the IAB (Internet Architecture Board), which is responsible for setting Internet standards and for managing the process of publishing the RFCs, and the IAB's two task forces: the IRTF (Internet Research Task Force) and the IETF.

Marshall Rose, now vice president of engineering at First Virtual Holdings, Inc., and Jeff Case, president of SNMP Research, are credited as the originators of SNMP. Fundamentally, SNMP consists of a simply composed set of network communication specifications that cover the basics of network management in a manner that introduces very little stress on the existing network. It works by exchanging messages containing network information, known as PDUs (Protocol Data Units). PDUs can be thought of as objects with variables that have titles and values. SNMP currently employs five types of PDUs: one, the "trap," is used to monitor startups and shutdowns; two deal with getting terminal information; and two others deal with setting terminal information.

The Advantages Of SNMP

The advantages of using SNMP as a network management protocol include the following:

➤ SNMP is a well understood and proven technology; it's easy to implement and does not strain the existing network.

➤ SNMP is widely accepted; most internetworking product vendors incorporate SNMP technology into their products, making it easier to implement.

➤ You don't need to develop a management user interface if tool development is not in your company's interest, because many are widely available.

➤ SNMP is easily integrated with other networking tools. Also, it's expandable, and its simplicity makes it easier to update for future use.

➤ SNMP can be easily incorporated into larger management frameworks.

➤ SNMP provides a mechanism by which management consoles can dynamically learn about new components and new component instrumentation; therefore, consoles that were written years ago are capable of managing components developed today.

The Disadvantages Of SNMP

SNMP is by no means a perfect network management tool, but it is cleverly designed, so some workarounds do exist. Its drawbacks include the following:

➤ SNMP has some major security holes that could give intruders access to secure information and potential shutdown capability over client computers.

➤ SNMP lacks sophistication (and the associated overhead), which prevents it from providing the detailed, high-level information that may be required by today's network managers.

Terminology

This book assumes that you are already familiar with the concepts of TCP/IP; however, network management is not always associated with that topic. To make sure that we're all on the same page, here is a brief glossary of network management terminology used in this chapter:

➤ **Host** Any network device, including workstations and servers. Hosts are not the only devices that can be managed using SNMP. WAN devices, such as DSU/CSUs, routers, hubs, switches, and so on, are commonly monitored with SNMP software.

➤ **Managed Objects** The hardware and software resources of the host that can be managed/monitored by someone at another computer on the network.

➤ **Management Information Base** Files located on the host that contain information about the manageable objects of that device.

➤ **Management Console** Any computer running the graphical user interface for SNMP manager software.

Agents

In the SNMP model, a software component resides on each network device being managed. This software component is referred to as the "agent," and it collects the related information about that device into a well-defined structure. The agent is responsible for responding to queries and carrying out requests to the network device. When an agent gets a request, it first checks to see if the request is from the community to which the agent belongs. If so, it consults the Management Information Base (MIB) for that request. It then replies with the requested value to the SNMP manager configured for that community and agent; otherwise, it changes the value, in the case of a **set** request. It may also send a message not requested, referred to as a "trap," to its SNMP manager to warn of unsolicited communications from an unauthorized SNMP manager. Failed passwords belong to the trap class of communication.

When an agent is started on a device, it waits for SNMP requests from the manager. Once received, the agent performs the **get, get… next**, and **set** operations that were requested. The only spontaneous operation is a trap, which alerts the manager that the device has started, stopped, or is under extraordinary stress, such as a full disk alert. By default, the computer listens to port 161 for messages and port 162 for traps. Note that in order to run multiple SNMP agents, a Registry edit is required for Win95- and NT-based computers.

Managers

The agent's counterpart is referred to as the "manager," or "management console," and is the software component that issues requests that are typically passed on to a textual, graphical, or object-oriented user interface. The results of the requests are passed on to a user interface that allows administrators to view data on the queried device. Normally, the agent software and the manager software are running on different networking components and are communicating via the network and a common protocol. Although Microsoft has made available basic SNMP management consoles, advanced organizations might require the power of HP's OpenView or Sun's Sun Net Manager as the SNMP management user interface. The beauty of SNMP is that it's possible to mix and match needs and budgets according to the demands of the organization.

In some cases, the manager may issue several requests to the agent without waiting for a response. In other cases, it may wait for a response after each request, operating in a lock-and-key fashion. Because SNMP is implemented on a wide variety of protocols with different degrees of reliability and transport mechanisms, the normal transmission method is the lowest common denominator: UDP. Because UDP is a connectionless transport method, each individual management application must set its own timeout strategy and verification scheme.

MIB (Management Information Base)

The SNMP agent is organized into collective units that are termed "Management Information Bases," or MIBs, for short. A MIB is basically a data file containing object values and managed object descriptions. MIBs are described via a precise definition language called "Abstract Syntax Notation" (ASN) that can be thought of as a compiled language like COBOL, FORTRAN, or C. An SNMP manager console uses the MIB that defines the data available on the SNMP agent to describe it to the user. Because of this relationship among agents, MIBs, and managers, the agents created today can work with management consoles that were written years ago.

ASN makes possible the definition of data types, structures, and arrays of structures of information on the managed device. Fundamentally, MIBs define the following for every entity in the agent:

➤ An association between a device's data entity and a name (object identifier, also known as an OID)

➤ A definition of the data type for that entity

➤ A textual description of the entity

➤ How the entity is indexed (if the entity is a member of a complex data type)

➤ How access is allowed for that entity

Several Windows NT–based MIBs are described in great detail in Appendix C of the "Networking Guide" of the *Windows NT Server Resource Kit*. These are the MIBs that ship with Microsoft-based products, by default. A short description of each follows.

Internet MIB II

Internet MIB II was created for Microsoft's Internet Information Server (IIS); it contains objects that provide information about network communications and performance on the IIS. It includes and expands Internet MIB I by defining 171 objects for configuration analysis and network fault isolation. Several MIBs branch from this node, including the FTP Server MIB, the Gopher Server MIB, and the HTTP Server MIB. The FTP Server MIB is concerned mostly with server statistics, such as total bytes sent and received, the number of anonymous users, the number of connections, and failed logon attempts. Because they're in the same server class, the Gopher MIB and HTTP MIB cover objects similar to those of the FTP MIB.

LAN Manager MIB II

Documented in *LAN Manager 2.0 Management Information Base, LAN Manager MIB Working Group, Internet Draft:LanMgr-Mib-II* by Microsoft, the object definitions for this MIB are contained in a file appropriately named LMMIB2.MIB. This MIB describes such objects as enterprises, servers, workstations, domains, and common groups. The MIB assigns such variables as syntax, access, status, and description.

DHCP MIB II

This MIB contains object types that are used to monitor the network traffic between remote hosts and a DHCP Server. It contains 14 parameters, including

DHCP start time, total number of discovers, total number of requests and declines, scope tables, and subnet addresses. The DHCP MIB is installed automatically with DHCP Server and is accessible from the remote DHCP manager.

WINS MIB

Similarly, the WINS MIB contains around 70 object types that are used to monitor the network traffic between the WINS server and remote hosts. It addresses applicable objects such as WINS push and pull services, Last Service Time, the handling of record conflicts, and how the database records should be treated. This MIB also includes such ghoulish topics as tombstones and planned scavenging. It is probably the most extensive sample MIB described. The WINS MIB is automatically installed with the WINS Server and can be remotely accessed using the WINS Manager.

Architecture Of Microsoft's SNMP

Now that we've discussed the various components of SNMP in general, let's take a look at Microsoft's SNMP implementation. Although Windows doesn't include a management console, it does include a Win32 SNMP API that conforms to the Windows Sockets API. The SNMP API can be used by developers for developing third-party management tools.

In addition, the MIB architecture is extensible to allow for third-party development of dynamic link libraries (DLLs). Each object in a MIB is identified by a hierarchical naming scheme (see Figure 14.1), governed by the IETF, that provides a universally unique label, known as the "object identifier" (or OID). This OID is accepted on a worldwide basis; it allows all developers and vendors to create new components and resources with unique identifiers. The IETF grants the authority for parts of the name space to individual organizations, such as Microsoft, for that use.

Microsoft's NT Server 4 runs SNMP version 1. It's implemented as a Windows 32-bit service on computers that use the TCP/IP and IPX protocols via Windows Sockets; TCP/IP must be installed before implementing SNMP on an NT-based computer. The agent programs that implement the additional MIBs for FTP, DHCP, WINS, and Internet services are called "extension agents." Extension agents work with the master NT-based agent program and are implemented as 32-bit DLLs.

SNMP.EXE is the Windows NT SNMP service. It's an extendible SNMP agent that allows developers to add additional DLLs to service third-party

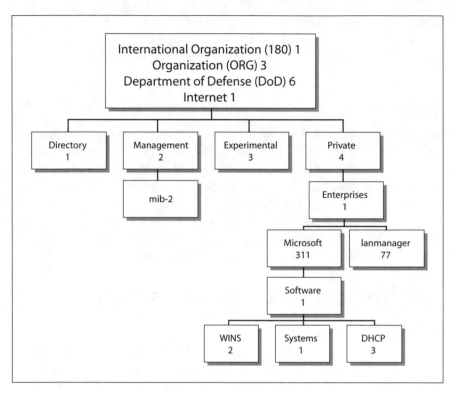

Figure 14.1 Example of a managed object name hierarchy.

MIBs. The agent is responsible for retrieving SNMP requests for the NT Workstation or Server and passing these requests on to the appropriate DLL for resolution. The response data is then returned to the agent, which in turn returns the request to the authenticated management station that initiated it. The extendible agent is also capable of issuing traps on behalf of any of the agent DLLs. Registry values under the Space HKEY_LOCAL_MACHINE\ SYSTEM\CurrentControlSet\Services\ SNMP\Parameters\ExtensionAgents key tell the extendible agent which agent DLLs to load.

The SNMP security service is referred to as an "authentication service," which means that a management request cannot be processed until it has been authenticated. SNMP uses community names as common passwords shared between the host and the manager to authenticate requests. All SNMP messages should contain a community name. If a message received at the host contains a known community name, the request is processed. Otherwise, the message is rejected, and the host may send a trap message to its designated management console of the failed attempt.

Whenever SNMP service is installed, the default community name is "Public." To completely open up the SNMP service, use the SNMP Service dialog box from the Network Services menu and remove all community names, including Public; the SNMP service will then process any and all messages. Whether or not this is desirable, it is expected behavior, as outlined in RFC 1157. Although intended to be a compromise, this feature seems to be the biggest security breach in SNMP. Many administrators accept the default community name "Public" when installing SNMP without a thought for how wide open this leaves their networks. This is not advisable under any circumstances.

Another executable, SNMPTRAP.EXE, receives SNMP traps from the SNMP agent and forwards them to the SNMP manager API on the management console. SNMPTRAP is a background process and, as such, is started only when the SNMP manager API receives a manager request for traps.

Installation And Configuration Of SNMP

To plan for an effective SNMP installation, the administrator must identify the following:

➤ The local administrator of the computer to be managed

➤ Community names to be shared by the network hosts

➤ The IP address, IPX address, or computer name of the SNMP management console

The administrator must plan for the community names and the manager for those communities. Figure 14.2 is an example of mixed community implementation taken from the July, 1997 edition of Microsoft's TechNet CD. In the example, two communities are used: Engineering and the default Public. Notice that agents and managers must belong to the same community to communicate.

In this example, Agent 1 can communicate only with Manager 2 because they are in the same community: Engineering. Likewise, Agents 2, 3, and 4 will send their replies and requests to Manager 1 in the Public community. There must be at least one community name.

The default community name for SNMP in Microsoft NT is Public.

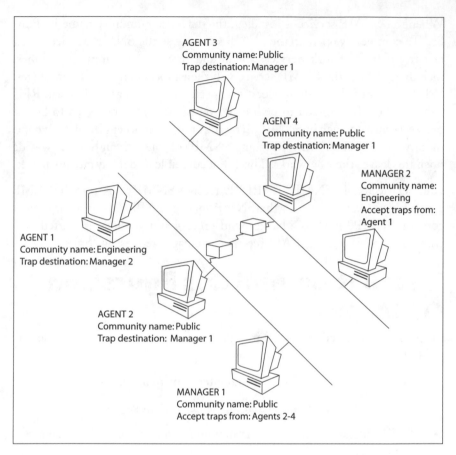

AGENT 3
Community name: Public
Trap destination: Manager 1

AGENT 4
Community name: Public
Trap destination: Manager 1

MANAGER 2
Community name:
Engineering
Accept traps from:
Agent 1

AGENT 1
Community name: Engineering
Trap destination: Manager 2

AGENT 2
Community name: Public
Trap destination: Manager 1

MANAGER 1
Community name: Public
Accept traps from: Agents 2-4

Figure 14.2 Sample implementation of mixed SNMP communities.

Once the planning phase has been completed, implementation can begin. TCP/IP must be installed in order for you to install the SNMP service (see Figure 14.3), even if IPX is installed as the main network protocol. On the client that will be receiving the traps, run IPCONFIG at the command prompt to determine the correct IP address for the local computer. Next, the agent must be installed on the client that will be sending the traps, using the Add option on the Network Services dialog box.

The computer must be restarted. Agents can then be configured by selecting the Agent tab on the Microsoft SNMP Properties page from the NT Network Services tab (see Figure 14.4). Windows 95 agents must be configured using the System Policy Editor or by editing the Registry. We strongly recommend that you consult the *Windows 95 Resource Guide*, be very knowledgeable, and back up the Registry before attempting any changes.

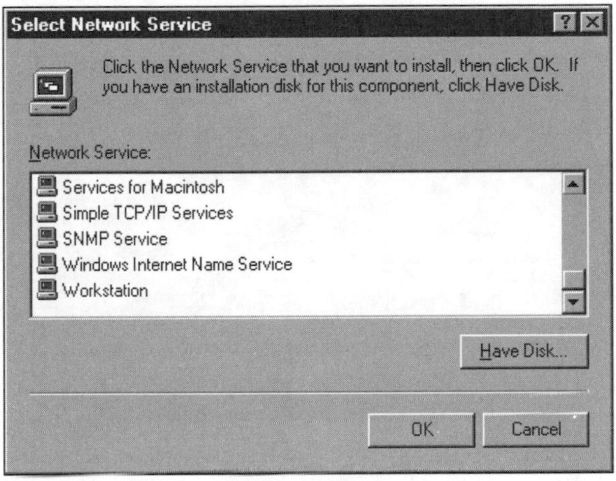

Figure 14.3   Installing the SNMP service.

SNMP properties that can be configured on NT-based computers are Agent, Traps (see Figure 14.5), and Security. If the default options are sufficient, the user only needs to add the contact name (for example, admin@microsoft.com)

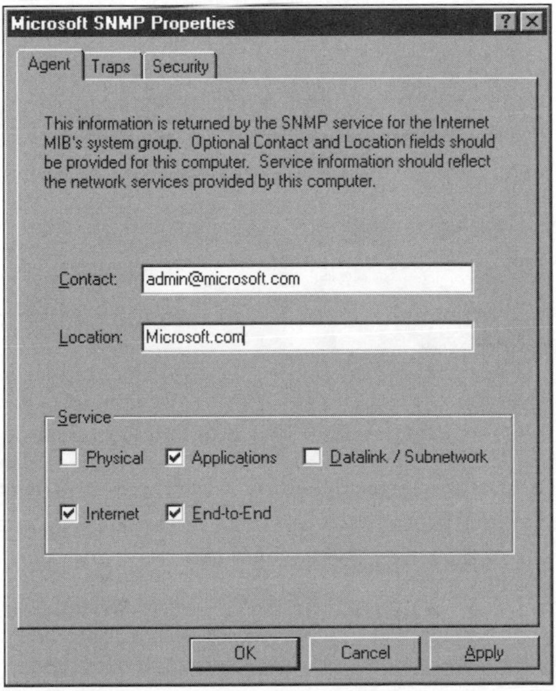

Figure 14.4   SNMP properties and default services.

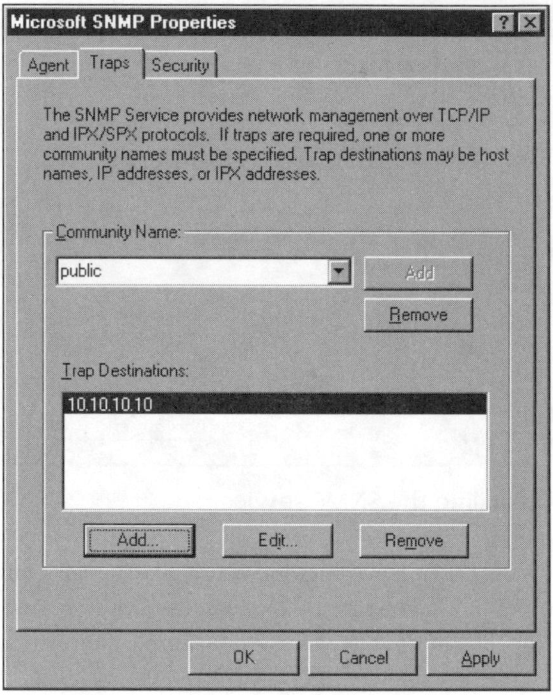

The SNMP Service provides network management over TCP/IP and IPX/SPX protocols. If traps are required, one or more community names must be specified. Trap destinations may be host names, IP addresses, or IPX addresses.

Community Name:

public

Add

Remove

Trap Destinations:

10.10.10.10

Add...   Edit...   Remove

OK   Cancel   Apply

Figure 14.5 The Windows NT SNMP Traps tab.

and the contact's location (microsoft.com). Service options include Physical, Applications, Datalink/Subnetwork, Internet, and End-to-End. The default options are shown in Figure 14.4.

You can use the Traps tab on the SNMP Properties page to configure the traps destinations on an NT-based computer.

 Trap destinations can be host names, IP addresses, or IPX addresses.

Traps may be configured differently for each community name and can be sent to a maximum of five hosts in each community. In the Send Traps With Community Name list box, type the IP or IPX address or DNS host name of the trap destination computer and then click on the Add button.

Community names are designated on the Security tab (see Figure 14.6).

 At least one community name must be specified in the Security tab.

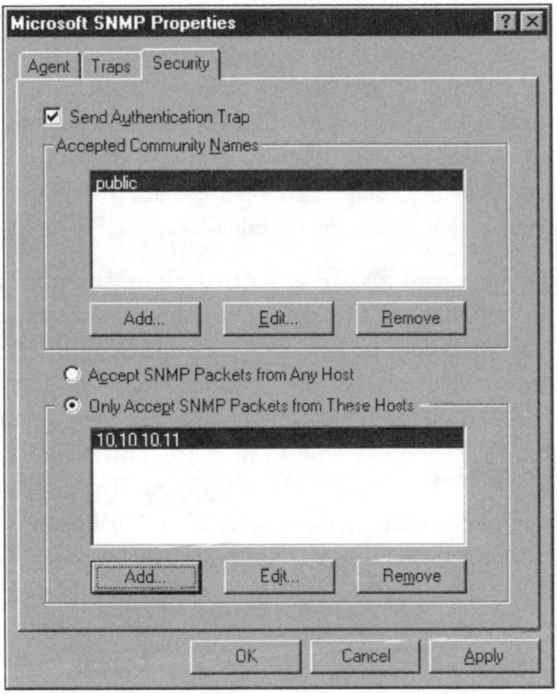

Figure 14.6   The Windows SNMP NT Security tab.

This tab also allows the end user to filter the type of packets the computer will accept and from which hosts.

Now that you know how SNMP is installed and configured for the agent and manager, let's see how it works in the Microsoft world.

SNMP In Action

The Microsoft implementation has four basic types of SNMP commands. The **get** command is a request for the value of a specific object in a MIB that resides on the agent. The **get-next** command is a request for the next MIB object's value and is used to obtain successive values in a branch or subset of a MIB. The **set** command may be issued to change the value of an object, provided the object has read-write access in the MIB. For security reasons, most objects in the MIB are read-only.

The SNMP agent also generates the trap messages that are sent to a trap destination: the SNMP management console. You can configure the trap destination, but which occurrences generate a trap message are identified internally by the agent. Results of an operation are sent to the manager program, which waits (listens) for the SNMP messages from the agent. The manager displays the information on the SNMP management console or saves the data in a specified file or database for later analysis. As discussed earlier, the Windows NT SNMP service is an SNMP agent that is part of the necessary framework needed for network management. However, a separate SNMP manager program is needed to perform management operations. An example of the SNMP communication process is shown in Figure 14.7.

What else can be done with SNMP other than simply monitor devices? After installation, the network administrator is able to monitor and configure parameters for any WINS server as well as monitor DHCP servers, due to the extension agents provided with NT. In addition, parameters in the LAN Manager and MIB II MIBs can be viewed and changed. The Performance Monitor will now monitor TCP/IP-related performance counters for TCMP, IP, Network Interface, TCP, UDP, DHCP, FTS, WINS, and IIS performance counters. These counters can be viewed using the Perf2MIB utility from the *Windows NT Server Resource Kit* to create a new MIB file for the counters in which you are interested. Simple SNMP manager functions can be found on the *Windows NT Server Resource Kit* CD-ROM, or you can use higher level, third-party products such as HP OpenView.

Once installed, SNMP will automatically start with the startup of the computer. Once stopped, however, SNMP must be manually restarted. Note that stopping a service cancels any network connections the service may be using, so choose this option with care. Starting and stopping the SNMP service

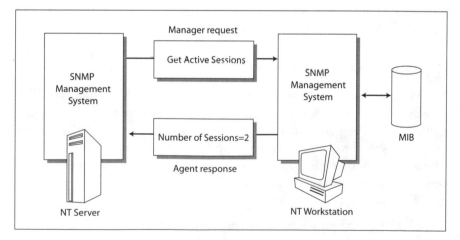

Figure 14.7 Graphical representation of an SNMP communication.

can be accomplished through the command prompt (**net start snmp** and **net stop snmp**), or you can use Control Panel|Services|SNMP|Start (or Stop). These actions are necessary whenever you're adding new extension agent DLLs and MIBs.

What should you do if you are having trouble with your SNMP installation? Fortunately, error handling has been improved in NT Server and Workstation 4. This improvement is obvious in the graphical interface provided by the Event Viewer (see Figure 14.8). You can filter the System Log events to display only those event details involving SNMP.

The Registry contains information about SNMP extension agent DLLs and parameters. You should use the appropriate user tools to change Registry information only after performing a confident Registry backup. For NT-based computers, these details can be found in the HKEY_LOCAL_ MACHINE\System\CurrentControlSet\services\SNMP\Parameters key. This key controls whether or not the SNMP service will send a trap to an unrecognized community name or host filter. It also controls information about the extension agent DLLs to load, valid community names, and host trap destinations, and where they are located.

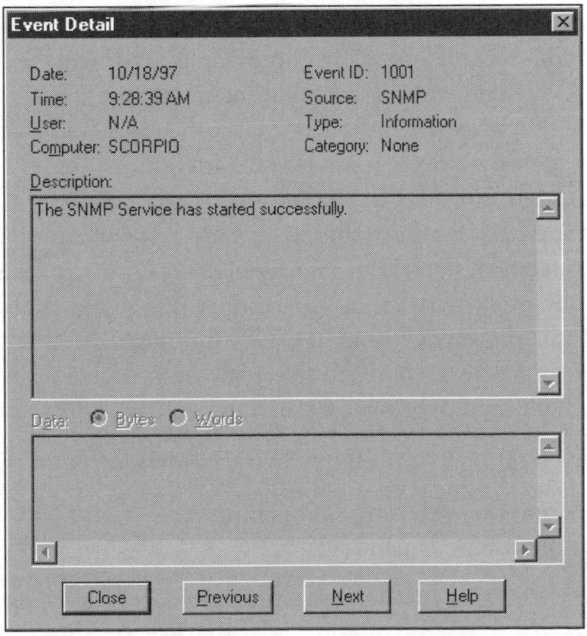

Figure 14.8   Example of an Event Viewer detail for SNMP actions.

You must be sure to enter the correct IPX address as a trap destination when installing the SNMP service. Otherwise, you might receive the Error 3 code when you restart your computer. This error indicates that the IPX address has been entered incorrectly. Be aware that the IPX address must conform to Microsoft's SNMP agent, which doesn't accept commas or hyphens (like some popular third-party management programs do). The address for the trap destination must use the "8.12" format for the network number and MAC address, where xxxxxxxx.yyyyyyyyyyyy gives the network number (represented with x's) and MAC address (represented with y's).

The Next Generation

In this chapter, you have been introduced to the basics of SNMP, as well as its agents, managers, and MIBs. You have learned about the Microsoft implementation of SNMP and how to install, configure, and troubleshoot SNMP. Even though it won't be included on the exam, we thought you might be interested in the future of SNMP and how that will affect your work.

The IETF working group for SNMPv2 has tried to implement better security and other needed improvements to SNMP, but it was never able to accommodate the different and strongly held views on the subject. Because of this, two different approaches have emerged (commonly called V2u and V2*). Because the IETF has not succeeded in vastly improving SNMP with SNMPv2, version 1 seems to have remained as the dominant force in today's industry. In order to rectify this situation in SNMPv3, the Security and Administrative Framework Evolution for SNMP Advisory Team (known simply as the Advisory Team) has been formed. The charter of this group is to provide a single, recommended approach for the evolution of SNMP. It will also work on defining MIBs for specifying targets of management operations, for notification filtering, and for proxy forwarding. Because it has recognized that timely completion of this project is crucial to the continuing success of SNMP, the Advisory Team hopes to accomplish the goals of updating SNMP to meet today's requirements and tightening security, while doing the following:

➤ Using as much of the work of the SNMPv2 Advisory Team as possible.

➤ Accommodating the wide range of operational environments with differing management demands.

➤ Facilitating the need to transition from previous, multiple protocols to SNMPv3.

➤ Providing for the ease of setup and maintenance activities.

What this means to you, the future Microsoft professional, is that an attempt is being made to ensure the survival of a simple, workable standard for monitoring and managing the networks of today for the internetworks of tomorrow. It also means that someone has finally recognized the beauty of simplicity and functionality in an increasingly complicated field.

Exam Prep Questions

Question 1

What types of transactions can be performed by an SNMP agent? [Check all correct answers]

❑ a. VARBIND

❑ b. GET

❑ c. GETALL

❑ d. Send trap

The correct answers are b and d. The agent responds only to requests, except in the case of an alarm condition, in which case it sends a trap to the trap destination. One example of this would be a host shutdown. **VarBind** is a data structure that consists of an OID and a value structure. Therefore, answer a is incorrect. There is no such command as **GetAll**. Therefore, answer c is incorrect.

Question 2

What types of devices can be monitored using SNMP? [Check all correct answers]

❑ a. Hubs

❑ b. Windows NT hosts

❑ c. Terminal servers

❑ d. Routers, bridges, and gateways

All of these answers are correct, assuming the device has the intelligence of SNMP incorporated into its design and assuming an MIB exists.

Question 3

A request is sent to an SNMP-managed device, but no response is obtained. Assume the community name is correct, the OID is correct, and a request with other OIDs does elicit a response. What could be the problem?

O a. This is not a manageable device.

O b. The network is unstable.

O c. The request is a SET request.

O d. There is no alarm condition.

The correct answer is c. A *set* request is a request for action on the part of the agent, and a reply is not mandated. Answer a is incorrect because the first condition of the question is that the device is manageable. Answer b is not plausible because other OIDs do elicit responses. If an alarm condition exists, a trap would be sent. Therefore, answer d is incorrect.

Question 4

What is an SNMP trap?

O a. PDU

O b. UDP

O c. Request

O d. Alarm

Answer d is correct. A trap message is sent to the trap destination to alert the SNMP manager of an unusual occurrence, such as startup, shutdown, low disk space, or password violation. By default, an SNMP agent sends no traps; it must be configured to do so. The PDU (Protocol Data Unit) is the SNMP message transport method. Therefore, answer a is incorrect. A UDP is a connectionless, unreliable transport protocol. Therefore, answer b is incorrect. A request may be an SNMP request for information or a request to perform some simple action. Therefore, answer c is incorrect.

Question 5

> Three attributes can be defined in the Only Accept SNMP Packets
> From These Hosts section of the SNMP Security tab. Which ones
> are they? [Check all correct answers]
>
> ❏ a. MAC address
>
> ❏ b. IP address
>
> ❏ c. IPX address
>
> ❏ d. Host name

The correct answers are b, c, and d. The MAC address is an IPX attribute, and
is not defined in the Only Accept SNMP Packets From These Hosts section
of the SNMP Security tab. Therefore, answer a is incorrect.

Question 6

> You are a network administrator in the Big Enormous Corpora-
> tion, and BEC policy dictates very strict data security. You want to
> monitor the Engineering PCs for unauthorized access, because
> very sensitive design data is kept on these computers. You set up
> the SNMP agent on each client and designate two SNMP trap des-
> tinations for the management console. You assign both of these
> SNMP servers to a single community known as Engineering and
> designate the host names of one of the two servers as the trap
> destination for the Engineering community. In the Security tab of
> the SNMP configuration at each client, you select the community
> name of Engineering and check the Accept SNMP Packets From
> Any Host box. How well does this solution fit the criteria?
>
> ○ a. Meets the requirements and is an outstanding solution
>
> ○ b. Meets the requirements and is an adequate solution
>
> ○ c. Meets the requirements but is not a desirable solution
>
> ○ d. Does not meet the requirements, although it appears
>   to work

Answer d is correct because this situation will work, but it will not meet the first objective of strict security. If the Accept SNMP Packets From Any Host box is checked, no SNMP packets will be rejected on the basis of the source host's ID, leaving your network open to intrusion. If the Accept SNMP Packets From These Hosts box is checked, access can be controlled somewhat and SNMP will be properly configured.

Question 7

Once SNMP service is installed, an administrator can do which of the following? [Check all correct answers]

❑   a. View and change parameters in the MIBs by using SNMP manager programs

❑   b. Monitor and configure parameters for any WINS server

❑   c. Monitor and configure parameters for any DHCP server

❑   d. Use the *Resource Kit* utilities to perform management functions

Only answers b and d are correct. After installing SNMP, administrators can monitor and configure WINS and use the utilities provided with the *Resource Kit*. Answer a is partially correct; once SNMP service is installed, the administrator can view and change parameters in the LAN Manager and MIB II MIBs only, not all MIBs. Answer c is incorrect because the administrator may monitor but not configure DHCP server parameters.

Question 8

> The network administrator can view performance counters on a computer after installing SNMP. How is this accomplished?
>
> ○ a. By editing the Registry key
> KEY\LOCAL_MACHINE\System\Current
> ControlSet\Services\Snmp\Parameter
>
> ○ b. By editing the Registry key
> HKEY_LOCAL_MACHINE\System\Current
> ControlSet\Services\Snmp\Parameter
>
> ○ c. By using the Perf2MIB utility to create new MIB files
>
> ○ d. By using the management console user interface

The correct answer is c. You use the Perf2MIB utility to create new MIB files to enumerate the counters in which the administrator is interested. Answer a is wrong because the incorrect syntax is being used; in addition, SNMP responses are determined by the MIB, not the Registry. The correct syntax is found in answer b. Answer b is incorrect because the responses to SNMP requests are determined by the contents of the MIB, not by the Registry, even though the Registry may contain the information required. Registry values under the HKEY_LOCAL_MACHINE\SYSTEM\CurrentControl Set\Services\SNMP\Parameters\ExtensionAgents key tell the extendible agent which agent DLLs to load. The management console user interface can display performance counters only after the appropriate MIB that describes the manageable objects on the host in question has been created. Therefore, answer d is incorrect.

Question 9

> How should the administrator troubleshoot SNMP errors?
>
> O a. By choosing Start|Programs|Event Viewer
>
> O b. By changing the Security parameters to Accept SNMP Requests From These Hosts
>
> O c. By editing the Registry key HKEY_LOCAL_ MACHINE\System\Current ControlSet\Services\Snmp\Parameter
>
> O d. By using the Performance Monitor to monitor TCP/IP- related counters

The correct answer is a. The key to troubleshooting SNMP-related errors is the Event Viewer, which has been improved in NT 4. If the Accept SNMP Packets From These Hosts box is checked, the agent will accept requests from and direct responses and traps to only the hosts specified. Therefore, answer b is incorrect. In order to run multiple SNMP agents, a Registry edit is required, but it's not needed for error determination. Therefore, answer c is incorrect. The Performance Monitor can be used for error troubleshooting only after the appropriate MIBs have been created. Therefore, answer d is incorrect.

Need To Know More?

 McLaren, Tim and Stephen Myers. *MCSE Study Guide: TCP/IP and Systems Management Servers*. New Riders Publishing, Indianapolis, IN, 1996. ISBN 1-56205-588-7. Chapter 15, "Simple Network Management Protocol," includes a brief overview of all the topics covered here with an additional section on testing the installation.

 The *Windows NT Server Resource Kit*. Microsoft Press. ISBN 1-57231-344-7. The "Networking Guide" contains numerous references to SNMP. In particular, Appendix C provides the managed objects definitions found in the MIBs shipped with Windows NT. Chapter 11 covers Microsoft's implementation of SNMP for Network Management.

Microsoft TechNet. July, 97. Volume 5, Issue 7. Contains numerous articles on SNMP. A simple query on SNMP is all that's required.

There are numerous newsgroups and Web sites that focus on SNMP. These include:

➤ comp.protocols.snmp

➤ www.iol.unh.edu/consortiums/netmgt/rfc-snmprel.html

➤ http://ds.internic.net/

➤ http://netman.cit.buffalo.edu/Papers.html

➤ ftp://SunSITE.unc.edu/pub/micro/pc-stuff/ms-windows/winsnmp/winsnmp_app

Performance, Tuning, And Optimization

15

· ·

Terms you'll need to understand:

√ Sliding window

√ TTL

√ Scope ID

Techniques you'll need to master:

√ Understanding the acknowledgment sequence

√ Understanding the Registry settings pertaining to TCP/IP performance

√ Knowing the tools available for TCP/IP monitoring

√ Knowing the implications of using Scope IDs

You must take a number of things into account regarding TCP/IP performance and tuning. First and foremost, you should note that TCP/IP, and especially Microsoft's implementation of TCP/IP, is for the most part self-tuning. However, for the exam, you'll need to know how to monitor and adjust TCP/IP and how to control NetBIOS traffic.

Basic Performance Factors

A number of things can affect TCP/IP performance—anything from the speed of the LAN or WAN link to the topology of the network. Even the type of data transfer (asynchronous or synchronous) being used has an effect on performance.

One of the biggest factors in TCP/IP's performance is that, by default, each segment transmitted must be acknowledged before the next segment can be sent. You can imagine how slow this process is when using Telnet asynchronous transfer (that is, one character at a time) over a 56 K link from a remote office. Frustrating, to say the least.

In an attempt to ease this problem, TCP/IP allows the user to specify the number of segments that can be received before sending an acknowledgment. The number of segments a computer has outstanding (without acknowledgment) is called the "window," or "sliding window." Don't worry; this will all make more sense in a minute. Let's look at how the acknowledgment process takes place.

The default configuration shown in Figure 15.1 has the windows size set to 1, causing the receiving computer to acknowledge (ACK) each packet. If you'll recall, the receiving computer acknowledges the packet by okaying the next packet.

In contrast, when the window is set to a larger number, the sending computer does not expect an ACK for each packet, but rather for a group of packets. In Figure 15.2, the sliding window is set to 4, which requires the recipient to acknowledge every fourth packet.

Of course, the whole reason TCP/IP expects an acknowledgment for each packet is to ensure reliable delivery. When each packet is acknowledged and one gets lost in the mail, the receiver simply requests that it be re-sent. Remember that a TCP/IP acknowledgment actually asks for the next number in line; therefore, if segment 3 doesn't make it to the destination, the receiving computer sends an acknowledgment that says "Send segment 3 again." The sender re-sends the segment, waits for acknowledgment that it has been

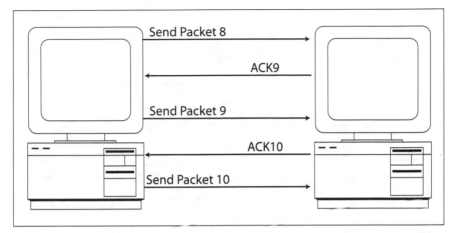

Figure 15.1   By default, computers using TCP/IP acknowledge each packet that is sent.

received, and then proceeds on to segment 4. What happens if the sliding window is set to more than 1 and a packet gets lost? As you might guess, this situation is treated a little differently. Figure 15.3 shows a situation in which a packet gets lost with the window set to 3.

In this example, segment 12 doesn't make it, but segment 13 does. As you can see from the figure, the receiving computer acknowledges that 11 arrived fine by asking for 12. Segment 12 is re-sent, and the computer acknowledges that 13 arrived by requesting segment 14 and continuing the conversation.

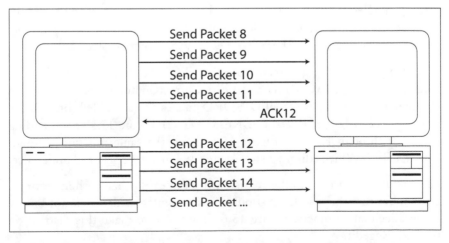

Figure 15.2   Increased window size requires fewer ACK packets.

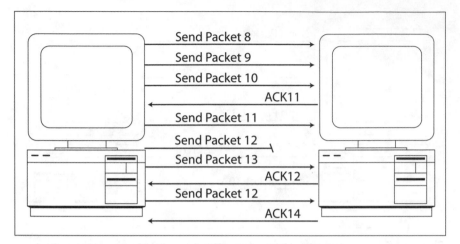

Figure 15.3 A lost packet is handled differently when the window is greater than 1.

The size of the send window on each computer is established during the initial TCP/IP handshake. The send window on either side is set to the size of the receive window on the opposite side.

Tuning Techniques

Windows NT includes a few Registry settings that can be used to adjust how TCP/IP reacts. However, as we mentioned earlier, TCP/IP is a self-tuning protocol, and the settings described in this section must be added manually through the Registry Editor. Remember that any changes will affect how TCP/IP performs as a whole, not just during one session or with one protocol type. We recommend you make these changes only if absolutely necessary.

The Registry settings used to tune TCP/IP are located in the HKEY_LOCAL_MACHINE\SYSTEM\CurrentControlSet\Services\Tcpip\ Parameters subkey. They are all DWORD entries and are added through the Registry Editor (either Regedit or REGEDT32). Figure 15.4 shows adding the entry through Regedit; Figure 15.5 shows the same function through REGEDT32. Which editor you use is entirely a matter of personal preference.

After adding the values to the Registry, you can easily change their settings. Remember that these settings should be represented as decimal, not binary or hexadecimal, numbers. Figure 15.6 shows how to make this distinction through Regedit.

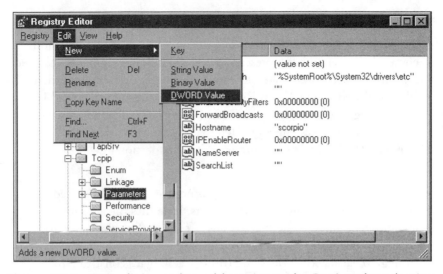

Figure 15.4   Regedit is used to add entries to the Registry by selecting DWORD Value from the New option of the Edit menu.

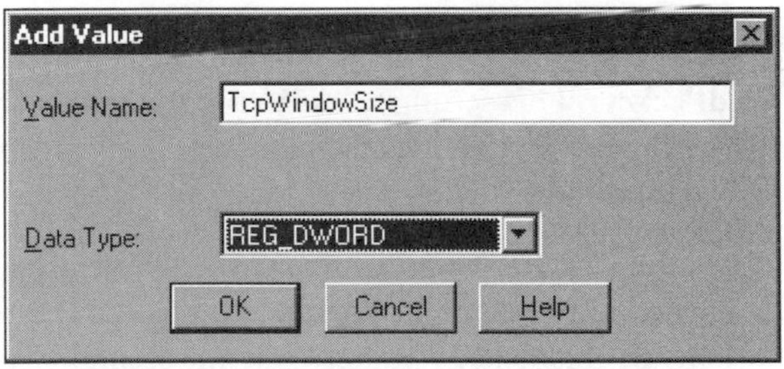

Figure 15.5   Adding entries to the Registry using REGEDT32 is accomplished by selecting Add Value from the Edit menu.

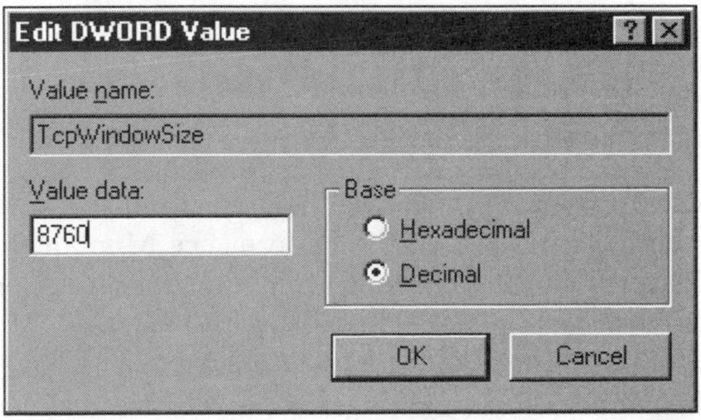

Figure 15.6   These Registry entries must be in decimal format.

The values that can be used to tune TCP/IP on a Windows NT system are:

➤ **TcpWindowSize** This is the size of the receive sliding window on the computer. This number represents not the number of segments accepted, but the number of data bytes accepted. This is because different media (that is, Ethernet and Token Ring) use different segment sizes. This number is generally no less that 8,192 (8 K) unless manually changed. For example, on a system connected to an Ethernet network, the default size is 8,760. This number represents the data portion (1,460 bytes) of 6 Ethernet packets.

➤ **ForwardBufferMemory** This setting is only used in multihomed systems that are routing TCP/IP packets. It defines the amount of memory the router queue is able to use. If the buffer value is too low, the computer will drop packets. The default value is 74,240, which allows storing 50 packets of 1,480 bytes (the extra 20 bytes constitute the difference between TCP and IP headers), plus a little extra. If the computer is continuously routing large transfers of data, it might be a good idea to increase this buffer size. If the IPEnableRouter setting is 0 (off), this parameter will be ignored.

➤ **NumForwardPackets** This setting works in conjunction with ForwardBufferMemory and defines the number of IP headers that can be stored in the router queue. The default value is 50 packets.

➤ **DefaultTTL** The TTL (time to live) of a packet defines the number of seconds it's allowed to live before it's discarded. Each router that receives a packet decrements this field by no less than one second, depending on the router's settings. The default setting for this field is 128 seconds. On a network with many slow links, this setting can be increased to ensure that communication between remote computers takes place.

Network Optimization Guidelines

TCP/IP is a very dynamic protocol and is generally able to adjust itself for optimum performance. However, the Performance Monitor included with Windows NT can assist you in making any optimization decisions. The Performance Monitor is automatically installed with Windows NT; it measures server- and network-related events. Also, it provides real-time graphing and report generation. The shortcut to access Performance Monitor (shown in Figure 15.7) is in the Start menu under Administrative Tools (Common).

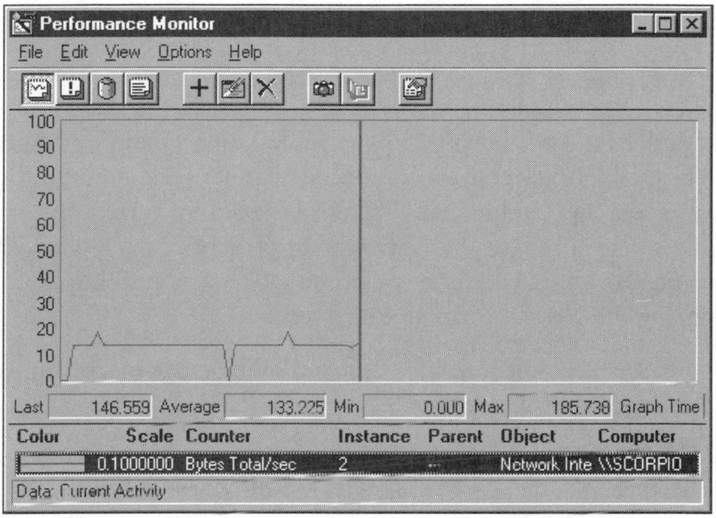

Figure 15.7   The Performance Monitor can be used to track network events.

The Performance Monitor is able to track a number of network events, including the total number of bytes transmitted each second, the number of TCP connection failures, IP datagrams received, and ICMP messages per second. To track a particular counter, select Add To Chart from the Edit menu. The window shown in Figure 15.8 will be invoked, which allows you to choose the object and the counter. Objects divide the counters logically. For example, by selecting the IP object, you can choose to monitor Datagrams Received, Datagrams Discarded, Datagrams Forwarded/sec, and many others. For more information on a particular counter, click the Explain button.

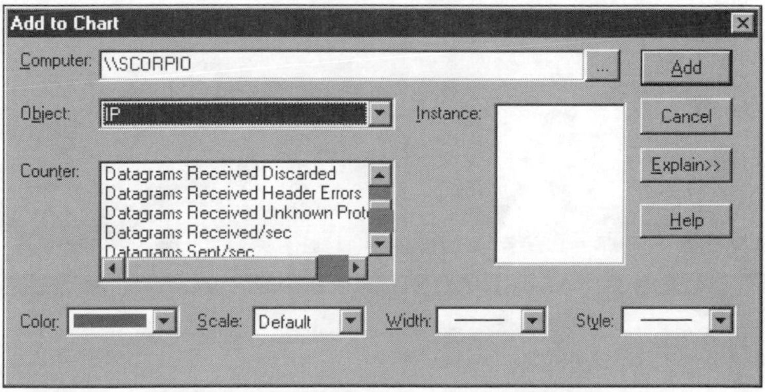

Figure 15.8   Many counters can be traced by Performance Monitor.

Bear in mind that although the Performance Monitor is a handy troubleshooting tool, it does tax the system. Because of this, it should not be run on a server, but on another Windows NT computer on the network.

The Network Monitor (shown in Figure 15.9) is an even more advanced tool that can be used to track conversations across the network, monitor total network utilization, and capture data. It's not installed by default, but it can be added as a service through the Network applet|Service tab. Again, this is a very powerful tool that taxes the system on which it is running. You should avoid running the Network Monitor on a server.

Once you have determined that changes need to be made in the way TCP/IP operates, it's a good idea to follow these guidelines:

➤ Make the changes one at a time. If you don't notice any difference in performance after a change, proceed on to the next one.

➤ Thoroughly document all changes that you make. A problem might not manifest itself for days or weeks after a change is made, and it could become necessary to back out of the updates.

When possible, test all changes on a machine that is not mission critical. If you're planning to change the TCP/IP settings on a server, you should always test them somewhere else first.

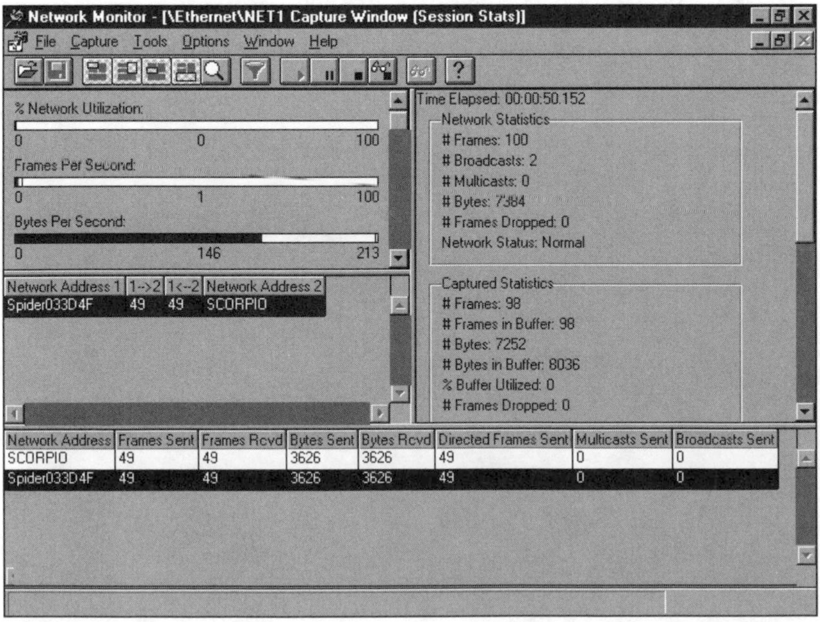

Figure 15.9 The Network Monitor can also be used to watch the network.

Managing NetBIOS Traffic

Due to the nature of NetBIOS, controlling how its traffic moves through the network is often difficult. Because of its use of broadcasts and name lookup, NetBIOS traffic can be extensive and can bog down computers and the network. NetBIOS Over TCP/IP (NBT) allows for an added level of authentication: the NetBIOS Scope. The Scope ID is appended to the NetBIOS computer name when network communications take place. Only computers with the same Scope ID are allowed to communicate with each other. Although this does not limit the amount of traffic on the network, it does provide a certain amount of filtering and, to some extent, added security.

NetBIOS Scopes are not recommended to be used on a network. However, NetBIOS Scopes may be addressed on the test. They are useful in workgroup, peer-to-peer situations where it's not necessary, or even not desirable, for two workgroups to communicate, even though they must share the same network medium. Figure 15.10 shows a situation where NetBIOS Scope would be used.

The Scope ID for a computer is assigned through the WINS tab of the TCP/IP Properties page of the Network applet, as shown in Figure 15.11. The Scope

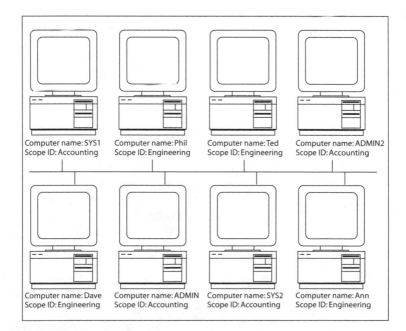

Figure 15.10   NetBIOS Scopes can be used to limit conversations between computers.

ID can consist of numbers or letters, but the entire NetBIOS name (computer name plus Scope ID) cannot exceed 256 characters.

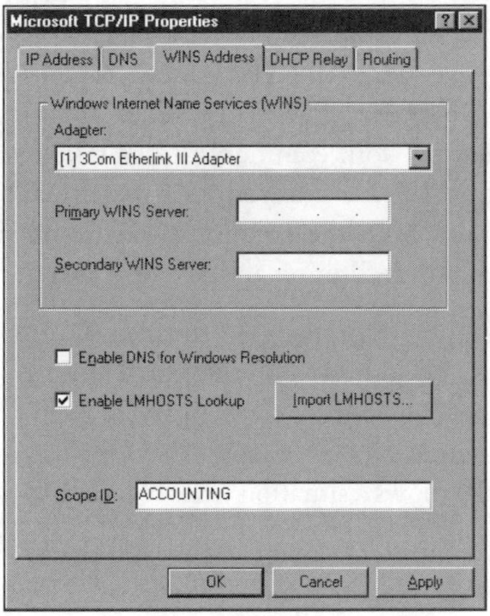

Figure 15.11 The Scope ID is configured through the WINS Address tab of the Network applet|TCP/IP Properties.

Exam Prep Questions

Question 1

> After monitoring your network for a week, you have concluded
> that your Windows NT Server, which is acting as a router, is drop-
> ping packets. Which of the following Registry settings can be used
> to correct this problem? [Check all correct answers]
>
> ❑ a. TcpWindowSize
>
> ❑ b. ForwardBufferMemory
>
> ❑ c. NumForwardPackets
>
> ❑ d. DefaultTTL

The correct answers for this question are b and c. Each of these settings
defines how routed packets are handled in memory. ForwardBufferMemory
defines how much data can be stored, whereas NumForwardPackets defines
the number of packets in the queue. TcpWindowSize defines the amount
of data that can be outstanding on the network before acknowledgment.
Therefore, answer a is incorrect. DefaultTTL defines the life of the packet.
Therefore, answer d is incorrect.

Question 2

> What type of communications does FTP use?
>
> ○ a. Synchronous
>
> ○ b. Asynchronous
>
> ○ c. Multisynchronous
>
> ○ d. Unisynchronous

The correct answer for this question is a, synchronous. Remember that synchronous communications send chunks of data, whereas asynchronous
communications send the data one character at a time. Answers c and d are
bogus; no such communications types exist.

Question 3

Which of the following utilities is used to monitor the network? [Check all correct answers]

❏ a. Performance Monitor

❏ b. Ethernet Monitor

❏ c. WINS Monitor

❏ d. Network Monitor

Answers a and d are correct. Both Performance Monitor and Network Monitor are able to trace network events. Answers b and c, although they would be handy, do not exist.

Question 4

What kind of data types are the Registry values that pertain to TCP/IP tuning? [Check all correct answers]

❏ a. DWORD

❏ b. STRING

❏ c. REG_DWORD

❏ d. REG_MULTI_SZ

The answers to this question are a and c. This is a trick question because although the values are all DWORD, the entry depends on which Registry editor is being used. They are REG_DWORD using REGEDT32, and DWORD using Regedit. Answers b and d do not apply to the settings discussed in this chapter.

Question 5

Which of the following protocols uses Scope ID to limit communications?

○ a. NWLink

○ b. NetBEUI

○ c. NBT

○ d. TCP

The correct answer to this question is c. NBT (NetBIOS over TCP/IP) is the
only protocol that supports this function.

Need To Know More?

Lammle, Todd, Monica Lammle, and James Chellis. *MCSE: TCP/IP Study Guide*. Sybex Network Press, San Francisco, CA, 1997. ISBN 0-7821-1969-7. Chapter 12, "Fine Tuning and Optimization," discusses many issues regarding optimizing your NT TCP/IP settings.

Microsoft TechNet. September, 97. PN99367. The document "MS Windows NT 3.5, 3.51, 4.0—TCP/IP Implementation Details" provides extensive information on these topics, or you can search TechNet (either CD or online version at www.microsoft.com) using the keywords "TcpWindowSize" and "NumForwardPackets" for more information.

The *Windows NT Server Resource Kit* contains a lot of useful information about TCP/IP and related topics. Also search the *Resource Kit* CD on any of these topics.

Troubleshooting

Terms you'll need to understand:

√ ARP

√ HOSTNAME

√ IPCONFIG

√ NSLOOKUP

√ NBTSTAT

√ NETSTAT

√ PING

√ ROUTE

√ TRACERT

Techniques you'll need to master:

√ Using the proper methods when troubleshooting TCP/IP problems

√ Using different switches for each diagnostic command to pinpoint problems

√ Troubleshooting "from the bottom up"

√ Troubleshooting with the Network Monitor and the Performance Monitor

√ Diagnosing TCP/IP performance problems

√ Troubleshooting connectivity problems

√ Troubleshooting naming resolution problems

The power of TCP/IP lends itself to complexity, which can lead to headaches when things go wrong. In this chapter, we'll provide an overview of trouble-shooting methodology and some specific first-line TCP/IP diagnostic tools. Not only will you find this overview helpful for the exam, you'll find these tools to be lifesavers in the real world. Next, we'll discuss various TCP/IP troubleshooting tasks and the specific tools that will assist you. Also, we'll briefly cover the use of the Performance Monitor and Network Monitor to analyze networking problems. Finally, we'll examine some common TCP/IP network-ing problems and their solutions.

TCP/IP Troubleshooting Tools

Table 16.1 gives you an overview of the diagnostic tools and utilities that are available in Microsoft's TCP/IP suite. As you can tell from the extensive list, troubleshooting IP networks can be tricky.

In addition to the tools mentioned in Table 16.1, don't forget the following:

➤ **Microsoft SNMP Service** Provides statistical information to SNMP management consoles. (See Chapter 14, "Implementing The SNMP Service.")

Table 16.1	**TCP/IP diagnostic utilities (in alphabetical order).**
Utility	**Description**
ARP	Views and modifies the physical address translation tables used by the Address Resolution Protocol (ARP) table. Can be used on the local machine to detect invalid address entries.
HOSTNAME	Prints the name of the current host to the screen.
IPCONFIG	Displays all current network configuration values. Especially useful on machines using DHCP.
NBTSTAT	Displays protocol statistics and current TCP/IP connections using NetBT. A very useful tool.
NETSTAT	Similar to NBTSTAT. Only displays TCP/IP network connection statistics and connections.
NSLOOKUP	Displays information about DNS servers. Available only if TCP/IP is installed.
PING	The most useful of all. Verifies basic connectivity to one or more remote computers.
ROUTE	Manipulates network routing tables.
TRACERT	Determines the route taken to a destination by sending ICMP echo packets and increments hops based on TTL (time to live) values.

➤ **Event Viewer** Tracks errors and events.

➤ **Performance Monitor** Analyzes server performance.

➤ **Network Monitor** Analyzes network protocols on a basic level.

➤ **Registry Editor** Views and edits Registry parameters.

Guidelines For Troubleshooting TCP/IP

As with any troubleshooting methodology, always employ a derivative of the scientific method. Remember, this is usually a reiterative process; you might not be successful on the first try. In the case of TCP/IP, a general method for troubleshooting might be:

1. Identify the problem, or at the least, symptoms of the problem. This may be the hardest part of all. Although the problem may appear at first to be caused by one element, the process of elimination and some detective work may point to something entirely different.

2. Eliminate what appears to work correctly to narrow the possibilities.

3. Examine the Physical layer first and then test each layer above it; 90 percent of all network problems are caused by faulty cabling.

4. Compose a hypothesis.

5. Test your hypothesis.

6. Analyze the data.

7. Take corrective action.

Compile a list of what works and what doesn't work; then study the list to isolate faults and failures. Remember to check the Event Viewer to determine the effects of any changes. In general, it's best to first verify that the machine's TCP/IP configuration is correct. Next, verify that a connection and a route exist between the machine and the network host, checking local network hardware first. Try a large number of PINGs of different sizes at random intervals and plot the success rate to verify link reliability. Then, resolve any IP addressing problems, followed by host name resolution and, finally, resolve any NetBIOS problems that may exist.

Using IPCONFIG To Verify Configuration

Using IPCONFIG to get the computer's configuration information at the host experiencing the problem is a good beginning for troubleshooting TCP/IP problems. Such helpful information as the IP address, subnet mask, and default gateway can be obtained by this command-line utility. When used with the /**all** switch, IPCONFIG produces a fairly detailed report for all bound interfaces, including any configured serial ports.

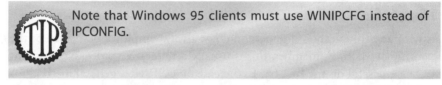

Note that Windows 95 clients must use WINIPCFG instead of IPCONFIG.

Once you learn the IPCONFIG command and its switches, and have practiced using it, you'll discover all sorts of useful tricks. Consider this: If your problem is a duplicate of an existing IP address, the subnet mask will be displayed as 0.0.0.0 by IPCONFIG. In Figure 16.1, you can see an example of the results of an **ipconfig /all** command.

Table 16.2 describes the three switches available for IPCONFIG.

Using PING To Test Connectivity

PING is your first line of defense when troubleshooting. PING is a tool that verifies IP-level connectivity by sending an ICMP echo request to an IP address or target NetBIOS name. You can use PING to isolate network

```
DOS Prompt                                                    _ □ ✕

D:\WINNT\system32>cd\

D:\>ipconfig /all

Windows NT IP Configuration

        Host Name . . . . . . . . . . : scorpio
        DNS Servers . . . . . . . . . :
        Node Type . . . . . . . . . . : Broadcast
        NetBIOS Scope ID. . . . . . . :
        IP Routing Enabled. . . . . . : No
        WINS Proxy Enabled. . . . . . : No
        NetBIOS Resolution Uses DNS : No

Ethernet adapter Elnk31:

        Description . . . . . . . . . : ELNK3 Ethernet Adapter.
        Physical Address. . . . . . . : 00-A0-24-09-22-06
        DHCP Enabled. . . . . . . . . : No
        IP Address. . . . . . . . . . : 101.101.101.101
        Subnet Mask . . . . . . . . . : 255.255.255.0
        Default Gateway . . . . . . . : 101.101.101.1

D:\>
```

Figure 16.1 The **ipconfig /all** command is used to display the TCP/IP settings for a Windows NT computer.

Table 16.2	IPCONFIG switches.
Switch	**Description**
all	Produces a full display; by default. Only the IP address, subnet masks, and default gateway values are given for each NIC.
Renew	Option available only to DHCP Client services; renews configuration parameters. Type an adapter name (which appears by default when using IPCONFIG without parameters) to target a specific adapter.
Release	Option available only to DHCP Client services; releases current configuration parameters. Type an adapter name (which appears by default when using IPCONFIG without parameters) to target a specific adapter. Useful for laptop computer users.

hardware problems, incompatible configurations, and flawed connectivity. Try PINGing the IP address of the target host first; this is the simplest case. The command syntax is:

```
ping IP-Address
```

To see what command-line options are available, type "ping -?". You can choose packet size, number of packets, record the route used, what TTL value to use, what host to target, type of service being used, an so on. As you can see, this is a very useful command-line diagnostic tool; it is also used with Unixtype systems.

In order to effectively use PING:

1. PING the default loopback address to verify the local installation and configuration.

2. PING 127.0.0.1.

3. PING the IP address of the local computer to make sure the network recognizes it.

4. PING the IP address of the local host.

5. Next, check connectivity of the default gateway. This will verify operation of the gateway (router) as well as communication between the host and the gateway.

6. PING the IP address of the default gateway.

7. PING the remote host's IP address to verify communications to the router.

8. PING the IP address of the remote host.

The default gateway must be located on the same logical subnetwork as the host IP address. If the default gateway is not on the same logical subnetwork, communications for that host are limited to the local logical network. In Figure 16.2, the result of PING (without switch parameters) gives you an idea of what results can be expected.

Notice that the switches for PING can help you adjust to almost any situation. For example, by default, PING waits only 750 milliseconds for each response to be returned before timing out. The -w (wait) switch can be used to specify a longer timeout. This is helpful in situations where the remote system being PINGed is across a high-delay link, such as a satellite link, on which responses could take longer to be returned. Table 16.3 lists the switches for PING, along with a brief explanation.

The PING utility can be used to test both the host name and IP address. If the IP address is verified but the host name is not, this may indicate a host name resolution problem that can be resolved by querying the local HOSTS file or the DNS database.

If you've determined by using PING that a name resolution problem exists, remember the order in which IP proceeds with NetBIOS name resolution: NetBIOS name cache, WINS, b-node broadcast, LMHOSTS, HOSTS, and DNS. This will reduce the amount of time you spend troubleshooting by giving you an indication of where to look first.

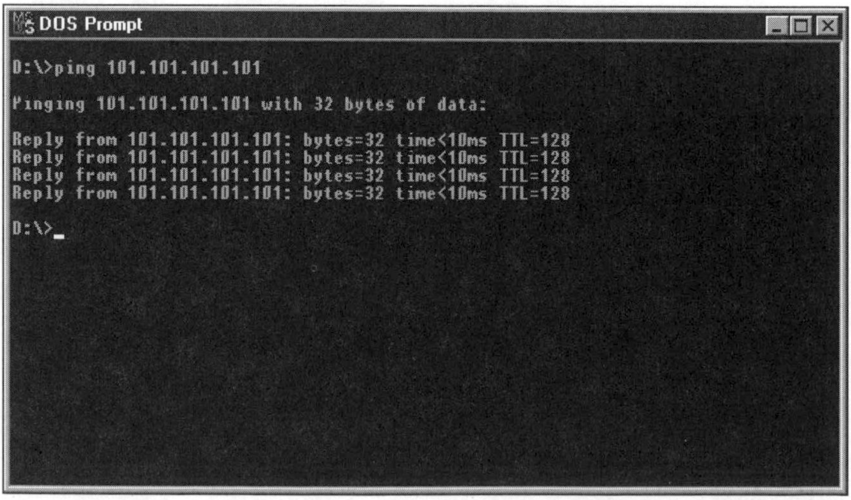

```
DOS Prompt                                    _ □ ✕

D:\>ping 101.101.101.101

Pinging 101.101.101.101 with 32 bytes of data:

Reply from 101.101.101.101: bytes=32 time<10ms TTL=128
Reply from 101.101.101.101: bytes=32 time<10ms TTL=128
Reply from 101.101.101.101: bytes=32 time<10ms TTL=128
Reply from 101.101.101.101: bytes=32 time<10ms TTL=128

D:\>_
```

Figure 16.2 The PING utility is used to check IP connectivity.

Table 16.3	PING switches.
Switch	**Description**
-t	PINGs the specified host until interrupted.
-a	Resolves address to host names.
-n *(count)*	Sends the number of echo packets specified by *count*. The default is 4.
-l *(length)*	Sends echo packets containing *length* amount of data. The default is 64; the maximum is 8,192.
-l ttl	Sets the TTL field to the value specified.
-v tos	Sets the type of service to the value specified.
-r *(count)*	Records the route in the record route field. A minimum of 1 to a maximum of 9 hosts must be specified by *count*.
-s *(count)*	Specifies the timestamp for *count* number of hops.
-j *(host-list)*	Routes packets via the list of hosts specified. The maximum allowed by IP is 9. Consecutive hosts can be separated by intermediate gateways (loose source routed).
-k *(host-list)*	Routes packets via the list of hosts specified. The maximum allowed by IP is 9. Consecutive hosts *cannot* be separated by intermediate gateways (strict source routed).
-w (timeout)	Timeout interval to wait in milliseconds.
destination	Pings a specific remote host.

Diagnostic Tools And Techniques

Now that you've gotten an idea of some powerful and effective first-line trouble-shooting utilities, let's consider some different diagnostic tools available in Microsoft's implementation of TCP/IP. If you've verified that cables are connected properly and have conducted initial tests with PING and IPCONFIG to verify configuration and connectivity, your problem may be the IP address or host name. To resolve IP addressing problems, you can use the ARP, ROUTE, and TRACERT utilities.

ARP

ARP is another very useful utility that allows you to view and modify ARP table entries on the local host, as well as to see the ARP cache and resolve any address resolution problems. As you know, in the Windows NT implementation of TCP/IP, networked devices communicate by way of an IP address, a host name in FQDN form, or a NetBIOS name. No matter which naming convention is used, that name must ultimately be resolved to the MAC address, a hardware address. The Address Resolution Protocol (ARP) allows a host to find the MAC address of the destination host. For efficiency, each host or router caches the IP-to-MAC address mappings for a given amount of time; the ARP utility queries this cache. This reduces repetitive ARP broadcast requests. Be aware, however, that by default, the caches are updated at 10-minute intervals for accuracy.

The switches for ARP are quite useful. For instance, if you want to target a specific host, use the **-a** switch. This displays the current ARP entries. The syntax is:

```
arp -a inet_addr -N if_addr
```

If **inet_addr** is specified in dotted-decimal notation, only the IP and physical address for the specified host are displayed. The **-N** switch specifies a network interface to display. **if_addr** specifies the IP address of the interface whose ARP table should be modified. If it's not present, the first applicable interface will be used.

In addition, you can use the following:

➤ **arp -d inet_addr [if_addr]** Deletes the entry specified by **inet_addr. arp.**

➤ **arp -s inet_addrether_addr [if_addr]** Adds an entry to the ARP cache that associates inet_addr with ether_addr, the physical MAC address in six hexadecimal bytes separated by hyphens.

The IP address is specified using the standard dotted-decimal notation. This entry is static and will not be removed automatically from the cache after the timeout expires; however, it will be lost if the machine is rebooted.

NSLOOKUP

NSLOOKUP is a very powerful tool that displays information from DNS servers. Obviously, NSLOOKUP is available only if TCP/IP is installed and a DNS server is available. The syntax is:

```
nslookup [-option] [hostname] - [server]
```

NSLOOKUP has two modes—interactive and noninteractive—depending on how much data you need. For a single piece of information, use the noninteractive mode by typing the IP address or name of the host to be looked up as the first argument. For the second argument, type the name or IP address of the DNS server. Omit the second argument and the default DNS will be used.

In the interactive mode, you can look up more than one piece of data. In this case, use the hyphen (-) as the first argument and either omit the second argument to use the default DNS server or type in an IP address or name to pinpoint a specific server. To get out of interactive mode, type Ctrl+C to interrupt and exit. Remember that in interactive mode, an unrecognized command is treated as a host name. To force NSLOOKUP to treat a built-in command as a host name, precede the command with the escape character (\). More than 25 command-line options are available to NSLOOKUP, but the total command-line length must be less than 256 characters. You'll probably not need to know any of these options for the exam; however, if you want to learn more, choose NSLOOKUP commands topic in the TCP/IP Procedure Help or consult Appendix A of the "Networking Guide" volume of the Microsoft *Windows NT Server Resource Kit*.

Routing Problems

In Windows NT 4, the MPR (MultiProtocol Router) was introduced; it can be used to support routing on single- and multihomed computers. MPR includes the Routing Information Protocol (RIP) for TCP/IP and IPX. In Chapter 6, "Implementing IP Routing," we examined routing and how it works in the Microsoft environment. Let's examine two utilities for troubleshooting routing problems: ROUTE and TRACERT.

ROUTE

The ROUTE utility is a diagnostic tool that works by manipulating the network routing tables. It uses the Networks file to convert destination names to addresses. For ROUTE to work correctly, the network numbers in the Networks file must be specified correctly; that is, all four octets must be in dotted-decimal notation. For example, a network number of 10.10.1 must be specified in the Networks file as 10.10.1.0, with trailing zeroes appended to make up the required number of octets.

To determine if the connectivity problem is due to faulty IP addressing, check the route taken to reach the packet's destination. The problem may be a fouled routing table somewhere or a faulty router. If you've PINGed a local host but can't ping the router, that can indicate router problems. If you can't PING beyond the router, router tables may be suspect. **ROUTE print** will display the routing tables on the screen. Other switches include **add, delete,** and **modify,** which are self-explanatory.

TRACERT

To check the health of routers in the path, use the TRACERT utility. If a destination can't be reached, this will show which router failed; if the network is slow, TRACERT will show time metrics from one router to another. In the following example, the default gateway has determined that there is no valid path for the host on 10.10.0.1. There is either a router configuration problem or the 10.10.0.0 network does not exist (or we've been given a bad IP address).

```
C:\>tracert 10.10.0.1
Tracing route to 10.10.0.1 over a maximum of 30 hops
192.54.48.1 reports: Destination net unreachable.
Trace complete.
```

Troubleshooting By Monitoring

Windows NT Server and Workstation include the Performance Monitor utility, which can be used to view many different TCP/IP-related counters. Once the SNMP service is installed, counters are available for NIC, IP, ICMP, UDP, TCP, and NetBT. One of the advantages of the Performance Monitor is that it allows you to monitor several counters from one management window. You can also set alert levels for the counters being monitored.

The Network Monitor is included with Windows NT Server to make troubleshooting complex network problems a little easier. Stations running the Network Monitor can attach to other stations running the agent software via the local area network (LAN) or by using RAS dial-up. This can be useful for remote monitoring or tracing remote segments.

The Network Monitor allows the capture of traffic to and from the local computer. Filters can be defined to narrow the scope of information obtained for later analysis. Filters can be based on source and destination NIC addresses, protocol addresses, and pattern matches. Display filters can be constructed in the query that further isolate potential problems and narrow the scope of information. The display report format includes a summary window, a detailed description window, and hex output.

Common TCP/IP Problems And Resolutions

Throughout this book, we've explored various types of TCP/IP issues, such as connectivity, name resolution, routing, address resolution, and faulty configuration. We've also taken a look at the many tools available for diagnosing problems when they occur. Before we put all this knowledge into practice, let's take a brief look at some examples of common TCP/IP problems and how to correct them.

If you cannot PING or otherwise connect to a remote host when connected to the LAN as a RAS client, you may not have Use Default Gateway On Remote Network selected under TCP/IP settings in the RAS Phonebook. This feature adds to the route table a route that allows IP addresses that are not resolved by other entries to be routed to the gateway on the RAS link. This feature must be enabled to use Internet utilities such as a Web browser or FTP.

Use the **ROUTE add** command to add the route of the subnet you're attempting to use and tie that route to the local gateway. For example, if the computer you're connecting to has an IP address of 11.1.0.3, use the following command to add the route to the table:

```
route add  11.0.0.0 MASK  255.0.0.0  199.199.41.1
```

This addition causes all frames bound for the 11.x.x.x subnet to be processed through the local LAN gateway (199.199.41.1) on the local network.

Use the **NBTSTAT -n** command to determine the cause of connectivity problems when specifying a particular server name. This tells you what name the server has registered on the network. The **NBTSTAT** command is also useful for displaying the cached entries for remote computers from either **#PRE** entries in LMHOSTS file or from recently resolved names.

If IP addresses work but host names do not when connecting to remote computers, make sure the appropriate HOSTS file and DNS Setup have been properly configured. To do this, check the host name resolution configuration in Control Panel|Network|DNS tab. Be sure the IP address of the DNS server is correct and in proper order. Use NSLOOKUP to determine if the DNS is working properly. PING to the remote computer by both host name and IP address to make sure the name is being properly resolved. If you're using a HOSTS file for name resolution, double-check for typing, spelling, and capitalization errors.

If your TCP/IP connection to a remote computer appears to be hung, use **NETSTAT -a** to show the status of all TCP and UDP port activity on the local machine. If the state of the TCP connection is good, it will usually be established with 0 bytes in the send and the receive queues. If data is blocked in either queue or if the state is not regular, a connection problem probably exists; otherwise, the problem is probably network or application related.

Obtaining Technical Support From Microsoft

The following list of resources may prove useful when you've completely run out of ideas:

➤ **Microsoft Frequently Asked Questions (FAQ)** Answers to the most common technical issues.

➤ **Microsoft Software Library** Contains free software add-ons, bug fixes, peripheral drivers, software updates, and programming aids.

➤ **Microsoft Knowledge Base** The database that Microsoft support engineers use to answer technical questions; a comprehensive collection of more than 70,000 detailed articles with technical information about Microsoft products, bug and fix lists, and answers to commonly asked technical questions.

➤ **Internet services (World Wide Web and FTP sites)** Microsoft's Web site is located at www.microsoft.com; the FTP site is located at ftp.microsoft.com.

➤ **The Microsoft Network (MSN) and other online services** To access Microsoft support services on MSN, choose Go To Other Location on the Edit menu and type "MSsupport."

➤ **Microsoft TechNet** Microsoft TechNet is the front-line resource for fast, complete answers to technical questions on Microsoft desktop and systems products. TechNet is $299 annually for a single-user license or $699 annually for a single-server, unlimited-users license. To subscribe to Microsoft TechNet, call 1-800-344-2121.

➤ **Microsoft Developer Network Library (MSDN)** To subscribe to the Microsoft Developer Network, call 1-800-759-5474. Even if you're not a developer, this is a great Web site. Now it's available to any Microsoft Certified Professional through the Microsoft Web site.

➤ **Microsoft Download Service (MSDL)** The Microsoft Download Service contains sample programs, device drivers, patches, software updates, and programming aids. Direct modem access to MSDL is available by dialing 1-206-936-6735. The service is available 24 hours a day, 365 days a year. Connect information: 1200, 2400, 9600, or 14400 baud, no parity, 8 data bits, and 1 stop bit.

➤ **Microsoft FastTips** Microsoft FastTips is an automated service that provides quick answers to common technical questions via an automated toll-free telephone number, fax, or mail. To access FastTips or to receive a map and catalog, call the FastTips number listed for your product of interest: Desktop applications, 1-800-936-4100; Development products, 1-800-936-4300; Personal Systems products, 1-800-936-4200; Business Systems, 1-800-936-4400.

➤ **Per-Incident Electronic Service Requests** This service is available to Premier, Priority Comprehensive 35 and 75, and Priority Developer 35 customers. You can directly submit electronic service requests to Microsoft support engineers who receive the requests and work with you to resolve your technical problem. This capability also allows you to access Microsoft support information to maintain and troubleshoot your Microsoft products independently. Contact your Microsoft Solution Provider for more information.

➤ **Standard Support** For the first 30 days after registering your product, you have access to unlimited, no-charge support from Microsoft support engineers on usability issues such as setup, usage, and troubleshooting error messages via a toll call between 6:00 A.M. and 6:00 P.M. Pacific time, Monday through Friday, excluding holidays. In the United States, call 1-206-635-7088. When you call, you should be at your computer and have the appropriate product documentation at hand. Be prepared to give the following information:

➤ The version number of the Microsoft product you're using

➤ The type of hardware you're using, including network hardware, if applicable

➤ The exact wording of any messages that appear on your screen

➤ A description of what happened and what you were doing at the time

➤ A description of how you tried to solve the problem

➤ **Priority Support** Microsoft Technical Support offers priority telephone access to Microsoft support engineers 24 hours a day, 7 days a week, excluding holidays, in the U.S. In the United States, call 1-900-555-2020; $55 (U.S.) per incident. Charges appear on your telephone bill.

➤ **Text Telephone** Microsoft text telephone (TT/TDD) services are available for the deaf or hearing impaired. In the United States, using a TT/TDD modem, dial 1-206-635-4948. In Canada, using a TT/TDD modem, dial 1-905-568-9641.

Exam Prep Questions

Question 1

> You have just received a new Windows NT workstation. You're
> able to connect to other IP machines on your local subnetwork
> using the UNC name of the targeted resource, but you seem to be
> having trouble mapping a drive to another Windows NT host that
> resides on a remote network. However, no one else is having prob-
> lems connecting to the remote Windows NT host. What is the first
> thing you should check?
>
> ○ a. Cabling
>
> ○ b. IP address of the remote host
>
> ○ c. IP address of the local host
>
> ○ d. IP address of the default gateway

**The correct answer is d. Remember that the default gateway must be located
on the same logical network as the host, and it must be configured properly in
the network configuration for the local host.** If the problem is cabling, most
likely the local host wouldn't be able to communicate at all or only with inter-
mittent results. Therefore, answer a is incorrect. The same is true if the IP
address of the local host is incorrect. Therefore, answer c is incorrect. If the IP
address of the remote system were incorrect, no one would be able to attach.
Therefore, answer b is incorrect.

Question 2

> You've added an entry to your LMHOSTS file and are now experi-
> encing long connect times. What could be causing the delay?
>
> ○ a. The delay is normal and will clear up the next time you
>   reboot.
>
> ○ b. There's a problem with the DNS.
>
> ○ c. There's a problem with the LMHOSTS file.
>
> ○ d. This indicates a cabling problem.

The correct answer is c. Long connect times can occur when there's a large LMHOSTS entry at the end of the file. Mark the entry in LMHOSTS as preloaded with the *#PRE* tag at the end of the mapping. Next, use the *nbtstat -R* command to immediately update the local name cache. Otherwise, place the mapping higher in the LMHOSTS file. Frequently used entries belong at the top of the file; preloaded entries belong at the bottom. Answer a is simply not correct. Answer b is incorrect because DNS problems would show up as lost connectivity. Answer d was included to throw you off, because slow response times can be attributed to cabling, but this is not the most likely source of the problem given the scenario.

Question 3

Mary has just taken over the desktop support for a different department of her company. She is setting up a new laptop on the local subnet for the CEO. During setup, she gets the following error message: "Your default gateway does not belong to one of the configured interfaces" What should Mary do?

O a. Check the cabling.

O b. Check the PCMCIA card and reinsert it.

O c. Run IPCONFIG.

O d. Check the spelling of the default gateway entry in the LMHOSTS file.

The correct answer is c. To find out whether the configured default gateway is located on the same logical network, run IPCONFIG (or WINIPFG if Win 95). Compare the Network ID portion of the gateway with the Network ID(s) of the PCMCIA network adapter. The network portion of the IP addresses must match in order for the default gateway to be on the same network. For example, if the IP address assigned to the default gateway is 192.89.x.y, then the network address of the NIC must match. If the problem were cabling, Setup probably wouldn't have been able to find the network. Therefore, answer a is incorrect; same for answer b. The LMHOSTS file is not used by the Setup program. Therefore, answer d is incorrect.

Question 4

You have established a Telnet session with a remote computer named "Sales," but the banner displays the name "Accnt." You check the IP address and it appears to be right. What should you check next? [Check all correct answers]

❏ a. Make sure the DNS name and HOSTS tables are current and correct

❏ b. Make sure two computers on the network don't have the same IP address

❏ c. arp -g

❏ d. This is not possible

The correct answers for this question are a, b, and c. By default, the ARP module believes the first response it receives. Therefore, an impostor's reply could reach the local computer before the intended computer's reply. If you have ruled out a faulty DNS name and have verified the HOSTS tables, use the *arp -g* command at the local computer to display the mappings in the ARP cache. If you know the Ethernet address of the remote computer, make sure it matches what's in the cache. If you don't, delete the entry using *arp -d*, force a new ARP by PINGing the same address, and then check the Ethernet address again to see if it matches the first one. If an impostor really does exist on the network, chances are good that you'll eventually find a mismatch. Use the Network Monitor for further troubleshooting to locate the owner or the system causing the problems.

Question 5

Mary is having some problems with her TCP/IP network. She tries PINGing her local machine, the local gateway (router), and a remote router with success on every occasion. However, when she tries to use the **NET USE** command to set up a drive mapping to the Engineering server's NetBIOS name, the command fails. She tries the **NET VIEW** command with the NetBIOS name and it also fails. Finally, she tries a PING to the NetBIOS name, and it succeeds. She calls the Engineering department and finds out that the computer is not hung and that she has typed the NetBIOS name correctly. What else can Mary do to troubleshoot this problem? [Check all correct answers]

❑   a. Check to make sure the server's service has started.

❑   b. Verify that a DNS is working properly and the HOSTS file is correct.

❑   c. Check to see whether the entry in question has been misspelled or entered incorrectly.

❑   d. Check to see whether there are two different machines with the same NetBIOS name with neither knowing if the other has responded, causing both machines to refuse the connection.

The correct answers for this question are a, b, and c. Answer a is correct because the server may respond to a PING even though the server's services haven't been started. The server's service is needed to establish the connection. Answer b is correct because commands such as *NET USE* may timeout before the HOSTS name resolution can take over, but PING will still be resolved. Answer c is correct because the NetBIOS name must be spelled correctly both at the command line and in the HOSTS file. Answer d is simply incorrect.

Question 6

George is working the Help Desk at 11:00 P.M. when he gets a call from a frantic engineer. She needs to access a server on the 128.131.0.0. network but can't. She's on the 10.10.0.0 network and can access resources on other networks. George instructs her on PINGing the local loopback address (127.0.0.1) and both sides of her default gateway, with successful results. PINGing a station on the remote network 128.131.0.0 fails. What should George check next?

○ a. The default gateway

○ b. The HOSTS file

○ c. Static routing

○ d. Her subnet mask

The correct answer is c. By PINGing the local loopback and both sides of the router successfully, George knows that the machine and the router are functioning. Furthermore, he knows that the subnet mask and the default gateway are properly configured. Therefore, answers a and d are incorrect. WINS resolves NetBIOS names to IP addresses. Therefore, if the PING to the remote network failed, the WINS is probably not the cause. **The probable cause is a bad static route address.** The **ROUTE print** command is what George should choose to troubleshoot this problem.

Question 7

John and Mary both start to work at the Big Enormous Company on the same day. Each is supplied with a laptop that is configured with NWLink and TCP/IP. Because they are both in the Engineering department, they decide they might need to share files in the future. However, when they try to do this, they discover they can communicate only with NWLink and not TCP/IP. When Mary types in "IPCONFIG," she notices that the subnet mask is 0.0.0.0. What could be the problem?

○ a. They use the same NetBIOS name.

○ b. They use the same default gateway.

○ c. They use the same IP address.

○ d. John configured his default gateway incorrectly.

The correct answer to this question is c. If two machines have the same IP address, TCP/IP will fail. Duplicate NetBIOS names are kicked out with an error notifying the user that a duplicate name exists. Therefore, answer a is incorrect. Because John and Mary are in the same department, chances are good that they're on the same network. Therefore, answer d is a highly unlikely to be the cause. For the same reason, answer b is incorrect: If they're on the same network, they must use the same gateway.

Need To Know More?

 Lammle, Todd, Monica Lammle, and James Chellis. *MCSE: TCP/IP Study Guide.* Sybex Network Press, San Francisco, CA, 1997. ISBN 0-7821-1969-7.

 McLaren, Tim and Myers, Stephen. *MCSE Study Guide: TCP/IP and Systems Management Server.* New Riders Publishing, Indianapolis, IN, 1996. ISBN 1-56205-588-7. Chapter 17, "Troubleshooting," examines the methodology, tools, and specific TCP/IP commands for problem resolution.

Microsoft TechNet. July, 97. Contains numerous articles on troubleshooting. Search on "NT," "TCP/ IP," and "trouble."

In addition to these references, you can also use the Microsoft NT 4's help topics (Control Panel|Help). Search for "TCP/IP Procedures Help." Also, see the lists of Microsoft technical resources earlier in this chapter in the section titled "Obtaining Technical Support From Microsoft."

Sample Test

The sections that follow provide a number of pointers for developing a successful test-taking strategy, including how to choose proper answers, how to decode ambiguity, how to work within the Microsoft framework, how to decide what to memorize, and how to prepare for the test. At the end, we provide a number of questions that cover subject matter that's likely to appear on the Internetworking Microsoft TCP/IP with Microsoft Windows NT 4 exam. Good luck!

Questions, Questions, Questions

You should have no doubt in your mind that you're facing a test full of questions. The TCP/IP exam is comprised of 58 questions; you are allotted 90 minutes to complete the exam. Remember, questions are of four basic types:

➤ Multiple choice with a single answer

➤ Multiple choice with multiple answers

➤ Multipart with a single answer

➤ Picking the spot on the graphic

Always take the time to read a question twice before selecting an answer. Also, be sure to look for an Exhibit button, which brings up graphics and charts used to help explain the question, provide additional data, or illustrate layout. You'll find it difficult to answer this type of question without looking at the exhibits.

Not every question has a single answer; a lot of questions require more than one answer. In fact, for some questions, all the answers should be marked. Read the question carefully so you know how many answers are necessary. Also, look for additional instructions for marking your answers. These instructions usually appear in brackets.

Picking Proper Answers

Obviously, the only way to pass any exam is by selecting the correct answers. However, the Microsoft exams are not standardized like SAT and GRE exams; they are more diabolical and convoluted. In some cases, questions are so poorly worded that deciphering them is nearly impossible. In those cases, you may need to rely on your answer-elimination skills. There is almost always at least one answer out of the possible choices that can be immediately eliminated because of any of the following scenarios:

➤ The answer doesn't apply to the situation.

➤ The answer describes a nonexistent issue.

➤ The answer is already eliminated by the question text.

Once obviously wrong answers are eliminated, you must rely on your retained knowledge to eliminate further answers. Look for items that sound correct but refer to actions, commands, or features not present or not available in the described situation.

If, after these phases of elimination, you're still faced with a blind guess between two or more answers, reread the question. Try to picture in your mind's eye the situation and how each of the possible remaining answers would alter the situation.

If you have exhausted your ability to eliminate answers and are still unclear about which of the remaining possible answers is the correct one—guess! An unanswered question offers you no points, but guessing gives you a chance of getting a question right; just don't be too hasty in making a blind guess. Wait until the last round of reviewing marked questions before you start to guess. Guessing should be a last resort.

Decoding Ambiguity

Microsoft exams have a reputation for including questions that are at times difficult to interpret, confusing, and ambiguous. In our experience with numerous exams, we consider this reputation to be completely justified. The Microsoft exams are difficult. They're designed specifically to limit the number of passing grades to around 30 percent of all who take the test; in other words, Microsoft wants 70 percent of test-takers to fail.

The only way to beat Microsoft at its own game is to be prepared. You'll discover that many exam questions test your knowledge of things that are not directly related to the issue raised by the question. This means that the answers offered to you, even the incorrect ones, are just as much part of the skill assessment as the question itself. If you don't know about all aspects of TCP/IP cold, you might not be able to eliminate obviously wrong answers because they relate to a different area of TCP/IP than the one being addressed by the question.

Questions often give away the answer, but you have to be better than Sherlock Holmes to see the clues. Often, subtle hints are included in the text in such a way that they seem like irrelevant information. You must realize that each question is a test in and of itself, and you need to inspect and successfully navigate each question to pass the exam. Look for small clues such as the mention of times, group names, configuration settings, and even local or remote access methods. Little items such as these can point out the right answer; if missed, they can leave you facing a blind guess.

Another common difficulty with the certification exams is that of vocabulary. Microsoft has an uncanny knack of naming utilities and features very obviously in some situations and completely inanely in others. This is especially so in the area of printing and remote access; be sure to brush up on the terms presented in Chapter 13. You may also want to review the Glossary before approaching the test.

Working Within The Framework

The test questions are presented to you in a random order, and many of the elements or issues are repeated in multiple questions. Often, you'll find that the correct answer to one question is the wrong answer to another. Take the time to read each answer, even if you know the correct one immediately. The incorrect answers might spark a memory that helps you on another question.

You can revisit any question as many times as you like. If you're uncertain of the answer to a question, make a mark in the box provided so that you can come back to it later. You should also mark questions you think might offer data you can use to solve other questions. We've marked 25 to 50 percent of the questions on exams we've taken. The testing software is designed to help you mark an answer for every question, so use its framework to your advantage. Everything you want to see again should be marked; the software will help you return to marked items.

Deciding What To Memorize

The amount of rote memorization you must do for the exams depends on how well you remember what you've read. If you're a visual learner and can see the drop-down menus and the dialog boxes in your head, you won't need to memorize as much as someone who is less visually oriented. The tests will stretch your recollection of commands related to TCP/IP.

The important types of information to memorize are:

➤ Where the protocols fit into the models (both TCP/IP and OSI)

➤ Registry keys that pertain to TCP/IP

➤ How to decode a subnet mask (128+64+32+16+8+4+2+1)

➤ The name resolution process for both WINS and DNS

If you work your way through this book while sitting at a Windows NT machine, you should have little or no problem interacting with most of these important items.

Preparing For The Test

The best way to prepare for the test—after you've studied—is to take at least one practice exam. We've included a practice exam in this chapter; the test questions are located after the following section. You should give yourself 90 minutes to take the practice test. Keep yourself on the honor system and don't cheat by looking at the text earlier in the book. Once your time is up or you finish, you can check your answers in Chapter 18, "Answer Key To Sample Test."

If you want additional practice exams, visit the Microsoft Training And Certification site (www.microsoft.com/train_cert/) and download the Self-Assessment Practice Exam utility.

Taking The Test

Relax. Once you're sitting in front of the testing computer, there's nothing more you can do to increase your knowledge or preparation. Take a deep breath, stretch, and attack the first question.

Don't rush; you have plenty of time to complete each question and to return to skipped questions. If you read a question twice and are clueless, mark it and move on. Both easy and difficult questions are dispersed throughout the test in a random order. Don't cheat yourself by spending so much time on a difficult question early on that it prevents you from answering numerous easy questions positioned near the end. Move through the entire test and before returning to the skipped questions, evaluate your time in light of the number of skipped questions. As you answer questions, remove the mark. Continue to review the remaining marked questions until your time expires or you complete the test.

That's it for pointers. Here are some questions for you to practice on.

Sample Test

Question 1

A DHCP-enabled client is moved from Subnet A to Subnet B. After the move, the users complain that they are no longer able to use TCP/IP. What is the possible cause for this problem?

○ a. DHCP cannot support multiple subnets.

○ b. The WINS server cannot see the client.

○ c. The default gateway was configured manually before the computer was moved.

○ d. The client did not terminate its lease before the computer was moved.

Question 2

A request is sent to an SNMP-managed device but no response is obtained. Assume the community name is correct, the OID is correct, and a request with other OIDs does elicit a response. What could be the problem?

○ a. The network is unstable.

○ b. The request is a **set** request.

○ c. There is no alarm condition.

○ d. This is not a manageable device.

Question 3

Which of the following describe a router? [Check all correct answers]

❑ a. A gateway

❑ b. An information service

❑ c. A specialized standalone device

❑ d. Software used to exchange email

Question 4

After monitoring your network for a week, you have concluded
that your Windows NT Server, which is acting as a router, is drop-
ping packets. Which of the following Registry settings can be used
to correct this problem? [Check all correct answers]

❏ a. TcpBufferSize

❏ b. TcpWindowSize

❏ c. ForwardBufferMemory

❏ d. NumForwardPackets

Question 5

By default, how many hosts will a Class B address support?

○ a. 65,534

○ b. 254

○ c. 2,097,152

○ d. 16,384

Question 6

By default, the first _____ octet(s) of a Class C address are used
to identify the network ID.

○ a. 1

○ b. 2

○ c. 3

○ d. 4

Question 7

Choose from the following options the answer that best describes the purpose of a subnet mask.

○ a. The subnet mask is used to help TCP/IP distinguish the network ID from the host ID. This aids in determining the IP address of other hosts.

○ b. The subnet mask aids in determining the location of other TCP/IP hosts.

○ c. The subnet mask is used to mask a portion of an IP address for TCP/IP.

○ d. The subnet mask is used to help TCP/IP distinguish the network ID from the host ID. This aids in determining the location of other TCP/IP hosts.

Question 8

Choose the option that best defines TCP/IP.

○ a. A suite of protocols designed by Microsoft to allow everyday people to access resources on the Internet

○ b. A suite of protocols that allows communication between different types of applications running on various platforms and in various network environments

○ c. A protocol designed by Microsoft to allow information to be routed between heterogeneous network environments

○ d A protocol designed by the IAB to allow many different hardware and software vendors to access the Internet

Question 9

Each of the following statements lists layers of the OSI Reference Model and the respective layers of the TCP/IP Reference Model. Which of the following statements correctly maps corresponding layers. [Check all correct answers]

❑ a. OSI Presentation and TCP/IP Application

❑ b. OSI Session and TCP/IP Transport

❑ c. OSI Network and TCP/IP Internet

❑ d. OSI Physical and TCP/IP Network Interface

Question 10

After checking its cache, what step does a computer take when resolving an address on the local network?

○ a. Sends a request to the router.

○ b. Sends a request to the ARP server.

○ c. Checks its HOSTS file for the information.

○ d. Sends a broadcast packet.

Question 11

As an administrator, you have recently implemented SNMP on your Windows NT system. However, you don't think it's working correctly. Which of the following applications can you use to troubleshoot SNMP errors?

○ a. Registry Editor

○ b. Event Viewer

○ c. Performance Monitor

○ d. Task Manager

Question 12

What is the binary value of the decimal number 213?

○ a. 11010101

○ b. 11100001

○ c. 11111000

○ d. 11111001

Question 13

UDP resides at which layer of the TCP/IP protocol stack? [Choose the best answer]

○ a. Network Interface

○ b. Internet

○ c. Transport

○ d. Application

Question 14

A new computer has been added to the network. Although you configured it yourself, the computer is having problems communicating. When you use IPCONFIG, you notice that the subnet mask is 0.0.0.0. What could be the problem?

○ a. There's another computer with the same DNS configuration.

○ b. There's another computer with the same WINS configuration.

○ c. There's another computer with the same NetBIOS name.

○ d. There's another computer with the same IP address.

Question 15

You have added a new **#PRE** entry to the LMHOSTS file to your computer and you want to verify that the changes you made are being used. Which of the following sets of commands will you use to test whether or not the file you edited is located in the correct directory and is being used for resolution?

○ a. **NBTSTAT -r**, followed by **NBTSTAT -c**

○ b. **NBTSTAT -R**, followed by **NBTSTAT -c**

○ c. **NETSTAT -r**, followed by **NBTSTAT -d**

○ d. **NETSTAT -R**, followed by **NBTSTAT -d**

Question 16

Juanita has just taken over the desktop support for her company. She is setting up a new laptop on the local subnet for the boss. During setup, she gets the following error message: "Your default gateway does not belong to one of the configured interfaces..." What should Juanita do?

○ a. Check the PCMCIA card and reinsert it.

○ b. Check the spelling of the default gateway entry in the LMHOSTS file.

○ c. Check the cabling.

○ d. Run IPCONFIG.

Question 17

Mary is having some problems with her TCP/IP network. She tries PINGing her local machine, the local gateway (router), and a remote router with success on every occasion. However, when she tries to use the **NET USE** command to set up a drive mapping to the Engineering server's NetBIOS name, the command fails. She tries the **NET VIEW** command with the NetBIOS name and it also fails. Finally, she tries a PING to the NetBIOS name and it succeeds. She calls the Engineering department and finds out that the computer is not hung and that she has typed the NetBIOS name correctly. What else can Mary do to troubleshoot this problem? [Check all correct answers]

❑ a. Check to make sure the Server service has started.

❑ b. Verify that a DNS is working properly and the HOSTS file is correct.

❑ c. Check to see whether the entry in question has been misspelled or entered incorrectly.

❑ d. Check to see whether there are two different machines with the same NetBIOS name and neither knows if the other has responded, so both machines refuse the connection.

Question 18

By using the Advanced IP Addressing properties sheet, how many addresses can be added to an interface?

○ a. 7

○ b. 8

○ c. 5

○ d. 6

Question 19

You have just installed the SNMP service on a Windows NT computer. Which of the following functions can you now perform? [Check all correct answers]

❏ a. Use the *Resource Kit* utilities to perform management functions.

❏ b. Monitor and configure parameters for any DHCP server.

❏ c. View and change parameters in the MIBs by using SNMP manager programs.

❏ d. Monitor and configure parameters for any WINS server.

Question 20

Shannon is getting ready to subnet his IP network and must determine the number of network IDs required before he can calculate an appropriate subnet mask for his network. Which of the following options would help him properly calculate the number of necessary network IDs? [Check all correct answers]

❏ a. Calculate a unique network ID for each network printer on a segment.

❏ b. Calculate a unique network ID for each segment of the network bordered by a router.

❏ c. Calculate only one unique network ID for network segments bordered by two or more routers.

❏ d. Calculate a unique network ID for each interface of a router.

Question 21

The Billington Steambath Company currently has nine divisions, and each one requires its own subnet. The company has been assigned the network ID 130.121.0.0. Billington anticipates the need to support up to 3,000 hosts in each division. Which subnet would you recommend that it use?

○   a.   255.255.240.0

○   b.   255.255.255.0

○   c.   255.255.224.0

○   d.   255.255.248.0

Question 22

Which of the following correctly states the order of the first four steps of the NetBIOS name resolution process?

○   a.   NetBIOS name cache, b-node broadcast, LMHOSTS, WINS

○   b.   WINS, NetBIOS name cache, b-node broadcast, LMHOSTS

○   c.   NetBIOS name cache, WINS, b-node broadcast, LMHOSTS

○   d.   B-node broadcast, WINS, NetBIOS name cache, LMHOSTS

Question 23

The following statements describe individual parts of the three-way handshake used to establish a session. Which of these statements is incorrect?

○   a.   "I have information for you, can we establish communication?"

○   b.   "Great, I received your response, here is the rest of the information."

○   c.   "Yes, I am available for communication. Continue with your transmission."

○   d.   "No, I am busy right now and don't have time for you. Try back in few minutes."

Question 24

The ROUTE utility can be used to perform what functions to a routing table? [Check all correct answers]

❑ a. Test a route.

❑ b. Add new routes.

❑ c. Remove entries.

❑ d. Display existing routes.

Question 25

Three attributes can be defined in the Only Accept SNMP Packets From These Hosts section of the SNMP Security tab. They are: [Check all correct answers]

❑ a. IPX address

❑ b. IP address

❑ c. MAC address

❑ d. Host name

Question 26

Using the default host name resolution order for Microsoft Windows NT, complete the following statement: "After checking the local _____, the _____ is consulted. If it cannot resolve the host name, TCP/IP will next consult the _____."

○ a. host name; the LMHOSTS file; NetBIOS name cache

○ b. HOSTS file; local DNS server; NetBIOS name cache

○ c. DNS server; NetBIOS name cache; local host name

○ d. NetBIOS name cache; WINS server; local HOSTS file

Question 27

What is the default time an entry will stay in the ARP cache?

○ a. 10 minutes

○ b. 20 minutes

○ c. 5 minutes

○ d. 1 minute

Question 28

What type of address resolution takes place with proxy ARP?

○ a. Remote address resolution

○ b. Local address resolution

○ c. Kinetic address resolution

○ d. Router address resolution

Question 29

What types of transactions can be performed by an SNMP agent? [Check all correct answers]

❑ a. Send trap

❑ b. **Get**

❑ c. **GetAll**

❑ d. **VarBind**

Question 30

Which items detailed in a routed packet are not the same when the packet reaches its destination as compared to their original values at the source host? [Check all correct answers]

☐ a. Source HWA

☐ b. Source IP address

☐ c. Destination HWA

☐ d. Destination IP address

Question 31

Which method of host name resolution uses a single static text file to resolve Internet names? [Choose the best answer]

○ a. LMHOSTS

○ b. HOSTS

○ c. Domain Name Space

○ d. Domain Name System

Question 32

Which of the following are benefits of subnetting a given network ID? [Check all correct answers]

☐ a. Subnetting allows the interconnection of networks that use different network technologies.

☐ b. Subnetting allows you to overcome the physical limitations of a network's capacity.

☐ c. Subnetting allows for an effective increase in network bandwidth by cutting down on the amount of broadcasts a network must process.

☐ d. Subnetting allows for the arbitrary allocation of IP addresses, regardless of host location.

Question 33

Which of the following are benefits of using DHCP? [Check all correct answers]

❑ a. Less chance of human error

❑ b. Centralized IP name resolution

❑ c. Dynamic NetBIOS name registration

❑ d. Dynamic IP configuration

Question 34

Which of the following are benefits of using WINS? [Check all correct answers]

❑ a. Dynamic NetBIOS name registration

❑ b. Dynamic IP configuration

❑ c. Reduction in broadcast traffic

❑ d. Increase in network throughput capacity

Question 35

Which of the following are items found in a static routing table? [Check all correct answers]

❑ a. Interface IP address

❑ b. Hop metric

❑ c. Network address

❑ d. Netmask

Question 36

Your Windows NT Workstation computer is attached to a network with numerous Unix machines. Which of the following utilities could you use to execute a command on one of those systems? [Check all correct answers]

❏ a. RPD

❏ b. REXEC

❏ c. RCP

❏ d. RSH

Question 37

Which of the following commands will not result in the HOSTS file being accessed?

○ a. **TRACERT**

○ b. **TFTP**

○ c. **NET VIEW**

○ d. **PING**

Question 38

Which of the following files contain DNS resource records for name resolution? [Check all correct answers]

❏ a. 12.122.205.IN-ADDR.ARPA.DNS

❏ b. Boot file

❏ c. CACHE.DNS

❏ d. LANW.COM.DNS

Question 39

In implementing your new TCP/IP network, you would like to use host names to identify computers on your network. Your boss, on the other hand, thinks that it's too much work to assign and keep track of the names. Which of the following arguments could you use to convince your boss to implement a host name system? [Check all correct answers]

❑ a. Host names are easier to remember than IP addresses.

❑ b. Host names allow you to assign several IP addresses to the same machine.

❑ c. Alphanumeric host names can convey more meaning than plain numeric IP addresses.

❑ d. The use of a host name to identify a machine allows the IP address and location of the machine to be transparent to the end user.

Question 40

Which of the following protocols uses Scope ID to limit communications?

○ a. NBT

○ b. TCP

○ c. NetBEUI

○ d. NWLink

Question 41

Which of the following statements about configuring a host name on a Windows NT machine are true? [Check all correct answers]

❑ a. You must change the default host name (that is, the original NetBIOS name) to some name other than the name that is currently being used as the NetBIOS name.

❑ b. By default, the NetBIOS name of the machine will be used as the host name.

❑ c. Any invalid characters in the NetBIOS name will be converted to dashes (-) in the host name.

❑ d. You can configure the host name and the DNS domain name in the DNS properties sheet of the TCP/IP properties.

Question 42

Which of the following statements are potential problems that can occur when using the LMHOSTS file? [Check all correct answers]

❑ a. The LMHOSTS file is not in the root directory of the system drive.

❑ b. The LMHOSTS file has been saved with an incorrect name or extension.

❑ c. The entry in question has been misspelled or entered incorrectly.

❑ d. There are two different entries for the same NetBIOS name, and the one that occurs first in the list is incorrect.

Question 43

Which of the following utilities can be used to administer the DHCP database?

○ a. IPCONFIG

○ b. JETPACK

○ c. DHCP Manager

○ d. Network applet

Question 44

Which of the following utilities is used to monitor printing on a remote Unix system?

○ a. LPD

○ b. LPS

○ c. LPQ

○ d. LPR

Question 45

Which of the following utilities is used to monitor the network? [Check all correct answers]

❑ a. WINS Monitor

❑ b. Ethernet Monitor

❑ c. Performance Monitor

❑ d. Network Monitor

Question 46

Which of the following utilities provide file transfer capabilities in a TCP/IP environment? [Check all correct answers]

❑ a. FTP

❑ b. RSH

❑ c. Telnet

❑ d. RCP

Question 47

Which types of names can WINS resolve for DNS?

- ○ a. Host
- ○ b. FQDN
- ○ c. Domain
- ○ d. Root

Question 48

Why is the dynamic routing protocol RIP limited to 15 hops?

- ○ a. To prevent infinite counting of looped paths.
- ○ b. To force large networks to be divided into smaller subnets.
- ○ c. No network system ever needs more than 15 hops.
- ○ d. The routing table uses hex codes to store hop values.

Question 49

You're attempting to resolve a communication problem with a computer named "bob15" on a remote subnet. You can successfully PING other computers on the same subnet as bob15; however, when you try to PING bob15, you get no response. Which of the following could be the problem? [Check all correct answers]

- ❑ a. Bob15 has a NetBIOS scope ID that is different from the other computers, including yours.
- ❑ b. Bob15 has an incorrect default gateway.
- ❑ c. Your default gateway is configured incorrectly.
- ❑ d. Bob15 is offline.

Question 50

You're getting ready to install and configure TCP/IP on your Windows NT Server. Which of the following items is not a requirement to complete the installation?

○ a. You must have a good understanding of the required settings and configurations.

○ b. You must be a member of the local administrators group for the machine you are configuring.

○ c. You must have some type of access to the original installation files.

○ d. You must be a domain administrator for the domain in which the machine is installed.

Question 51

You're thinking about creating an application that will require a constant end-to-end connection with another machine that is running a corresponding service. You do not want to include code in your program that ensures the data is arriving at its destination in an orderly and timely fashion. With these requirements in mind, which of the following protocols is most appropriate for use with your application?

○ a. TCP

○ b. UDP

○ c. ARP

○ d. ICMP

Question 52

You have been asked to configure several Windows NT workstations for your company's network that uses DNS and WINS for name resolution.

Required Result:

- The computers must be able to communicate with each other via a computer name, Internet-style name, or IP address.

Optional Desired Results:

- Keep the broadcast traffic to a minimum.

- Give the clients a level of fault tolerance for name resolution if the primary WINS server is unavailable.

Proposed Solution:

- Place an LMHOSTS file on each computer that has mappings for the computer names and IP addresses.

Which results does the proposed solution produce?

- O a. The proposed solution produces the required result and produces both of the optional desired results.

- O b. The proposed solution produces the required result and produces only one of the optional results.

- O c. The proposed solution produces the required result but does not produce any of the optional desired results.

- O d. The proposed solution does not produce the required result.

Question 53

You have been asked to provide dynamic name resolution for your entire network. Your network is configured as shown in the following graphic. What is the minimum number of WINS Proxy Agents you require and where would you put them?

- O a. None

- O b. Two, one for segment H and one for segment B

- O c. Seven, one for each segment except segment A

- O d. One, for segment H

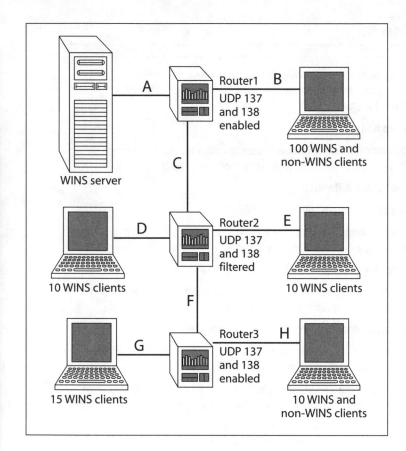

Question 54

You have just received a new Windows NT Workstation and you seem to be having trouble mapping a drive to a Windows NT host that resides on a remote network. Your network does not currently have a WINS server providing NetBIOS name resolution. Which of the following files should you modify to enable Windows NT to correctly resolve the name of the Windows host to which you are trying to connect?

○ a. HOSTS

○ b. LMHOST

○ c. LMHOSTS

○ d. HOST

Question 55

You have just received a new Windows NT Workstation. You are able to connect to other IP machines on your local subnetwork using the UNC name of the targeted resource, but you seem to be having trouble mapping a drive to a Windows NT host that resides on a remote network. However, no one else is having problems connecting to the remote Windows NT host. What is the first thing you should check?

○ a. Your default gateway setting

○ b. The other machine's default gateway setting

○ c. The other machine's IP address

○ d. Your IP address

Question 56

You manage a network of 1,500 Microsoft clients, all configured to use DHCP. You have been asked to implement WINS on your network for NetBIOS name resolution. What is the easiest way to configure these client computers to use WINS?

○ a. Configure the DHCP server with option 44 WINS/NBNS only.

○ b. Configure each client with the address of the WINS server manually.

○ c. Configure the DHCP server with options 44 WINS/NBNS and 46 WINS/NBT.

○ d. Configure the DHCP server with option 46 WINS/NBT only.

Question 57

Your company has configured seven different Internet-style domains for your network. You are responsible for the South-western domain. Which of the following could you implement to distribute the name resolution load on your domain? [Check all correct answers]

❏ a. Caching-only server

❏ b. Primary name server

❏ c. DNS Round-Robin

❏ d. Secondary zone

Question 58

You have established a Telnet session with a remote computer named "Sales," but the banner displays the name "Accnt." You check the IP address, and it appears to be right. What should you check next? [Check all correct answers]

❏ a. The DNS name and HOSTS tables to make sure they are current and correct

❏ b. The two computers on the network to make sure they don't have the same IP address

❏ c. **arp -g**

❏ d. This is not possible

Answer Key
To Sample Test

1. c
2. b
3. a,c
4. c,d
5. a
6. c
7. d
8. b
9. a,c,d
10. d
11. b
12. a
13. c
14. d
15. b
16. d
17. a,b,c
18. c
19. a,d
20. b,c

21. a
22. c
23. d
24. b,c,d
25. a,b,d
26. b
27. a
28. a
29. a,b
30. a,c
31. b
32. a,b,c
33. a,d
34. a,c
35. a,b,c,d
36. b,d
37. c
38. a,c,d
39. a,c,d
40. a

41. b,c,d
42. b,c,d
43. b
44. c
45. c,d
46. a,d
47. a
48. a
49. a,b,d
50. d
51. a
52. d
53. d
54. c
55. a
56. c
57. a,d
58. a,b,c

Question 1

The correct answer is c. If anything was configured manually, the DHCP configuration would not override it. Regardless of whether the client terminated its lease, the lease process will begin again when the computer is booted on the new subnet. Therefore, answer d is incorrect. DHCP does support multiple subnets if the router is able to act as a relay agent. Therefore, answer a is incorrect. The WINS server has nothing to do with the computer's TCP/IP configuration. Therefore, answer b is incorrect.

Question 2

The correct answer is b, because a *set* request does not require a response. Answer a is not plausible because other OIDs do elicit responses. If an alarm condition existed, a trap would be sent. Therefore, answer c is incorrect. Answer d is incorrect because the first condition of the question is that the device is manageable.

Question 3

A router can be a gateway or a standalone device. Therefore, answers a and c are correct. A router is not an information service. Therefore, answer b is incorrect. And, although they may sometimes be described this way, email exchange programs are generally gateways, not routers. Therefore, answer d is incorrect.

Question 4

The correct answers for this question are c and d. Each of these settings defines how routed packets are handled in memory. ForwardBufferMemory defines how much data can be stored, whereas NumForwardPackets defines the number of packets in the queue. TcpWindowSize defines the amount of data that can be outstanding on the network before acknowledgment. Therefore, answer b is incorrect. TcpBufferSize is a bogus, nonexistent Registry setting. Therefore, answer a is incorrect.

Question 5

The correct answer for this question is a. The formula for determining the host IDs any number of bits will support is 2^n-2, where n is the number of bits available for use in the host ID. By default, a Class B address uses 16 bits for the host ID. Thus, $2^{16}-2$ equals 65,534. The number of hosts that a Class C address supports, by default, is 254; the number of network IDs available in the

Class C address space, by default, is 2,097,152; and the number of network IDs available in the Class B address space, by default, is 16,384. Therefore, answers b, c, and d are all incorrect.

Question 6

The correct answer for this question is c. By default, the first three octets of a Class C address represent the network ID. The default for a Class A address is the first octet, and the default for a Class B address is the first two octets. Although you can change the number of octets that represent the network ID by changing the subnet mask, this question is asking for the default values Therefore, answers a, b, and d are incorrect.

Question 7

The best answer for this question is d. The subnet mask is used by a TCP/IP host to help it determine its own network ID during initialization. It then uses this information to determine whether the destination host resides on the local network or a remote network. Answer b is partially correct, but it's not the best answer because it does not give enough information. Answer c is not correct for the same reason. Answer a is incorrect because the subnet mask does not help TCP/IP determine the IP address of another host. The remote host's IP address must be known before the subnet mask will be of any use.

Question 8

The correct answer for this question is b. TCP/IP allows for network communication between applications and services running on almost any platform, including Unix, Windows, Macintosh, and others. TCP/IP was not designed by Microsoft, although it created its implementation of this protocol. Therefore, answers a and c are incorrect. And, although the IAB and its subcommittee, the IETF, are involved in the TCP/IP standards process, they did not design TCP/IP themselves. Therefore, answer d is incorrect.

Question 9

The correct answers for this question are a, c, and d. The TCP/IP Application layer encompasses the Session, Presentation, and Applications layers of the OSI Model; the Network layer corresponds to the Internet layer of the TCP/IP Model; and the TCP/IP Network Interface layer handles the functions of both the Physical and Data Link layers in OSI. As you can see by the answer, the functions of the Session layer of the OSI model are actually handled by the Application layer in TCP/IP. Therefore, answer b is incorrect.

Question 10

The correct answer for this question is d. If the computer does not find the destination hardware address in its cache, it sends a broadcast packet to the network. Answer a is incorrect because it's a local address resolution; the router is queried only for remote resolutions. Answer b is incorrect because there's no such creature as an ARP server. The HOSTS file does not contain address resolution information. Therefore, answer c is incorrect.

Question 11

The correct answer for this question is b. The Event Viewer, more than any other application, can easily identify problems sending or receiving SNMP packets.

Question 12

The correct answer is a. To answer this question correctly, you must be able to convert decimal numbers to binary digits. This can be done by memorizing the sequence 128+64+32+16+8+4+2+1 and then choosing the largest number that will go into the decimal number without exceeding it. In this question, the number you would select first is 128. Now, choose the largest number remaining that, when added to the original selection, will not exceed the decimal value being sought. Continue this operation from left to right (largest to smallest values) until you obtain the decimal value you're seeking. For this question, the value would be 128+64+0+16+0+4+0+1, which equals 213. Now that you have the decimal value being sought, replace each nonzero number with a 1. What you are left with is the binary value for the decimal number with which you began. Here, this would be 11010101, which makes a the correct answer.

Question 13

The correct answer is c. The User Datagram Protocol (UDP) resides at the Transport layer of the TCP/IP Reference Model.

Question 14

The correct answer to this question is d. TCP/IP uses ARP to resolve IP addresses to MAC addresses. Therefore, if two machines have the same IP address, TCP/IP will fail. DNS and WINS configurations have no affect on the IP address of a machine. Therefore, answers a and b are incorrect. Duplicate NetBIOS names are kicked out with an error notifying the user that a duplicate name exists. Therefore, answer c is incorrect.

Question 15

The correct answer for this question is b. This is because NBTSTAT (NetBIOS utility) allows you to purge the NetBIOS name cache and reload it with entries from the LMHOSTS file with the use of the *-R* option. Once the name cache has been successfully purged and reloaded from the LMHOSTS file, you can use the *NBTSTAT -c* (cache) option to view the new contents of the NetBIOS name cache. The presence of the newly added preloaded (*#PRE*) NetBIOS name in the NetBIOS name cache indicates that the LMHOSTS file was found in the correct directory and is being used for NetBIOS name resolution.

The lowercase **-r** option for NBTSTAT shows a list of statistics relating to registered and resolved NetBIOS names and the method used to resolve the name (either WINS or broadcast). Therefore, answer a is incorrect. The NETSTAT command does not provide NetBIOS information. Therefore, answers c and d are incorrect. In addition, there's no documented **-d** option for the NBTSTAT utility. Therefore, any answers containing these options are wrong.

Question 16

The correct answer is d. To find out whether the configured default gateway is located on the same logical network, run IPCONFIG (or WINIPCFG if using Windows 95). Compare the network ID portion of the gateway with the network ID(s) of the PCMCIA network adapter. The network portion of the IP addresses must match in order for the default gateway to be on the same network. If the problem were cabling, Setup probably wouldn't have been able to find the network. Therefore, answer a is incorrect; same for answer c. The LMHOSTS file is not used by the Setup program. Therefore, answer b is incorrect.

Question 17

The correct answers for this question are a, b, and c. Answer a is correct because the server may respond to a PING even though the Server service hasn't been started. The Server service is needed to establish the connection. Answer b is correct because commands such as NET USE may time-out before the HOSTS name resolution can take over, but PING will still be re-solved. Answer c is correct because the NetBIOS name must be spelled correctly both at the command line and in the HOSTS file. Answer d is simply incorrect.

Question 18

The correct answer for this question is c. Windows NT will allow you to configure up to five IP addresses through the Advanced IP Addressing interface. It's possible to add more, but this must be done through the Registry. Therefore, answers a, b, and d are incorrect.

Question 19

Only answers a and d are correct. Answer c is partially incorrect: The administrator may monitor but not configure DHCP server parameters. Answer b is partially correct: once the SNMP service is installed, the administrator can view and change parameters in the LAN Manager and MIB-II MIBs only, not in all MIBs.

Question 20

The correct answers to this question are b and c. When determining the number of unique network IDs needed for a network, you need to calculate one unique network ID for each segment of your network bordered by at least one router. However, a closed network (one without outside access) that has two routers with two interfaces each would require three separate network IDs (answer c must be used in conjunction with answer b). Answer a is incorrect because each network printer or host on a network segment requires a unique host ID, but they all share the same network ID. Some of those interfaces might be attached to a single segment in multiple routers, and all of them would share an identical network address, even though each one must have a unique host address. Therefore answer d is incorrect.

Question 21

The correct answer for this question is a. The ".240" value in the third octet of the subnet mask allows for a total of 14 subnets on this network. This subnet mask meets the requirements of the currently needed network IDs and allows for future growth. Additionally, this subnet allows for a maximum of 4,094 hosts per subnet. This subnet meets the requirements of the Billington Steambath Company. Answers b and d are incorrect because, although they provide the required number of subnets, they do not allow for the anticipated number of hosts per subnet. Answer c is incorrect because it does not provide enough subnets to meet the current needs of the company.

Question 22

The correct answer to this question is c. By default, a Windows NT machine that's configured to contact at least a primary WINS server uses h-node resolution. The hybrid form of resolution first checks the NetBIOS name cache and then the WINS server. If WINS cannot resolve the requested name, the sending host initiates a broadcast to the local network in order to locate a machine that responds to the name being resolved. If no response is received, the sending host then checks for the presence of an entry in the local LMHOSTS file, assuming that it has been configured to do so.

Question 23

The correct answer for this question is d. The three-way handshake does not include a "No" response from the recipient machine. If the machine is unavailable, it simply doesn't respond. If it is available but is getting bogged down with other transmissions, it uses a flow-control mechanism such as "source quench" to ask the sending client to slow the transmission of data. Answers a, c, and d are the correct format of the handshake messages.

Question 24

The ROUTE utility can add new routes (with the *add* command), remove gateway entries (with -*f* parameter), and display existing routes (with the *print* command). Therefore, answers b, c, and d are correct. The ROUTE utility cannot test a route—TRACERT is used for that function. Therefore, answer a is incorrect.

Question 25

The correct answers are a, b, and d. The MAC address cannot be used to specify a host. Therefore, answer c is incorrect.

Question 26

The correct answer to this question is b. The configuration of a particular Windows NT machine can cause one or several of the default name resolution steps to be skipped. Therefore, several of the proposed answers will appear to be correct at first glance. However, only b has three steps of the process in the correct order. Remember that host name resolution has the following order, by default: Local host name>HOSTS file>DNS>NetBIOS name cache>WINS>Broadcast>LMHOSTS. Answer a is incorrect because right after checking the local host name, TCP/IP checks the HOSTS file. Answer c is incorrect because, by default, TCP/IP on Windows NT tries the local host name before it tries any other method of name resolution. Answer d is incorrect because, by default, the HOSTS file is consulted before any type of NetBIOS name resolution is attempted.

Question 27

The correct answer for this question is a. Unless configured otherwise, an entry will stay in the ARP cache for 10 minutes.

Question 28

The correct answer to this question is a. Proxy ARP is another term for remote address resolution, because the default gateway or router acts as a Proxy Agent for the local computer. Local address resolution does not involve a proxy of any kind. Therefore, answer b is incorrect. Kinetic address resolution sounds good, but does not exist. Router address resolution is also a fictional term. Therefore, answers c and d are incorrect as well.

Question 29

The correct answers are a and b. The agent performs *get* requests, except in the case of an alarm condition, when it sends a trap to the trap destination. One example of this would be a host shutdown. There's no such command as **GetAll**. Therefore, answer c is incorrect. **VarBind** is a data structure that consists of an OID and a value structure. Therefore, answer d is incorrect.

Question 30

The source and destination hardware addresses (HWA) change each time a packet traverses a router or makes a hop. Therefore, answers a and c are correct. The source and destination IP addresses remain the same throughout the transmission of routed packets. Therefore, answers b and d are incorrect.

Question 31

The correct answer here is b. The tricky part to this question is listing the LMHOSTS file, which is a static name-resolution file. However, the LMHOSTS file is primarily used to resolve NetBIOS names, not host names. Therefore, a is incorrect. Domain Name Space and Domain Name System are used in a distributed name resolution system and not a single text file. Therefore, c and d are incorrect.

Question 32

The correct answers for this question are a, b, and c. Because routers can often transfer information from Ethernet networks to Token Ring networks, and vice versa, subnetting your network can allow hosts that use different network technologies to communicate with one another. Subnetting also allows you to overcome the inherent physical limitations of a particular network technology such as Ethernet, which can support only a limited number of hosts per physical network segment. If you currently have more hosts than Ethernet can support on a single network segment, subnetting allows you to spread those hosts out over multiple physical network segments. Finally, on a related issue, because subnetting physically isolates each segment of a network from the other segments, the number of broadcasts that must be processed by any one network is reduced substantially. This effectively increases the available bandwidth of each subnet. Answer d is incorrect because the act of subnetting requires that IP addresses be assigned to hosts in a very specific manner, according to which subnet the host resides on.

Question 33

The correct answers for this question are a and d. One of the major reasons for choosing DHCP is its capability to dynamically configure hosts (hence its name). Because configuration is centralized at the server, a smaller chance exists that someone will screw up. Centralized IP name resolution is done by DNS, not DHCP. Therefore, answer b is incorrect. DHCP does not concern itself with NetBIOS name registration, even though WINS server addresses can be assigned by DHCP. Therefore, answer c is incorrect.

Question 34

The correct answers for this question are a and c. WINS also provides dynamic (automatic) name registration, release, and discovery services. WINS does reduce broadcast traffic on the network because WINS clients use the WINS server for name resolution instead of broadcasting. DHCP provides dynamic IP configuration, not WINS. Therefore, answer b is incorrect. Although fewer broadcasts can, in essence, increase capacity, answer d is incorrect; this usually requires a hardware upgrade and has nothing to do with WINS or name resolution.

Question 35

A static routing table is comprised of five items: network address, netmask, gateway address, interface IP address, and hop metric. Therefore, all the answers are correct.

Question 36

The correct answers for this question are b and d. Both RSH (remote shell) and REXEC (remote execute) can be used to run a command on a remote system. However, remember that a password is required for REXEC. RCP will copy files, but nothing more. Therefore, answer c is incorrect. RPD is a bogus acronym. Therefore, answer a is incorrect.

Question 37

The correct answer for this question is c because *NET VIEW* is one of the many NetBIOS network commands that can be used with Windows NT. This command results in a list of currently available NetBIOS resources, such as servers and network shares. TFTP, TRACERT, PING, Telnet, FTP, and even Web browsers are all applications that access the HOSTS file when they are given a host name (assuming that the host is properly configured to access this file).

Question 38

The correct answers for this question are a, c, and d. The boot file contains only information that is used when starting DNS. Each of the other files listed is used for name resolution. The CACHE.DNS file is used to point your name server to the root servers at the InterNIC that are used for name resolution. The file name 12.122.205.IN-ADDR.ARPA.DNS indicates that this file is for the Class C address 205.122.12.0 and is used for inverse name queries. LANW.COM.DNS is a file that would hold resource records name resolution on the lanw.com domain.

Question 39

Answers a, c, and d are all valid arguments for host names. Answer b, on the other hand, is not a true statement when dealing with host names. Therefore, it's incorrect.

Question 40

The correct answer to this question is a. NBT (NetBIOS over TCP/IP) is the only protocol that supports this function. Some people may be confused because TCP is involved in this process, but it does not support Scope ID.

Question 41

The correct answers for this question are b, c, and d. By default, Windows NT uses its NetBIOS name as the host name for TCP/IP. Windows NT converts any nonvalid characters in the NetBIOS name to dashes in the host name. If you want to change the host name to something other than the default, you may do so in the Network Control Panel|Protocols|TCP/IP Properties|DNS tab. Answer a is incorrect because it's not mandatory that you change the default host name.

Question 42

The correct answers for this question are b, c, and d. Answer b is correct because, while editing the LMHOSTS file, it's possible that you might save the file with the wrong name (for example, LMHOST) or save it with an extension such as ".SAM" or ".TXT." The correct name for this file is LMHOSTS. Typos and spelling mistakes are quite common when editing text files such as the LMHOSTS file. Therefore, answer c is correct. Answer d is correct because the LMHOSTS file is parsed from top to bottom, a line at a time. When a matching entry is found, the NetBIOS name resolution process stops, whether there's another entry in the file or not. This problem occurs most often in environments where large LMHOSTS files must be maintained. Answer a is incorrect because the LMHOSTS file is supposed to reside in the *systemroot*\system32 \drivers\etc directory, not the root of the drive that contains the system files.

Question 43

The correct answer to this question is b. JETPACK is used to compress the DHCP database. IPCONFIG is used to view configuration information and to renew or release a DHCP lease, but it cannot administer the database. The DHCP Manager can be used to modify the database, but administration generally refers to backup, restoring, and compression, rather than management. The Network applet is used to install DHCP, but that is where its usefulness ends.

Question 44

The answer to this question is c. Remember that LPQ is used to check the print queue on a remote system. LPD is the daemon that enables printing from remote systems. Therefore, answer a is incorrect. LPR sends the job to a remote printer. Therefore, answer d is incorrect. Finally, LPS is an acronym for Lilly's Publishing Service, but not for TCP/IP printing. Therefore, answer b is incorrect.

Question 45

Answers c and d are correct. Both Performance Monitor and Network Monitor are able to trace network events. Answers a and b, although they would be handy, do not exist.

Question 46

The correct answers to this question are a and d. FTP provides full file transfer with security via user names and passwords, whereas RCP copies files to a remote system using user names assigned in the. RHOSTS file. Telnet is a terminal emulation application, but it does not provide file transfer. Therefore, answer c is incorrect. RSH is able to execute a command on a remote system, but it's not able to transfer files. Therefore, answer b is incorrect.

Question 47

The correct answer here is a. Probably the only trick here is knowing that even though DNS resolves FQDNs, it sends only the host portion of the name to the WINS server. Domain names and root names would not be handled by the WINS server because they are outside of the scope of WINS.

Question 48

RIP is limited to 15 hops to prevent infinite counting of looped paths. Therefore, answer a is correct. The 15-hop limitation encourages larger single networks, not several small ones; many network systems, such as the Internet, use more than 15 hops; and routing tables do not use hex codes to store hop values. Therefore, answers b, c, and d are incorrect.

Question 49

The correct answers are a, b, and d. Your default gateway must be configured correctly if the other computers on the same subnet as bob15 can respond to you. Therefore, answer c is incorrect. However, if bob15 has an incorrect default gateway, the reply from the PING could not be returned to you. **Bob15 could have a NetBIOS scope ID set in its WINS configuration tab that is different than yours. Only computers with the same NetBIOS scope ID can communicate with one another. Therefore, if bob15 were configured with one Scope ID and the other computers' Scope IDs were left blank (or configured with a different set of characters than bob15), bob15 could not communicate with the others. Of course, if a computer is offline or shut down, it will also not be able to communicate on the network.**

Question 50

The correct answer for this question is d. You don't need to be a domain administrator when installing or configuring TCP/IP on a standard NT Workstation or Server. However, the statements made in a, b, and c are all necessary requirements.

Question 51

The correct answer for this question is a. The Transmission Control Protocol (TCP) provides a "reliable" connection-oriented session, over IP, with another client or server on the network. Answer b is incorrect because User Datagram Protocol (UDP) is "unreliable" and makes only a "best-effort" attempt when sending information. Answers c and d are also incorrect. ARP is used by IP to resolve IP addresses to hardware addresses, and it does not provide for the reliable transmission of data. ICMP is also used by IP to send error and flow-control messages to a client, and it does not provide for the reliable transmission of data.

Question 52

The answer to this question is d; this solution does not meet the required result. An LMHOSTS file is not used to resolve Internet-style names, such as www.microsoft.com; you would need a DNS server or HOSTS file for that purpose. Remember, if a solution in a question like this does not meet the required results, you don't have to worry about the optional results!

Question 53

The correct answer to this question is d; only segment H requires a WINS Proxy Agent. If you thought a was the correct answer, look again at Router 2. Router 2 is going to filter broadcasts from the non-WINS clients on segment H before they reach the WINS server on segment A. Segment B does not require a WINS Proxy Agent because Router 1 will forward broadcasts to segment A. Only subnets B and H contain non-WINS clients. Therefore, only those subnets should be considered candidates for WINS Proxy Agent.

Question 54

The correct answer for this question is c. Remember that both the HOSTS file and the LMHOSTS file can contain multiple friendly-name-to-IP-address mappings. Therefore, the names of each of these files take the plural and not the singular form.

Question 55

The correct answer is a. Remember that the default gateway must be located on the same logical network as the host, and it must be configured properly in the network configuration for the local host. If the other system's default gateway setting is incorrect, no one would be able to communicate with it. Therefore, answer b is incorrect. The same applies if the IP address of the remote system is incorrect. Therefore, answer c is incorrect. If your IP address is incorrect, you would not be able to communicate at all. Therefore, answer d is incorrect.

Question 56

The best answer for this question is c. There are 1,500 computers, so you don't want to run around and configure the clients manually if you are using DHCP. You cannot add option 44 without option 46 on the DHCP server.

Question 57

The correct answers to this question are a and d. DNS Round-Robin does not allow you to distribute the name resolution load. Instead, this is a method for DNS to distribute the load of client requests to your network servers by resolving names to alternating addresses. A primary name server will not help because it would handle name resolution for another domain rather than the one on which you're presently working. The options you have are to configure a secondary zone or add a caching-only name server to your existing zone.

Question 58

The correct answers for this question are a, b, and c. By default, the ARP module believes the first response it receives, so an impostor's reply could reach the local computer before the intended computer's reply. If you have ruled out a faulty DNS name and verified the HOSTS tables, use the arp-g command at the local computer to display the mappings in the ARP cache. If you know the Ethernet address of the remote computer, make sure it matches what's in the cache. If you don't, delete the entry using arp -d, force a new ARP by PINGing the same address, and check the Ethernet address again to see if it matches the first one. If there really is an impostor on the network, chances are good that you'll eventually find a mismatch. Use Network Monitor for further trouble-shooting to locate the owner or the system causing the problems.

Glossary

. . . .

#DOM tag—In an LMHOSTS file entry, the **#DOM** tag represents a particular domain controller for a particular domain.

#PRE tag—In NetBIOS-name-to-IP-address mapping, indicates that the preceding entry should be preloaded into the name cache.

administrator—The person responsible for the upkeep, management, and security of a network. Also, when capitalized (Administrator), a built-in user in Windows NT that has full control of the system.

agents—In TCP/IP, software in SNMP-managed devices that responds to **get** and **set** requests and can send trap messages.

alphanumeric host names—A host name that contains letters and numbers.

ANDing—The process used by TCP/IP to determine whether the destination host is on a local or remote subnet.

API (Application Programming Interface)—A message and language format that allows programmers to use functions within another program.

Application layer—Layer 7 of the OSI Model. It's responsible for allowing applications to gain network access. User applications and system services generally gain network access by interacting with a process running at this layer of the OSI Model.

architecture—The term used to describe how a network is set up and how the network's components are connected to each other.

ARP (Address Resolution Protocol)—The Internet layer protocol responsible for determining the hardware address (also called a *MAC address*) that corresponds to a particular IP address.

ARP cache—The storage area for the IP-address-to-hardware-address information for hosts on the network.

ARPANet (Advanced Research Project Agency Network)—A packet-switching network, funded by ARPA, that served as the central Internet backbone for a number of years.

ASCII (American Standard Code for Information Interchange)—A way of coding that translates letters, numbers, and symbols into digital form.

ASN (Abstract Syntax Notation)—A precise definition language that describes MIBs. ASN can be thought of as a compiled language like COBOL, FORTRAN, or C.

assessment exam—Similar to the certification exam, this type of exam gives you the opportunity to answer questions at your own pace. It also uses the same tools as the certification exam.

ATEC (Authorized Technical Education Center)—The location where you can take a Microsoft Official Curriculum course taught by Microsoft Certified Trainers.

ATM (Asynchronous Transfer Mode)—A high-speed transmission technology that supports data, real-time voice, and real-time video.

BDC (Backup Domain Controller)—A backup server that protects the integrity and availability of the SAM database. BDCs are not able to make changes or modifications, but they can use the database to authenticate users.

beta exam—A trial exam that is given to participants at a Sylvan Prometric Testing Center before the development of the Microsoft Certified Professional certification exam is finalized. The final exam questions are selected based on the results of the beta exam. For example, if all beta exam participants get an answer correct or wrong, that question generally will not appear in the final version.

binary—The way data is rendered on a computer; everything is either on or off, true or false, ones or zeros.

BIND (Berkeley Internet Name Domain)—A specification of the DNS that came from the University of California at Berkeley.

b-node broadcast—A broadcast initiated by the local host to the local network if the WINS server is unable to provide NetBIOS name resolution.

boot disk—A hard drive or floppy drive that has bootstrap files on it. The bootstrap files enable an operating system to launch.

boot file—A startup configuration file that contains the information required to resolve names outside of official domains.

BOOTP (Bootstrap Protocol)—A protocol that allows the startup and automatic configuration of TCP/IP by diskless clients. BOOTP is the basis for DHCP.

bottlenecks—The effect of trying to force too much information through a system with inadequate bandwidth, which causes the system to slow significantly.

browsing—The ability to view the presence of and use NetBIOS network resources without having previous knowledge of their existence or location.

cache—A specified area of high-speed memory used to contain data that is going to be, or recently has been, accessed.

cache-only name server—A name server that caches name resolutions.

CIDR (Classless Inter-Domain Routing)—A method used to expand the number of subnetworks available within the current IP address length. CIDR defines the host and subnet portions of an IP address according to the number of bits used.

classes—A method of network addressing that easily establishes the distinction between host and subnet by making the delineation at octet breaks.

CNAMEs (canonical name records)—Aliases for host names. These records allow you to associate more than one host name with an IP address.

community names—Used by SNMP to define access to software agents.

computername—The name of a computer on a LAN that is specific to an individual workstation or server.

Control Panel—In Windows, the area where you modify settings such as fonts, screen color, SCSI hardware, and printers.

CPU (Central Processing Unit)—The brains of your computer—the area where all functions are performed.

cut score—On the Microsoft Certified Professional exam, the lowest score a person can receive and still pass.

daemon—A Unix program that provides services such as FTP or TFTP to clients.

Data Link layer—Layer 2 of the OSI Model. It's comprised of two sublayers: the Logical Link Control (LLC) sublayer and the Media Access Control (MAC) sublayer. Together, these two sublayers are responsible for moving packets onto and off of the network.

database—A collection of information arranged and stored so that data can be accessed quickly and accurately.

datagram—Another term for a packet of data, usually associated with connectionless services such as UDP.

default—A setting that is factory set and used until the user specifies otherwise.

DHCP (Dynamic Host Configuration Protocol)—A service that enables the assignment of dynamic TCP/IP network addresses, based on a specified pool of available addresses.

DHCP Relay—The process used to enable the routers in your network, between the DHCP server and DHCP clients, to forward the DHCP (BOOTP) broadcast packets.

DNS (Domain Name System)—A distributed database of host- and domain-name-to-IP-address mappings that is used to provide name resolution services for TCP/IP client applications.

domain—A group of computers and peripheral devices sharing a common security database.

Domain Master Browser—In Windows NT networks, a browser that communicates resource lists across subnets within the same domain.

domain name—The name of a group of workstations and servers on a network.

Domain Name Space—The structure and data that create the distributed Domain Name System used on the Internet.

DOS (Disk Operating System)—The most popular of all PC operating systems. It provides a primitive command-line driven, runtime environment for x86-based computers.

dotted-decimal notation—The way of representing an IP address as four groups of numbers, called *octets*, each separated by a dot (.).

DWORD entries—One type of Registry entry.

dynamic routing—Routing that automatically accommodates any changes in the network traffic or topology.

echo packets—Packets used by ICMP in response to PING requests.

encryption—A method of coding data in which a person has to have a decoding key to decipher the information.

Ethernet—The most widely used type of LAN; developed by Xerox.

Exam Preparation Guides—Guides that provide information specific to the material covered on Microsoft Certified Professional exams to help students prepare for the exam.

Exam Study Guide—Short for Microsoft Certified Professional Program Exam Study Guide, this contains information about the topics covered on more than one of the Microsoft Certified Professional exams.

fault tolerance—The capability of a computer to work continuously, even when system failure occurs.

firewall—A barrier (made of software and/or hardware) between two networks, permitting only authorized communication to pass.

FQDN (fully qualified domain name)—The complete site name of an Internet computer system.

FTP (File Transfer Protocol)—A protocol that transfers files to and from a local hard drive to an FTP server located on another TCP/IP-based network (such as the Internet).

gateway—A dedicated computer or router that has a more complete list of the surrounding networks than does each host device within a single network.

gateway address—The column of data in the routing table that represents the IP address of the entrance point (router interface) for each network.

Gopher service—An Internet service that provides text-only information over the Internet. A Gopher service is most suited to large documents with little or no formatting or images.

GUI (graphical user interface)—A computer setup that uses graphics, windows, and a trackball or mouse as the method of interaction with the computer.

hard drive—The permanent storage area for data. It is also called the *hard disk*.

hardware—The physical components of a computer system.

hexadecimal value—A numbering system that includes 16 characters—6 letters and 10 digits. It's used to condense large binary numbers.

host—A computer system or device connected to an internetwork.

host ID—An IP address that identifies a specific host on a network.

host name—A name or alias assigned to a TCP/IP host that is easier to remember than the numeric IP address.

host name resolution—A mechanism used to convert host names or domain names into numeric IP addresses.

HOSTS file—A file containing a list of host names and their corresponding IP addresses.

HTML (Hypertext Markup Language)—Based on SGML, the markup language used to create Web pages.

HTTP (Hypertext Transfer Protocol)—The World Wide Web protocol that allows for the transfer of HTML documents over the Internet or intranets and responds to actions (such as a user clicking on hypertext links).

HWA (hardware address)—In networks, the low-level address associated with hardware devices. The HWA is associated with the number on the network interface card.

IAB (Internet Architecture Board)—The organization responsible for individual or company submissions of RFCs.

ICMP (Internet Control Message Protocol)—A protocol used by IP and other higher level protocols to send and receive status reports about the information being transmitted.

IGMP (Internet Group Management Protocol)—The protocol used for IP multicasting. Used to establish a group to which to send multicasts.

IIS (Internet Information Server)—Web server software by Microsoft; included and implemented with Windows NT Server.

INETSTP—The name of the EXE file that installs the IIS program; it's located in the *processor*\INETSRV directory.

input/output system—A system that requires input into an input device (such as a keyboard) and outputs.

interface—The column of data in the routing table that represents the HWA assigned to the network's interface point.

Internet—The collection of publicly accessible TCP/IP-based networks around the world.

Internet layer—The layer of the DoD's TCP/IP networking model that roughly corresponds to the Network layer of the OSI Model. IP resides at this layer.

InterNIC (Internet Network Information Center)—The organization responsible for allocating and assigning IP addresses to those who want to connect their networks with the Internet.

intranet—An internal, private network that uses the same protocols and standards as the Internet.

IP address—Four sets of numbers, separated by decimal points, that represent the numeric address of a computer attached to a TCP/IP network, such as the Internet.

IPCONFIG—A Windows NT command-line utility that provides you with most TCP/IP configuration information, without requiring you to access the Network Control Panel.

IPX/SPX (Internetwork Packet eXchange/Sequenced Packet eXchange)—Novell's NetWare protocol, reinvented by Microsoft and implemented in Windows NT under the name NWLink. It's fully compatible with Novell's version and, in many cases, is a better implementation than the original.

ISM (Internet Service Manager)—A utility used to monitor and configure IIS services.

ISO (International Standards Organization)—An international body that was formed to develop network protocol standards and created the Open Systems Interconnection (OSI) Reference Model.

ISP (Internet Service Provider)—An organization that charges a fee for providing your Internet connection and other related services.

iterative name query—A query used between name servers to obtain partial name resolutions.

JETPACK—The utility used to compact Windows NT databases, including the WINS and DHCP databases.

job function expert—A person with extensive knowledge about a particular job function and the software products/technologies related to that job. Typically, a job function expert is currently performing the job, has recently performed the job, or is training people to do this job.

LAN (local area network)—A network confined to a single building or geographic area and comprised of servers, workstations, peripheral devices, a network operating system, and a communications link.

leased line—A communication line leased from a communications provider, such as an ISP or a telephone company.

LFN (long file names)—File names of up to 256 characters.

LLC (Logical Link Control) sublayer—One of the sublayers of the Data Link layer of the OSI Model; it's responsible for moving packets onto and off of the network.

LMHOSTS—The predecessor to WINS, LMHOSTS is a static list of NetBIOS names mapped to IP addresses.

LMHOSTS file—A static text file kept on and used by the local machine to resolve friendly (NetBIOS) names to IP addresses.

logoff—The process by which a user quits a computer system.

logon—The process by which a user gains access or signs on to a computer system.

loopback address—An IP address, with a first octet of 127. It cannot be used as the address for a host on a network. It's used to test the TCP/IP protocol stack within a computer without sending information out onto the network.

LPD (Line Printer Daemon)—The TCP/IP printer service.

LPQ (Line Printer Queue)—The utility used to display the status of a remote print queue.

LPR (Line Printer Remote) clients—Clients that send print jobs to LPD servers.

management console—Any computer running the graphical user interface for an SNMP manager software.

managers—Also called *management consoles*. An SNMP agent's counterpart that's the software component that issues requests typically passed on to a textual, graphical, or object-oriented user interface.

master name server—Any name server that provides a zone list to a secondary name server.

MCI (multiple-choice item)—An item (within a series of items) that's the answer to a question (single-response MCI) or one of the answers to a question (multiple-response MCI).

MCP (Microsoft Certified Professional)—An individual who has taken and passed at least one certification exam and has earned one or more of the following certifications: Microsoft Certified Trainer, Microsoft Certified Solution Developer, Microsoft Certified Systems Engineer, or Microsoft Certified Product Specialist.

MCPS (Microsoft Certified Product Specialist)—An individual who has passed at least one of the Microsoft operating system exams.

MCSD (Microsoft Certified Solution Developer)—An individual who is qualified to create and develop solutions for businesses using the Microsoft development tools, technologies, and platforms.

MCSE (Microsoft Certified Systems Engineer)—An individual who is an expert on Windows NT and the Microsoft BackOffice integrated family of server software. This individual also can plan, implement, maintain, and support information systems associated with these products.

MCT (Microsoft Certified Trainer)—An individual who is qualified by Microsoft to teach Microsoft Education courses at sites authorized by Microsoft.

Media Access Control (MAC) sublayer—One of the sublayers of the Data Link layer of the OSI Model responsible for moving packets onto and off of the network.

metric—The column of data in the routing table that represents the number of hops to reach the destination network.

MIB (Management Information Base)—A data file containing object values and managed-object descriptions.

Microsoft certification exam—A test created by Microsoft to verify a test-taker's mastery of a software product, technology, or computing topic.

Microsoft Certified Professional Certification Update—A newsletter for Microsoft Certified Professional candidates and Microsoft Certified Professionals.

Microsoft official curriculum—Microsoft education courses that support the certification exam process and are created by the Microsoft product groups.

Microsoft Roadmap to Education and Certification—An application, based on Microsoft Windows, that takes you through the process of deciding what your certification goals are and informs you of the best way to achieve them.

Microsoft Sales Fax Service—A service through which you can obtain Exam Preparation Guides, fact sheets, and additional information about the Microsoft Certified Professional Program.

Microsoft Solution Provider—An organization, not directly related to Microsoft, that provides integration, consulting, technical support, and other services related to Microsoft products.

Microsoft Technical Information Network (TechNet)—A service provided by Microsoft that provides helpful information via a monthly CD-ROM disk. TechNet is the primary source of technical information for people who support and/or educate end users, create automated solutions, or administer networks and/or databases.

MOLI (Microsoft Online Institute)—An organization that makes training materials, online forums and user groups, and online classes available.

MPR (Multiprotocol Router)—A service that can dynamically route TCP/IP traffic between different subnets as well as support IPX routing and DHCP Relay Agents.

MRI (multiple-rating item)—An item that gives you a task and a proposed solution. Every time the task is set, an alternate solution is given and the candidate must choose the answer that gives the best results produced by one solution.

MSDN (Microsoft Developer Network)—The official source for Software Development Kits (SDKs), Device Driver Kits (DDKs), operating systems, and programming information associated with creating applications for Microsoft Windows and Windows NT.

multihomed computer—A system with two or more network interfaces installed.

name registration—The process a computer uses to ensure it has a unique NetBIOS name.

NBTSTAT—A utility that provides statistical information specifically for NetBIOS over TCP/IP (NBT).

NDIS (Network Device Interface Specification)—An API designed to facilitate communication between transport protocol drivers and the underlying network interface drivers. It provides the ability to use more than one protocol over a single network card. Microsoft's version of TCP/IP has extended support for this interface.

negative name—In a name registration request, a registration response sent when a name is already in use.

NetBIOS—Originally developed by IBM in the 1980s, this protocol provides the underlying communication mechanism for some basic NT functions, such as browsing and interprocess communications between network servers.

NetBIOS name—A name used by NetBIOS applications and processes to establish communication with other NetBIOS applications on remote hosts.

NetBIOS name cache—A storage area that contains valid IP address mapping for a NetBIOS name. The NetBIOS name cache does not contain host names, because host names and NetBIOS names can be the same.

netmask—The column of data in the routing table that represents the subnet mask used for each network.

NETSTAT—A utility that displays protocol (TCP, IP, ICMP, or UDP) statistics and IP connection information.

network ID—The particular network (or segment) on which a host physically resides.

network address—The column of data in the routing table that represents the address of each known network, including the local address (0.0.0.0) and broadcasts (255.255.255.255).

Network layer—Layer 3 of the OSI Model. This layer is responsible for routing packets through multiple networks.

Network Neighborhood—Within Explorer or My Computer, the area in which you access other computers on the network.

NSLOOKUP—A utility use to troubleshoot the Domain Name Service database.

NWLink—Microsoft's implementation of the Internetwork Packet eXchange/Sequenced Packet eXchange (IPX/SPX) protocols.

octet—Eight bits used to represent an IP address.

OS (operating system)—A software program that controls the operations on a computer system.

OSI (Open Systems Interconnection) Reference Model—An ideal created by the International Standards Organization (ISO) that defines the steps that must take place for networked communications. Most modern protocols are based on this model.

OSPF (Open Shortest Path First)—A second-generation TCP/IP routing protocol that uses link-state rather than distance-vector algorithms to compute its best route.

PDC (Primary Domain Controller)—The central storage and management server for the SAM database on a Windows NT network.

Performance Monitor—A graphical application that lets you set, graph, log, and report alerts.

peripheral device—A hardware device connected to a computer.

Physical layer—Layer 1 of the OSI Model. The layer where hardware, connectors, cable length, and signaling specifications are defined.

PING—A TCP/IP command used to verify the existence of and connection to remote hosts over a network.

PPP (Point-To-Point Protocol)—An industry-standard protocol used to establish network-protocol-supporting links over telephone lines using modems.

PPTP (Point-To-Point Tunneling Protocol)—A protocol that enables "tunneling" of IPX, NetBEUI, or TCP/IP inside PPP packets in such a way as to establish a secure link between a client and server over the Internet.

Presentation layer—Layer 6 of the OSI model. It ensures that data being passed up to the Application layer is either converted to, or is already in, a format that will be understood by the Application layer's processes.

primary name server—The name server that creates and maintains a given zone and is said to have authority for that zone. The primary name server also answers name resolution requests that come from clients.

protocol—In networking, a set of rules that defines how information is transmitted over a network.

Proxy ARP—The process by which a router assists in the ARP process by forwarding requests for destination hardware addresses.

PTR (Pointer Record)—A type of resource record that is used for IP-address-to-name resolution in reverse lookup zones (IN-ADDR.ARPA).

pull partner—A WINS server configured to "pull" requested database changes from its partner on a fixed interval.

push partner—A WINS server that's configured to send its database changes to its partner.

RARP (Reverse Address Resolution Protocol)—The reverse of ARP; it provides an IP address when given a physical address. Used to provide IP addresses to diskless workstations.

RAS (Remote Access Service)—A Windows NT service that provides network communication for remote clients over telecommunication lines. RAS connections are different from standard direct network connections only in relation to speed.

RCP (Remote Copy)—A utility that copies files from one TCP/IP-enabled computer to another and does not require user validation.

recursive name query—A query issued by resolvers. The client (resolver) wants an absolute name resolution, meaning that it needs a complete IP address returned from the name server.

Registry Editor—A utility that views and edits Registry parameters.

relay agent—A utility that relays DHCP messages between DHCP server and clients that are not on the same network.

remote host—An IP host not on the local subnet.

reserved client—A client that's always assigned the same IP address whenever it requests an IP address from a DHCP server.

resolver—In the DNS name resolution process, a resolver is the client computer attempting to resolve a name.

Resource Kit—The additional documentation and software utilities distributed by Microsoft to provide information and instruction on the proper operation and modification of its software products.

REXEC (Remote Execution)—The utility that executes a process on a remote computer that's running an REXEC service.

RFC (Request For Comments)—TCP/IP standards that are publicly available and published.

RIP (Routing Internet Protocol)—A protocol that enables communication between routers on a network to facilitate the exchange of routing tables.

router—A device or a software implementation that enables interoperability and communication across networks.

routing table—A database that correlates network segment IP addresses with the IP addresses of the router's interfaces.

RSH (Remote Shell)—A utility that allows users to issue commands on a remote system without logging in to that system.

scope—The range of IP addresses a DHCP server can assign.

Scope ID—An ID appended to the NetBIOS computer name when network communications take place. Only computers with the same Scope ID are able to communicate with each other.

secondary name server—A name server that maintains a copy of the zone information that it receives from the primary server or another secondary server.

Session layer—Layer 5 of the OSI Model. This layer is responsible for establishing, maintaining, and terminating communications among applications or processes running across a network.

set—A request for action on the part of the agent; a reply is not mandated.

sliding window—A term used to describe the variable sizes of the sending and receiving TCP buffers and the mechanism used to control how full each of these buffers gets.

SNMP (Simple Network Management Protocol)—A protocol used to monitor remote hosts over a TCP/IP network.

sockets—An addressing technique used by services and applications that need to establish a connection with another host(s).

static routing—A method for populating routing tables in which the information is manually added.

subnet—A portion or segment of a network.

subnet mask—A 32-bit address that indicates how many bits in an address are being used for the network ID.

supernetting—A function of CIDR; it's a process used to combine a number of Class C addresses into one subnet by changing the number of bits used in the subnet mask.

System Policy Editor—The administrative tool used to create and modify system policies for computers, groups, and users.

TCP/IP—The most widely used protocol suite in networking today because it's the most flexible of the transport protocols and is able to easily span wide areas.

TCP/IP Model—Also known as the *DoD Model*. It's the four layers of the TCP/IP protocol suite: Network Interface layer, Internet layer, Transport layer, and the Application layer.

Telnet—A very useful remote terminal emulation application that has its own protocol for transport (defined in RFC 854).

topology—The basic configuration and layout of a network. Star and Bus are two common network topologies.

TRACERT—The TCP/IP diagnostic utility that determines the route taken to a destination by sending ICMP echo packets and increments hops based on TTL (time to live) values.

Transport layer—Layer 4 of the OSI model. This layer is responsible for the transmission of messages from the sending host to the final receiving destination.

traps—An SNMP alert sent by an agent when a threshold is exceeded.

TTL (time to live)—The number of seconds a packet is allowed to traverse the network.

UDP (User Datagram Protocol)—A TCP/IP transport protocol that transmits data through a connectionless service.

UNC (Universal Naming Convention)—A standardized naming method for networks that takes the form of \\servername\sharename.

Unix—An interactive, time-sharing operating system developed in 1969 by a hacker to play games. This system developed into the most widely used industrial-strength computer operating system in the world, and it ultimately supported the birth of the Internet.

user name—The user-friendly name of a user account. The user name is one of the two data items used to log on to NT. NT does not recognize an account by the user name, but rather by the SID.

WAN (wide area network)—A network that spans geographically distant segments. Often a distance of two or more miles is used to define a WAN. Microsoft, however, considers that any RAS connection establishes a WAN.

Windows NT Workstation—A Microsoft OS product that is a client version of the NT system. It's the same as NT Server, but without the capability to host multiple services and resources for a network.

WINS (Windows Internet Name Service)—A Windows network service used to resolve NetBIOS names to IP addresses.

WINS Proxy Agent—A Windows NT computer configured to allow the forwarding of name resolution broadcasts of non-WINS clients to a WINS server.

WinSock (Windows Sockets)—A networking API designed to facilitate communication among different TCP/IP applications and protocol stacks.

World Wide Web—An information distribution system hosted on TCP/IP networks. The Web supports text, graphics, and multimedia. The IIS component of NT is a Web server that can distribute Web documents.

zone—A piece of the Domain Name Space hierarchy that is used to manage the DNS service.

Index

Order Practice Tests from the
Authors of the *Exam Cram* Series

LANWrights offers diskette copies of practice tests for these MCSE exams:

70-058 Networking Essentials   70-073 NT Workstation 4
70-063 Windows 95   70-059 TCP/IP for NT 4
70-067 NT Server 4   TBD Exchange Server 5.5*
70-068 NT Server 4 in the Enterprise TBD   IIS 4*

*available Q2/98

Each diskette includes the following:

√ Two practice exams consisting of 50-60 questions, designed to help you prepare for the certification test. One test automates the test that appears in each *Exam Cram* book; the other is new material.

√ Feedback on answers, to help you prepare more thoroughly.

√ Access to the LANWrights Question Exchange, an online set of threaded discussion forums aimed at the topics for each of these books, where you can ask for help and get answers within 72 hours.

Note: These tests are written in HTML and use Java and JavaScript tools, so you must use Navigator 3.02 or Internet Explorer 3.02 or higher.

Fees for practice exam diskettes:

$25 for single diskette $100 for any five
$45 for any two $115 for any six
$65 for any three $135 for all eight
$85 for any four   All amounts are US$

To order, please send a check or money order drawn on a U.S. bank. Please include complete delivery information with your order: Name, Company, Street Address, City, State, Postal Code, Country. Send all orders to LANWrights Exams, P.O. Box 26261, Austin, TX, USA 78755-0261. For orders from Mexico or Canada, please add US$5; for orders outside North America, please add US$10. For expedited delivery, online orders, or other information, please visit www.lanw.com/examcram/order.htm.